GOVERNMENT PROCEDURES AND OPERATIONS

U.S. INTERNATIONAL TAX SYSTEM

ANALYSIS AND REFORM PROPOSALS

GOVERNMENT PROCEDURES AND OPERATIONS

Additional books in this series can be found on Nova's website
under the Series tab.

Additional e-books in this series can be found on Nova's website
under the e-book tab.

GOVERNMENT PROCEDURES AND OPERATIONS

U.S. INTERNATIONAL TAX SYSTEM: ANALYSIS AND REFORM PROPOSALS

HOLLY LANFORD
EDITOR

nova publishers
New York

For permission to use material from this book please contact us:
Telephone 631-231-7269; Fax 631-231-8175
Web Site: http://www.novapublishers.com

Library of Congress Cataloging-in-Publication Data

ISBN: 978-1-63321-976-2

Published by Nova Science Publishers, Inc. † New York

CONTENTS

Preface		**vii**
Chapter 1	Present Law and Background Related to Proposals to Reform the Taxation of Income of Multinational Enterprises *Joint Committee on Taxation*	**1**
Chapter 2	Opening Statement of Ron Wyden, Chairman, Senate Committee on Finance. Hearing on "The U.S. Tax Code: Love It, Leave It or Reform It!" *Ron Wyden*	**81**
Chapter 3	Testimony of Robert B. Stack, Deputy Assistant Secretary for International Tax Affairs, U.S. Department of the Treasury. Hearing on "The U.S. Tax Code: Love It, Leave It or Reform It!" *Robert B. Stack*	**83**
Chapter 4	Testimony of Pascal Saint-Amans, Director, Centre for Tax Policy and Administration, Organisation for Economic Co-operation and Development (OECD). Hearing on "The U.S. Tax Code: Love It, Leave It or Reform It!" *Pascal Saint-Amans*	**89**
Chapter 5	Testimony of Mihir A. Desai, Professor of Finance, Harvard University. Hearing on "The U.S. Tax Code: Love It, Leave It or Reform It!" *Mihir A. Desai*	**97**
Chapter 6	Statement of Peter R. Merrill, Principal, National Economics and Statistics Group, PricewaterhouseCoopers LLP. Hearing on "The U.S. Tax Code: Love It, Leave It or Reform It!" *Peter R. Merrill*	**101**
Chapter 7	Testimony of Leslie Robinson, Associate Professor of Business Administration, Dartmouth College. Hearing on "The U.S. Tax Code: Love It, Leave It or Reform It!" *Leslie Robinson*	**117**

Chapter 8 Statement of Allan Sloan, Senior Editor at Large, Fortune. Hearing on "The U.S. Tax Code: Love It, Leave It or Reform It!" **127**
Allan Sloan

Index **135**

PREFACE

On July 22, 2014, the Senate Committee on Finance held a public hearing on the taxation of cross-border income. This document, prepared by the staff of the Joint Committee on Taxation for the hearing, includes a description of present law, background on recent global activity related to the taxation of cross-border income, and descriptions and a comparison of recent proposals to reform the U.S. international tax system.

In: U.S. International Tax System
Editor: Holly Lanford

ISBN: 978-1-63321-976-2

Chapter 1

PRESENT LAW AND BACKGROUND RELATED TO PROPOSALS TO REFORM THE TAXATION OF INCOME OF MULTINATIONAL ENTERPRISES*

Joint Committee on Taxation

INTRODUCTION AND SUMMARY

The Senate Committee on Finance has scheduled a public hearing for July 22, 2014 on the taxation of cross-border income. This document,[1] prepared by the staff of the Joint Committee on Taxation, includes a description of present law, background on recent global activity related to the taxation of cross-border income, and descriptions and a comparison of recent proposals to reform the U.S. international tax system.

The U.S. international tax rules provide worldwide taxation of all U.S. persons on all income, whether derived in the United States or abroad, but allow deferral of U.S. taxation of much foreign business income derived by foreign subsidiaries of U.S. companies. The rules provide territorial-based taxation of U.S.-source income of nonresident aliens and foreign entities. Part I of this document describes in more detail the rules applicable to inbound investment (the U.S. activities of foreign persons) and outbound investment (the foreign activities of U.S. persons).

The U.S. rules for the taxation of cross-border income have been the subject of much criticism. Critics have had a few broad, sometimes conflicting policy concerns. On the one hand, critics have argued that the U.S. tax burden on the foreign business income of U.S. companies is too high, particularly when U.S. multinational companies are competing in foreign markets with foreign multinational firms that are subject to little or no home-country tax on foreign income. Commentators also have argued that the U.S. tax rules discourage U.S. companies from investing foreign earnings in the United States and favor reinvestment of the earnings abroad, even when the pre-tax rate of return on the potential U.S. investment is higher than the pre-tax rate of return on the potential foreign investment. On the other hand,

* This is an edited, reformatted and augmented version of a document, JCX-90-14, issued July 21, 2014.

critics have expressed concern that under the U.S. rules for taxing cross-border income, both U.S. and foreign multinational companies reduce the amount of U.S. tax they pay by shifting profits reported for income tax purposes outside the United States and, in some cases, by shifting manufacturing, headquarters, and other business activities outside the United States. Policy makers and commentators in countries other than the United States have expressed similar concerns about the competitiveness of home country firms, about profit shifting by U.S. and home country firms, and about the erosion of the corporate tax bases of those countries by U.S. and home country firms. Part II of this document describes these policy concerns.

Governments around the world have responded to these policy concerns in various ways. The Organisation for Economic Co-operation and Development ("OECD") has undertaken an initiative on base erosion and profit shifting. The European Union and several of its member states have introduced proposals or enacted laws that deny tax benefits in arrangements in which companies might otherwise derive low-tax or zero-tax cross-border income. Some countries have legislation intended to attract intellectual property development or ownership. In the United States, the Administration's budget proposals include a number of proposals intended to restrict profit shifting, particularly in respect of intangible property income, by U.S. multinational companies and to reduce erosion of the U.S. tax base by foreign multinational companies.[2] Members of the U.S. Congress, including Senate Finance Committee Chairman Ron Wyden, former Senate Finance Committee Chairman Max Baucus, Senator Mike Enzi, and House Ways and Means Chairman Dave Camp, have made public or have introduced legislation to reform the U.S. international tax rules.[3] These reform proposals replace deferred U.S. taxation of the business earnings of foreign subsidiaries of U.S. companies with either full current U.S. taxation of foreign subsidiary earnings or a mix of current U.S. taxation of the earnings and exemption from U.S. taxation.[4] Parts III and IV of this document describe recent global (Part III) and U.S. (Part IV) policy responses, and Part V of this document compares the recent U.S. proposals across several dimensions.

I. Present Law

A. General Overview

1. International tax principles and their application in the U.S. system

International law recognizes the right of each sovereign nation to regulate conduct based on a nexus of the conduct to the territory of the nation or to a person (whether natural or juridical) whose status links the person to the nation, subject to limitations based on evaluating the reasonableness of the regulatory action.[5] In turn, these two broad bases of jurisdiction, i.e., territoriality and nationality of the person whose conduct is regulated, have been refined and, in varying combinations, form the bases of most systems of income taxation. A number of commonly accepted principles have developed to minimize the extent to which conflicts arise as a result of extraterritorial or overlapping exercise of taxing authority. In addition to general acceptance of some variation of territorial or national nexus as a basis for taxing jurisdiction, most systems also comport with international norms by respecting reasonableness as a limit on extraterritorial enforcement, providing an enforcement mechanism such as withholding tax at source of a payment, and establishing guidelines for determining how to resolve duplicative assertions of authority.[6]

Exercise of taxing authority based on a person's status as a national, resident, or domiciliary of a jurisdiction reaches worldwide activities of such persons and is the broadest assertion of taxing authority. A more limited exercise of taxation occurs when taxation is imposed only to the extent that activities occur or property is located in the territory of the taxing jurisdiction. If a person conducts business or owns property in a jurisdiction, or if a transaction occurs in whole or in part in a jurisdiction, the resulting limited basis of taxation is a territorial application. Whether the broader or narrower basis of taxation is used by a jurisdiction, identification of the tax base depends upon establishing rules for determining the source of income and its proper allocation among related parties, as well as the status of all persons, that is, their residency for tax purposes.

The same income may be subject to taxation in two jurisdictions if those jurisdictions adopt different standards for determining residency of persons, source of income, or other basis for taxation. To the extent that the rules of two or more countries overlap, rules to mitigate potential double taxation generally apply, either by operation of bilateral treaties to avoid double taxation or in the form of legislative relief, such as credits for taxes paid to another jurisdiction.

Present law combines the worldwide taxation of all U.S. persons[7] on all income, whether derived in the United States or abroad, with limited deferral for foreign income earned by foreign subsidiaries of U.S. companies, and provides territorial-based taxation of U.S.-source income of nonresident aliens and foreign entities. This combination is sometimes described as the U.S. hybrid system. Under this system, the application of the Code to outbound investment (the foreign activities of U.S. persons) differs somewhat from its rules applicable to inbound investment (foreign persons with investment in U.S. assets or activities).

With respect to outbound activities, U.S. citizens, resident individuals, and domestic corporations generally are taxed on all income, whether derived in the United States or abroad.[8] Income earned by a domestic parent corporation from foreign operations conducted by foreign corporate subsidiaries generally is subject to U.S. tax when the income is distributed as a dividend to the domestic parent corporation. Until that repatriation, the U.S. tax on the income generally is deferred. However, certain U.S. anti-deferral regimes may cause the domestic parent corporation to be taxed currently in the United States on certain categories of passive or highly mobile income earned by its foreign corporate subsidiaries, regardless of whether the income has been distributed as a dividend to the domestic parent corporation. The main anti-deferral regimes in this context are the controlled foreign corporation ("CFC") rules of subpart F[9] and the passive foreign investment company ("PFIC") rules.[10]

By contrast, with respect to inbound activities, nonresident aliens and foreign corporations are generally subject to U.S. tax only on their U.S.-source income. Thus, the source and type of income received by a foreign person generally determines whether there is any U.S. income tax liability, and the mechanism by which it is taxed (either by gross-basis withholding , as described below in subpart IV.B.1, or on a net basis through tax return filing as described in subpart IV.B.2).

To mitigate double taxation of foreign-source income, the United States allows a credit for foreign income taxes paid.[11] As a consequence, even though resident individuals and domestic corporations are subject to U.S. tax on all their income, both U.S.- and foreign-source, source of income remains a critical factor to the extent that it determines the amount of credit available for foreign taxes paid. The foreign tax credit generally is available to offset, in whole or in part, the U.S. tax owed on foreign-source income, whether the income is earned directly by the domestic corporation, repatriated as an actual dividend, or included in the domestic parent corporation's income under one of the anti-deferral regimes.[12] In addition to the statutory relief afforded by the credit, the U.S. network of bilateral income tax treaties provides a system for removing double taxation and ensuring reciprocal treatment of taxpayers from treaty countries.

Category-by-category rules determine whether income has a U.S. source or a foreign source. Additionally, present law provides detailed rules for the allocation of deductible expenses between U.S.-source income and foreign-source income. These rules do not, however, affect the timing of the expense deduction. A domestic corporation generally is allowed a current deduction for its expenses (such as interest and administrative expenses) that support income that is derived through foreign subsidiaries and on which U.S. tax is deferred. Instead, the expense allocation rules apply to a domestic corporation principally for determining the corporation's foreign tax credit limitation.

U.S. tax law includes rules intended to prevent reduction of the U.S. tax base, whether through excessive borrowing in the United States, migration of the tax residence of domestic corporations from the United States to foreign jurisdictions through corporate inversion transactions,[13] or aggressive intercompany pricing practices, particularly with respect to intangible property.

2. Principles common to inbound and outbound taxation

Although the U.S. tax rules often differ depending upon whether the activity in question is inbound or outbound, there are certain concepts that are not readily characterized as inbound or outbound investment. Such areas include the transfer pricing rules, entity classification, the rules for determination of source, and whether a corporation is foreign or domestic.

Transfer pricing

A basic U.S. tax principle applicable in dividing profits from transactions between related taxpayers is that the amount of profit allocated to each related taxpayer must be measured by reference to the amount of profit that a similarly situated taxpayer would realize in similar transactions with unrelated parties. The transfer pricing rules of section 482 and the accompanying Treasury regulations are intended to preserve the U.S. tax base by ensuring that taxpayers do not shift income properly attributable to the United States to a related foreign company through pricing that does not reflect an arm's-length result.[14] Similarly, the domestic laws of most U.S. trading partners include rules to limit income shifting through transfer pricing. The arm's-length standard is difficult to administer in situations in which no unrelated party market prices exist for transactions between related parties. When a foreign person with U.S. activities has transactions with related U.S. taxpayers, the amount of income attributable to U.S. activities is determined in part by the same transfer pricing rules of section 482 that apply when U.S. persons with foreign activities transact with related foreign taxpayers.

Section 482 authorizes the Secretary of the Treasury to allocate income, deductions, credits, or allowances among related business entities[15] when necessary to clearly reflect income or otherwise prevent tax avoidance, and comprehensive Treasury regulations under that section adopt the arm's-length standard as the method for determining whether allocations are appropriate.[16] The regulations generally attempt to identify the respective amounts of taxable income of the related parties that would have resulted if the parties had been unrelated parties dealing at arm's length. For income from intangible property, section 482 provides "in the case of any transfer (or license) of intangible property (within the meaning of section 936(h)(3)(B)), the income with respect to such transfer or license shall be commensurate with the income attributable to the intangible." By requiring inclusion in income of amounts commensurate with the income attributable to the intangible, Congress was responding to concerns regarding the effectiveness of the arm's-length standard with respect to intangible property—including, in particular, high-profit-potential intangibles.[17]

Entity classification

A business entity is generally eligible to choose how it is classified for Federal tax law purposes, under the "check-the-box" regulations adopted in 1997.[18] Those regulations simplified the entity classification process for both taxpayers and the Internal Revenue Service ("IRS"), by making the entity classification of unincorporated entities explicitly elective in most instances.[19] Whether an entity is eligible and the breadth of its choices depends upon whether it is a "per se corporation" and the number of beneficial owners.

Certain entities are treated as "per se corporations" for which an election is not permitted. Generally, these are domestic entities formed under a State corporation statute. A number of specific types of foreign business entities are identified in the regulations as per se corporations. These entities are generally corporations that are not closely held and the shares of which can be traded on a securities exchange.[20]

An eligible entity with two or more members may elect, however, to be classified as a corporation or a partnership. If an eligible entity fails to make an election, default rules apply. A domestic entity with multiple members is treated as a partnership. A foreign entity with multiple members is treated as a partnership, if at least one member does not have limited liability, but is treated as a corporation if all members have limited liability.

The regulations also provide explicitly that a single-member unincorporated entity may elect either to be treated as a corporation or to be disregarded (treated as not separate from its owner). A disregarded entity owned by an individual is treated in the same manner as a sole proprietorship. In the case of an entity owned by a corporation or partnership, the disregarded entity is treated in the same manner as a branch or division. The default treatment for an eligible single-member domestic entity is as a disregarded entity. For an eligible single-member foreign entity, the default treatment depends upon whether the single-member entity has limited liability. If it does, the foreign entity is treated as a corporation; otherwise, its default treatment is that of a disregarded entity.

The regulations extended elective classification to foreign, as well as domestic, entities on the basis that the complexities and resources devoted to classification of domestic unincorporated business entities were mirrored in the foreign context. As a result, it is possible for an entity that operates cross-border to elect into a hybrid status. "Hybrid entities" refers to entities that are treated as flow-through or disregarded entities for U.S. tax purposes but as corporations for foreign tax purposes; for "reverse hybrid entities," the opposite is true. The existence of hybrid and reverse hybrid entities can affect whether the taxpayer can use foreign tax credits attributable to deferred foreign-source income or income that is not taxable in the United States, as well as whether income is currently includible under subpart F.

Source of income rules

The rules for determining the source of certain types of income are specified in the Code and described briefly below. Various factors determine the source of income for U.S. tax purposes, including the status or nationality of the payor, the status or nationality of the recipient, the location of the recipient's activities that generate the income, and the situs of the assets that generate the income. If a payor or recipient is an entity that is eligible to elect its classification for Federal tax purposes, its choice of whether to be recognized as legally separate from its owner in another jurisdiction can affect the determination of the source of the income and other tax attributes, if the hybrid entity is disregarded in one jurisdiction, but recognized in the other. To the extent that the source of income is not specified by statute, the Treasury Secretary may promulgate regulations that explain the appropriate treatment. However, many items of income are not explicitly addressed by either the Code or Treasury regulations. On several occasions, courts have determined the source of such items by applying the rule for the type of income to which the disputed income is most closely analogous, based on all facts and circumstances.[21]

Interest

Interest is derived from U.S. sources if it is paid by the United States or any agency or instrumentality thereof, a State or any political subdivision thereof, or the District of Columbia. Interest is also from U.S. sources if it is paid by a resident or a domestic corporation on a bond, note, or other interest-bearing obligation.[22] Special rules apply to treat as foreign-source certain amounts paid on deposits with foreign commercial banking branches of U.S. corporations or partnerships and certain other amounts paid by foreign branches of domestic financial institutions.[23] Interest paid by the U.S. branch of a foreign corporation is also treated as U.S.- source income.[24]

Dividends

Dividend income is generally sourced by reference to the payor's place of incorporation.[25] Thus, dividends paid by a domestic corporation are generally treated as entirely U.S.-source income. Similarly, dividends paid by a foreign corporation are generally treated as entirely foreign-source income. Under a special rule, dividends from certain foreign corporations that conduct U.S. businesses are treated in part as U.S.-source income.[26]

Rents and royalties

Rental income is sourced by reference to the location or place of use of the leased property.[27] The nationality or the country of residence of the lessor or lessee does not affect the source of rental income. Rental income from property located or used in the United States (or from any interest in such property) is U.S.-source income, regardless of whether the property is real or personal, intangible or tangible.

Royalties are sourced in the place of use of (or the place of privilege to use) the property for which the royalties are paid.[28] This source rule applies to royalties for the use of either tangible or intangible property, including patents, copyrights, secret processes, formulas, goodwill, trademarks, trade names, and franchises.

Income from sales of personal property

Subject to significant exceptions, income from the sale of personal property is sourced on the basis of the residence of the seller.[29] For this purpose, special definitions of the terms "U.S. resident" and "nonresident" are provided. A nonresident is defined as any person who is not a U.S. resident,[30] while the term "U.S. resident" comprises any juridical entity which is a U.S. person, all U.S. citizens, as well as any individual who is a U.S. resident without a tax home in a foreign country or a nonresident alien with a tax home in the United States.[31] As a result, nonresident includes any foreign corporation.[32]

Several special rules apply. For example, income from the sale of inventory property is generally sourced to the place of sale, which is determined by where title to the property passes.[33] However, if the sale is by a nonresident and is attributable to an office or other fixed place of business in the United States, the sale is treated as U.S.-source without regard to the place of sale, unless it is sold for use, disposition, or consumption outside the United States and a foreign office materially participates in the sale.[34] Income from the sale of inventory property that a taxpayer produces (in whole or in part) in the United States and sells outside the United States, or that a taxpayer produces (in whole or in part) outside the United States and sells in the United States is treated as partly U.S.-source and partly foreign-source.[35]

In determining the source of gain or loss from the sale or exchange of an interest in a foreign partnership, the IRS applies the asset-use test and business activities test at the partnership level to determine whether there is a U.S. business and, if so, the extent to which income derived is effectively connected with that U.S. business. To the extent that there is unrealized gain attributable to partnership assets that are effectively connected with the U.S. business, the foreign person's gain or loss from the sale or exchange of a partnership interest is effectively connected gain or loss to the extent of the partner's distributive share of such unrealized gain or loss. Similarly, to the extent that the partner's distributive share of unrealized gain is attributable to a permanent establishment of the partnership under an applicable treaty provision, it may be subject to U.S. tax under a treaty.[36]

Gain on the sale of depreciable property is divided between U.S.-source and foreign-source in the same ratio that the depreciation was previously deductible for U.S. tax purposes.[37] Payments received on sales of intangible property are sourced in the same manner as royalties to the extent the payments are contingent on the productivity, use, or disposition of the intangible property.[38]

Personal services income

Compensation for labor or personal services is generally sourced to the place-of-performance. Thus, compensation for labor or personal services performed in the United States generally is treated as U.S.-source income, subject to an exception for amounts that meet certain de minimis criteria.[39] Compensation for services performed both within and without the United States is allocated between U.S.- and foreign-source.[40]

Insurance income

Underwriting income from issuing insurance or annuity contracts generally is treated as U.S.-source income if the contract involves property in, liability arising out of an activity in, or the lives or health of residents of, the United States.[41]

Transportation income

Generally, income from furnishing transportation that begins and ends in the United States is U.S.-source income.[42] Fifty percent of other income attributable to transportation that begins or ends in the United States is treated as U.S.-source income.

Income from space or ocean activities or international communications

In the case of a foreign person, generally no income from a space or ocean activity or from international communications is treated as U.S.-source income.[43] With respect to the latter, an exception is provided if the foreign person maintains an office or other fixed place of business in the United States, in which case the international communications income attributable to such fixed place of business is treated as U.S.-source income.[44] For U.S. persons, all income from space or ocean activities and 50 percent of international communications is treated as U.S.-source income.

Amounts received with respect to guarantees of indebtedness

Amounts received, directly or indirectly, from a noncorporate resident or from a domestic corporation for the provision of a guarantee of indebtedness of such person are income from U.S. sources.[45] This includes payments that are made indirectly for the provision of a guarantee. For example, U.S.-source income under this rule includes a guarantee fee paid by a foreign bank to a foreign corporation for the foreign corporation's guarantee of indebtedness owed to the bank by the foreign corporation's domestic subsidiary, where the cost of the guarantee fee is passed on to the domestic subsidiary through, for instance, additional interest charged on the indebtedness. In this situation, the domestic subsidiary has paid the guarantee fee as an economic matter through higher interest costs, and the additional interest payments made by the subsidiary are treated as indirect payments of the guarantee fee and, therefore, as U.S.-source.

Such U.S.-source income also includes amounts received from a foreign person, whether directly or indirectly, for the provision of a guarantee of indebtedness of that foreign person if the payments received are connected with income of such person that is effectively connected with the conduct of a U.S. trade or business. Amounts received from a foreign person, whether directly or indirectly, for the provision of a guarantee of that person's debt, are treated as foreign- source income if they are not from sources within the United States under section 861(a)(9).

Place of incorporation effect on taxation

Place of incorporation determines whether a corporation is treated as domestic or foreign for purposes of U.S. tax law, irrespective of other factors that might be thought to bear on a corporation's "nationality," such as the location of the corporation's management activities, employees, business assets, operations, revenue sources, the exchanges on which the corporation's stock is traded, or the residence of the corporation's shareholders. [46] The ability of a domestic corporation to expatriate and thus avoid taxation on its worldwide income is limited by section 7874 to the Code, which denies certain tax benefits of a typical inversion transaction by deeming the new top-tier foreign corporation to be a domestic corporation for all Federal tax purposes. This sanction generally applies to a transaction in which, pursuant to a plan or a series of related transactions: (1) a U.S. corporation becomes a subsidiary of a foreign-incorporated entity or otherwise transfers substantially all of its properties to such an entity in a transaction completed after March 4, 2003; (2) the former shareholders of the U.S. corporation hold (by reason of the stock they had held in the U.S. corporation) 80 percent or more (by vote or value) of the stock of the foreign-incorporated entity after the transaction; and (3) the foreign- incorporated entity, considered together with all companies connected to it by a chain of greater than 50 percent ownership (that is, the "expanded affiliated group"), does not have substantial business activities in the entity's country of incorporation, compared to the total worldwide business activities of the expanded affiliated group.[47]

B. U.S. Tax Rules Applicable to Nonresident Aliens and Foreign Corporations (Inbound)

Nonresident aliens and foreign corporations are generally subject to U.S. tax only on their U.S.-source income. Thus, the source and type of income received by a foreign person generally determines whether there is any U.S. income tax liability and the mechanism by which it is taxed. The U.S. tax rules for U.S. activities of foreign taxpayers apply differently to two broad types of income: U.S.-source income that is "fixed or determinable annual or periodical gains, profits, and income" ("FDAP income") or income that is "effectively connected with the conduct of a trade or business within the United States" ("ECI"). FDAP income generally is subject to a 30-percent gross-basis withholding tax, while ECI is generally subject to the same U.S. tax rules that apply to business income derived by U.S. persons. That is, deductions are permitted in determining taxable ECI, which is then taxed at the same rates applicable to U.S. persons. Much FDAP income and similar income is, however, exempt from withholding tax or is subject to a reduced rate of tax under the Code[48] or a bilateral income tax treaty.[49]

1. Gross-basis taxation of U.S.-source income

Non-business income received by foreign persons from U.S. sources is generally subject to tax on a gross basis at a rate of 30 percent, which is collected by withholding at the source of the payment. As explained below, the categories of income subject to the 30-percent tax and the categories for which withholding is required are generally coextensive, with the result that determining the withholding tax liability determines the substantive liability.

The income of non-resident aliens or foreign corporations that is subject to tax at a rate of 30-percent includes FDAP income that is not effectively connected with the conduct of a U.S. trade or business.[50] The items enumerated in defining FDAP income are illustrative; the common characteristic of types of FDAP income is that taxes with respect to the income may be readily computed and collected at the source, in contrast to the administrative difficulty involved in determining the seller's basis and resulting gain from sales of property.[51] The words "annual or periodical" are "merely generally descriptive" of the payments that could be within the purview of the statute and do not preclude application of the withholding tax to one-time, lump sum payments to nonresident aliens.[52]

Types of FDAP income

FDAP income encompasses a broad range of types of gross income, but has limited application to gains on sales of property, including market discount on bonds and option premiums.[53] Capital gains received by nonresident aliens present in the United States for fewer than 183 days are generally treated as foreign source and are thus not subject to U.S. tax, unless the gains are effectively connected with a U.S. trade or business; capital gains received by nonresident aliens present in the United States for 183 days or more[54] that are treated as U.S.- source are subject to gross-basis taxation.[55] In contrast, U.S-source gains from the sale or exchange of intangibles are subject to tax, and subject to withholding if they are contingent upon productivity of the property sold and are not effectively connected with a U.S. trade or business.[56]

Interest on bank deposits may qualify for exemption on two grounds, depending on where the underlying principal is held on deposit. Interest paid with respect to deposits with domestic banks and savings and loan associations, and certain amounts held by insurance companies, are U.S. source but are not subject to the U.S. withholding tax when paid to a foreign person, unless the interest is effectively connected with a U.S. trade or business of the recipient.[57] Interest on deposits with foreign branches of domestic banks and domestic savings and loan associations is not treated as U.S.-source income and is thus exempt from U.S. withholding tax (regardless of whether the recipient is a U.S. or foreign person).[58] Similarly, interest and original issue discount on certain short-term obligations is also exempt from U.S. withholding tax when paid to a foreign person.[59] Additionally, there is generally no information reporting required with respect to payments of such amounts.[60]

Although FDAP income includes U.S.-source portfolio interest, such interest is specifically exempt from the 30 percent withholding tax. Portfolio interest is any interest (including original issue discount) that is paid on an obligation that is in registered form and for which the beneficial owner has provided to the U.S. withholding agent a statement certifying that the beneficial owner is not a U.S. person.[61] For obligations issued before March 19, 2012, portfolio interest also includes interest paid on an obligation that is not in registered form, provided that the obligation is shown to be targeted to foreign investors under the conditions sufficient to establish deductibility of the payment of such interest.[62] Portfolio interest, however, does not include interest received by a 10-percent shareholder,[63] certain contingent interest,[64] interest received by a controlled foreign corporation from a related person,[65] or interest received by a bank on an extension of credit made pursuant to a loan agreement entered into in the ordinary course of its trade or business.[66]

Imposition of gross-basis tax and reporting by U.S. withholding agents

The 30-percent tax on FDAP income is generally collected by means of withholding.[67] Withholding on FDAP payments to foreign payees is required unless the withholding agent,[68] i.e., the person making the payment to the foreign person receiving the income, can establish that the beneficial owner of the amount is eligible for an exemption from withholding or a reduced rate of withholding under an income tax treaty.[69] The principal statutory exemptions from the 30-percent withholding tax apply to interest on bank deposits, and portfolio interest, described above.[70]

In many instances, the income subject to withholding is the only income of the foreign recipient that is subject to any U.S. tax. No U.S. Federal income tax return from the foreign recipient is required with respect to the income from which tax was withheld, if the recipient has no ECI income and the withholding is sufficient to satisfy the recipient's liability. Accordingly, although the 30-percent gross-basis tax is a withholding tax, it is also generally the final tax liability of the foreign recipient.

A withholding agent that makes payments of U.S.-source amounts to a foreign person is required to report and pay over any amounts of U.S. tax withheld. The reports are due to be filed with the IRS by March 15 of the calendar year following the year in which the payment is made. Two types of reports are required: (1) a summary of the total U.S.-source income paid and withholding tax withheld on foreign persons for the year and (2) a report to both the IRS and the foreign person of that person's U.S.-source income that is subject to reporting.[71] The nonresident withholding rules apply broadly to any financial institution or other payor, including foreign financial institutions.[72]

To the extent that the withholding agent deducts and withholds an amount, the withheld tax is credited to the recipient of the income.[73] If the agent withholds more than is required, and results in an overpayment of tax, the excess may be refunded to the recipient of the income upon filing of a timely claim for refund.

Excise tax on foreign reinsurance premiums

An excise tax applies to premiums paid to foreign insurers and reinsurers covering U.S. risks.[74] The excise tax is imposed on a gross basis at the rate of one percent on reinsurance and life insurance premiums, and at the rate of four percent on property and casualty insurance premiums. The excise tax does not apply to premiums that are effectively connected with the conduct of a U.S. trade or business or that are exempted from the excise tax under an applicable income tax treaty. The excise tax paid by one party cannot be credited if, for example, the risk is reinsured with a second party in a transaction that is also subject to the excise tax.

Many U.S. tax treaties provide an exemption from the excise tax, including the treaties with Germany, Japan, Switzerland, and the United Kingdom.[75] To prevent persons from inappropriately obtaining the benefits of exemption from the excise tax, the treaties generally include an anti-conduit rule. The most common anti-conduit rule provides that the treaty exemption applies to the excise tax only to the extent that the risks covered by the premiums are not reinsured with a person not entitled to the benefits of the treaty (or any other treaty that provides exemption from the excise tax).[76]

2. Net-basis taxation of U.S. source income

Income from a U.S. business

The United States taxes on a net basis the income of foreign persons that is "effectively connected" with the conduct of a trade or business in the United States.[77] Any gross income derived by the foreign person that is not effectively connected with the person's U.S. business is not taken into account in determining the rates of U.S. tax applicable to the person's income from the business.[78]

U.S. trade or business

A foreign person is subject to U.S. tax on a net basis if the person is engaged in a U.S. trade or business. Partners in a partnership and beneficiaries of an estate or trust are treated as engaged in the conduct of a trade or business within the United States if the partnership, estate, or trust is so engaged.[79]

The question whether a foreign person is engaged in a U.S. trade or business is factual and has generated much case law. Basic issues include whether the activity constitutes business rather than investing, whether sufficient activities in connection with the business are conducted in the United States, and whether the relationship between the foreign person and persons performing functions in the United States in respect of the business is sufficient to attribute those functions to the foreign person.

The trade or business rules differ from one activity to another. The term "trade or business within the United States" expressly includes the performance of personal services within the United States.[80] If, however, a nonresident alien individual performs personal services for a foreign employer, and the individual's total compensation for the services and period in the United States are minimal ($3,000 or less in total compensation and 90 days or fewer of physical presence in a year), the individual is not considered to be engaged in a U.S. trade or business.[81] Detailed rules govern whether trading in stocks or securities or commodities constitutes the conduct of a U.S. trade or business.[82] A foreign person who trades in stock or securities or commodities in the United States through an independent agent generally is not treated as engaged in a U.S. trade or business if the foreign person does not have an office or other fixed place of business in the United States through which trades are carried out. A foreign person who trades stock or securities or commodities for the person's own account also generally is not considered to be engaged in a U.S. business so long as the foreign person is not a dealer in stock or securities or commodities.

For eligible foreign persons, U.S. bilateral income tax treaties restrict the application of net-basis U.S. taxation. Under each treaty, the United States is permitted to tax business profits only to the extent those profits are attributable to a U.S. permanent establishment of the foreign person. The threshold level of activities that constitute a permanent establishment is generally higher than the threshold level of activities that constitute a U.S. trade or business. For example, a permanent establishment typically requires the maintenance of a fixed place of business over a significant period of time.

Effectively connected income

A foreign person that is engaged in the conduct of a trade or business within the United States is subject to U.S. net-basis taxation on the income that is "effectively connected" with the business. Specific statutory rules govern whether income is ECI.[83]

In the case of U.S.-source capital gain and U.S.-source income of a type that would be subject to gross basis U.S. taxation, the factors taken into account in determining whether the income is ECI include whether the income is derived from assets used in or held for use in the conduct of the U.S. trade or business and whether the activities of the trade or business were a material factor in the realization of the amount (the "asset use" and "business activities" tests).[84] Under the asset use and business activities tests, due regard is given to whether the income, gain, or asset was accounted for through the U.S. trade or business. All other U.S.-source income is treated as ECI.[85]

A foreign person who is engaged in a U.S. trade or business may have limited categories of foreign-source income that are considered to be ECI.[86] Foreign-source income not included in one of these categories (described next) generally is exempt from U.S. tax.

A foreign person's foreign-source income generally is considered to be ECI only if the person has an office or other fixed place of business within the United States to which the income is attributable and the income is in one of the following categories: (1) rents or royalties for the use of patents, copyrights, secret processes or formulas, good will, trade-marks, trade brands, franchises, or other like intangible properties derived in the active conduct of the trade or business; (2) interest or dividends derived in the active conduct of a banking, financing, or similar business within the United States or received by a corporation the principal business of which is trading in stocks or securities for its own account; or (3) income derived from the sale or exchange (outside the United States), through the U.S. office or fixed place of business, of inventory or property held by the foreign person primarily for sale to customers in the ordinary course of the trade or business, unless the sale or exchange is for use, consumption, or disposition outside the United States and an office or other fixed place of business of the foreign person in a foreign country participated materially in the sale or exchange.[87] Foreign-source dividends, interest, and royalties are not treated as ECI if the items are paid by a foreign corporation more than 50 percent (by vote) of which is owned directly, indirectly, or constructively by the recipient of the income.[88]

In determining whether a foreign person has a U.S. office or other fixed place of business, the office or other fixed place of business of an agent generally is disregarded. The place of business of an agent other than an independent agent acting in the ordinary course of business is not disregarded, however, if the agent either has the authority (regularly exercised) to negotiate and conclude contracts in the name of the foreign person or has a stock of merchandise from which he regularly fills orders on behalf of the foreign person.[89] If a foreign person has a U.S. office or fixed place of business, income, gain, deduction, or loss is not considered attributable to the office unless the office was a material factor in the production of the income, gain, deduction, or loss and the office regularly carries on activities of the type from which the income, gain, deduction, or loss was derived.[90]

Special rules apply in determining the ECI of an insurance company. The foreign-source income of a foreign corporation that is subject to tax under the insurance company provisions of the Code is treated as ECI if the income is attributable to its United States business.[91]

Income, gain, deduction, or loss for a particular year generally is not treated as ECI if the foreign person is not engaged in a U.S. trade or business in that year.[92] If, however, income or gain taken into account for a taxable year is attributable to the sale or exchange of property, the performance of services, or any other transaction that occurred in a prior taxable year, the determination whether the income or gain is taxable on a net basis is made as if the income were taken into account in the earlier year and without regard to the requirement that the taxpayer be engaged in a trade or business within the United States during the later taxable year.[93] If any property ceases to be used or held for use in connection with the conduct of a U.S. trade or business and the property is disposed of within 10 years after the cessation, the determination whether any income or gain attributable to the disposition of the property is taxable on a net basis is made as if the disposition occurred immediately before the property ceased to be used or held for use in connection with the conduct of a U.S. trade or business and without regard to the requirement that the taxpayer be engaged in a U.S. business during the taxable year for which the income or gain is taken into account.[94]

Allowance of deductions

Taxable ECI is computed by taking into account deductions associated with gross ECI. For this purpose, the apportionment and allocation of deductions is addressed in detailed regulations. The regulations applicable to deductions other than interest expense set forth general guidelines for allocating deductions among classes of income and apportioning deductions between ECI and non-ECI. In some circumstances, deductions may be allocated on the basis of units sold, gross sales or receipts, costs of goods sold, profits contributed, expenses incurred, assets used, salaries paid, space used, time spent, or gross income received. More specific guidelines are provided for the allocation and apportionment of research and experimental expenditures, legal and accounting fees, income taxes, losses on dispositions of property, and net operating losses. Detailed regulations under section 861 address the allocation and apportionment of interest deductions. In general, interest is allocated and apportioned based on assets rather than income.

3. Special rules

FIRPTA

The Foreign Investment in Real Property Tax Act of 1980 ("FIRPTA")[95] generally treats a foreign person's gain or loss from the disposition of a U.S. real property interest ("USRPI") as ECI and, therefore, as taxable at the income tax rates applicable to U.S. persons, including the rates for net capital gain. A foreign person subject to tax on this income is required to file a U.S. tax return under the normal rules relating to receipt of ECI.[96] In the case of a foreign corporation, the gain from the disposition of a USRPI may also be subject to the branch profits tax at a 30-percent rate (or lower treaty rate).

The payor of income that FIRPTA treats as ECI ("FIRPTA income") is generally required to withhold U.S. tax from the payment. Withholding is generally 10 percent of the sales price, in the case of a direct sale by the foreign person of a USRPI, and 35 percent of the amount of a distribution to a foreign person of proceeds attributable to such sales from an entity such as a partnership, real estate investment trust ("REIT") or regulated investment company ("RIC").[97] The foreign person can request a refund with its U.S. tax return, if appropriate, based on that person's total ECI and deductions (if any) for the taxable year.

Branch profits taxes

A domestic corporation owned by foreign persons is subject to U.S. income tax on its net income. The earnings of the domestic corporation are subject to a second tax, this time at the shareholder level, when dividends are paid. As described previously, when the shareholders are foreign, the second-level tax is imposed at a flat rate and collected by withholding. Unless the portfolio interest exemption or another exemption applies, interest payments made by a domestic corporation to foreign creditors are likewise subject to U.S. withholding tax. To approximate these second-level withholding taxes imposed on payments made by domestic subsidiaries to their foreign parent corporations, the United States taxes a foreign corporation that is engaged in a U.S. trade or business through a U.S. branch on amounts of U.S. earnings and profits that are shifted out of, or amounts of interest that are deducted by, the U.S. branch of the foreign corporation. These branch taxes may be reduced or eliminated under an applicable income tax treaty.[98]

Under the branch profits tax, the United States imposes a tax of 30 percent on a foreign corporation's "dividend equivalent amount."[99] The dividend equivalent amount generally is the earnings and profits of a U.S. branch of a foreign corporation attributable to its ECI.[100] Limited categories of earnings and profits attributable to a foreign corporation's ECI are excluded in calculating the dividend equivalent amount.[101]

In arriving at the dividend equivalent amount, a branch's effectively connected earnings and profits are adjusted to reflect changes in a branch's U.S. net equity (that is, the excess of the branch's assets over its liabilities, taking into account only amounts treated as connected with its U.S. trade or business).[102] The first adjustment reduces the dividend equivalent amount to the extent the branch's earnings are reinvested in trade or business assets in the United States (or reduce U.S. trade or business liabilities). The second adjustment increases the dividend equivalent amount to the extent prior reinvested earnings are considered remitted to the home office of the foreign corporation.

Interest paid by a U.S. trade or business of a foreign corporation generally is treated as if paid by a domestic corporation and therefore is subject to U.S. 30-percent withholding tax (if the interest is paid to a foreign person and a Code or treaty exemption or reduction would not be available if the interest were actually paid by a domestic corporation).[103] Certain "excess interest" of a U.S. trade or business of a foreign corporation is treated as if paid by a U.S. corporation to a foreign parent and, therefore, is subject to U.S. 30-percent withholding tax.[104] For this purpose, excess interest is the excess of the interest expense of the foreign corporation apportioned to the U.S. trade or business over the amount of interest paid by the trade or business.

Earnings stripping

A foreign multinational enterprise with U.S. business operations may reduce the U.S. tax on the income derived from its U.S. business by arranging to have its U.S. subsidiary pay deductible amounts such as interest, rents, royalties, premiums, and management service fees to foreign affiliates that are not subject to U.S. tax on the receipt of such payments.[105] Generating excessively large U.S. tax deductions in this manner is known as "earnings stripping."

Although the term "earnings stripping" may be broadly applied to the generation of excessive deductions for interest, rents, royalties, premiums, management fees, and similar types of payments in the circumstances described above, more commonly it refers only to the generation of excessive interest deductions. In general, earnings stripping provides a net tax benefit only to the extent that the foreign recipient of the interest income is subject to a lower amount of foreign tax on such income than the net value of the U.S. tax deduction applicable to the interest, i.e., the amount of U.S. deduction times the applicable U.S. tax rate, less the U.S. withholding tax. That may be the case if the country of the interest recipient provides a low general corporate tax rate, a territorial system with respect to interest, or reduced taxes on financing structures.

Taxpayers are limited in their ability to reduce the U.S. tax on the income derived from their U.S. operations through certain earnings stripping transactions involving interest payments. If the payor's debt-to-equity ratio exceeds 1.5 to 1 (a debt-to-equity ratio of 1.5 to 1 or less is considered a "safe harbor"), a deduction for disqualified interest paid or accrued by the payor in a taxable year is generally disallowed to the extent of the payor's excess interest expense.[106] Disqualified interest includes interest paid or accrued to related parties when no Federal income tax is imposed with respect to such interest;[107] to unrelated parties in certain instances in which a related party guarantees the debt ("guaranteed debt"); or to a REIT by a taxable REIT subsidiary of that REIT. Excess interest expense is the amount by which the payor's net interest expense (that is, the excess of interest paid or accrued over interest income) exceeds 50 percent of its adjusted taxable income (generally taxable income computed without regard to deductions for net interest expense, net operating losses, domestic production activities under section 199, depreciation, amortization, and depletion). Interest amounts disallowed under these rules can be carried forward indefinitely and are allowed as a deduction to the extent of excess limitation in a subsequent tax year. In addition, any excess limitation (that is, the excess, if any, of 50 percent of the adjusted taxable income of the payor over the payor's net interest expense) can be carried forward three years.

C. U.S. Tax Rules Applicable to Foreign Activities of U.S. Persons (Outbound)

1. In general

The United States has a worldwide tax system under which U.S. citizens, resident individuals, and domestic corporations generally are taxed on all income, whether derived in the United States or abroad. The U.S. does not impose an income tax on foreign corporations on income earned from foreign operations, whether or not some or all its shareholders are U.S. persons. Income earned by a domestic parent corporation from foreign operations conducted by foreign corporate subsidiaries generally is subject to U.S. tax when the income is distributed as a dividend to the domestic parent corporation. Until that repatriation, the U.S. tax on the income generally is deferred. U.S. shareholders of foreign corporations are taxed by the U.S. when the foreign corporation distributes its earnings as dividends or when a U.S. shareholder sells it stock at a gain. Thus, the U.S. tax on foreign earnings of foreign corporations is "deferred" until distributed to a U.S. shareholder or a U.S. shareholder recognizes gain on its stock.

However, certain anti-deferral regimes may cause the domestic parent corporation to be taxed on a current basis in the United States on certain categories of passive or highly mobile income earned by its foreign corporate subsidiaries, regardless of whether the income has been distributed as a dividend to the domestic parent corporation. The main anti-deferral regimes in this context are the CFC rules of subpart F[108] and the PFIC rules.[109] A foreign tax credit generally is available to offset, in whole or in part, the U.S. tax owed on foreign-source income, whether the income is earned directly by the domestic corporation, repatriated as an actual dividend, or included in the domestic parent corporation's income under one of the anti-deferral regimes.[110]

2. Anti-deferral regimes

Subpart F

Subpart F,[111] applicable to CFCs and their shareholders, is the main anti-deferral regime of relevance to a U.S.-based multinational corporate group. A CFC generally is defined as any foreign corporation if U.S. persons own (directly, indirectly, or constructively) more than

50 percent of the corporation's stock (measured by vote or value), taking into account only those U.S. persons that own at least 10 percent of the stock (measured by vote only).[112] Under the subpart F rules, the United States generally taxes the 10-percent U.S. shareholders of a CFC on their pro rata shares of certain income of the CFC (referred to as "subpart F income"), without regard to whether the income is distributed to the shareholders.[113] In effect, the United States treats the 10-percent U.S. shareholders of a CFC as having received a current distribution of the corporation's subpart F income.

With exceptions described below, subpart F income generally includes passive income and other income that is readily movable from one taxing jurisdiction to another. Subpart F income consists of foreign base company income,[114] insurance income,[115] and certain income relating to international boycotts and other violations of public policy.[116]

Foreign base company income consists of foreign personal holding company income, which includes passive income such as dividends, interest, rents, and royalties, and a number of categories of income from business operations, including foreign base company sales income, foreign base company services income, and foreign base company oil-related income.[117]

Insurance income subject to current inclusion under the subpart F rules includes any income of a CFC attributable to the issuing or reinsuring of any insurance or annuity contract in connection with risks located in a country other than the CFC's country of organization. Subpart F insurance income also includes income attributable to an insurance contract in connection with risks located within the CFC's country of organization, as the result of an arrangement under which another corporation receives a substantially equal amount of consideration for insurance of other country risks.

In the case of insurance, a temporary exception from foreign personal holding company income applies for certain income of a qualifying insurance company with respect to risks located within the CFC's country of creation or organization. Temporary exceptions from insurance income and from foreign personal holding company income also apply for certain income of a qualifying branch of a qualifying insurance company with respect to risks located within the home country of the branch, provided certain requirements are met under each of the exceptions. Further, additional temporary exceptions from insurance income and from foreign personal holding company income apply for certain income of certain CFCs or branches with respect to risks located in a country other than the United States, provided that the requirements for these exceptions are met. In the case of a life insurance or annuity contract, reserves for such contracts are determined under rules specific to the temporary exceptions. Present law also permits a taxpayer in certain circumstances, subject to approval by the IRS through the ruling process or in published guidance, to establish that the reserve of a life insurance company for life insurance and annuity contracts is the amount taken into account in determining the foreign statement reserve for the contract (reduced by catastrophe, equalization, or deficiency reserve or any similar reserve). IRS approval is to be based on whether the method, the interest rate, the mortality and morbidity assumptions, and any other factors taken into account in determining foreign statement reserves (taken together or separately) provide an appropriate means of measuring income for Federal income tax purposes.

Special rules apply under subpart F with respect to related person insurance income.[118] Enacted in 1986, these rules address the concern that "the related person insurance income of many offshore 'captive' insurance companies avoided current taxation under the subpart F rules of prior law because, for example, the company's U.S. ownership was relatively dispersed."[119] For purposes of these rules, the U.S. ownership threshold for CFC status is reduced to 25 percent or more. Any U.S. person who owns or is considered to own any stock in a CFC, whatever the degree of ownership, is treated as a U.S. shareholder of such corporation for purposes of this 25- percent U.S. ownership threshold and exposed to current tax on the corporation's related person insurance income. Related person insurance income is defined for this purpose to mean any insurance income attributable to a policy of insurance or reinsurance with respect to which the primary insured is either a U.S. shareholder (within the meaning of the provision) in the foreign corporation receiving the income or a person related to such a shareholder.

Investments in U.S. property

The 10-percent U.S. shareholders of a CFC also are required to include currently in income for U.S. tax purposes their pro rata shares of the corporation's untaxed earnings invested in certain items of U.S. property.[120] This U.S. property generally includes tangible property located in the United States, stock of a U.S. corporation, an obligation of a U.S. person, and certain intangible assets, such as patents and copyrights, acquired or developed by the CFC for use in the United States.[121] There are specific exceptions to the general definition of U.S. property, including for bank deposits, certain export property, and certain trade or business obligations.[122] The inclusion rule for investment of earnings in U.S. property is intended to prevent taxpayers from avoiding U.S. tax on dividend repatriations by repatriating CFC earnings through non-dividend payments, such as loans to U.S. persons.

Subpart F exceptions

A provision colloquially referred to as the "CFC look-through" rule and applicable for taxable years beginning after 2005 and before 2014, excludes from foreign personal holding company income dividends, interest, rents, and royalties received or accrued by one CFC from a related CFC (with relation based on control) to the extent attributable or properly allocable to non-subpart-F income of the payor.[123] The exclusion has been extended most recently to apply for taxable years of the foreign corporation beginning before 2014.[124]

There is also an exclusion from subpart F income for certain income of a CFC that is derived in the active conduct of banking or financing business ("active financing income").[125] The exception from subpart F for active financing income now applies to taxable years of foreign corporations starting before January 1, 2014 (and to taxable years of 10-percent U.S. shareholders with or within which those corporate taxable years end). With respect to income derived in the active conduct of a banking, financing, or similar business, a CFC is required to be predominantly engaged in such business and to conduct substantial activity with respect to such business in order to qualify for the active financing exceptions. In addition, certain nexus requirements apply, which provide that income derived by a CFC or a qualified business unit ("QBU") of a CFC from transactions with customers is eligible for the exceptions if, among other things, substantially all of the activities in connection with such transactions are conducted directly by the CFC or QBU in its home country, and such income is treated as earned by the CFC or QBU in its home country for purposes of such country's tax laws. Moreover, the exceptions apply to income derived from certain cross border transactions, provided that certain requirements are met.

In the case of a securities dealer, the temporary exception from foreign personal holding company income applies to certain income. The income covered by the exception is any interest or dividend (or certain equivalent amounts) from any transaction, including a hedging transaction or a transaction consisting of a deposit of collateral or margin, entered into in the ordinary course of the dealer's trade or business as a dealer in securities within the meaning of section 475. In the case of a QBU of the dealer, the income is required to be attributable to activities of the QBU in the country of incorporation, or to a QBU in the country in which the QBU both maintains its principal office and conducts substantial business activity. A coordination rule provides that this exception generally takes precedence over the exception for income of a banking, financing or similar business, in the case of a securities dealer.

Income is treated as active financing income only if, among other requirements, it is derived by a CFC or by a qualified business unit of that CFC. Certain activities conducted by persons related to the CFC or its qualified business unit are treated as conducted directly by the CFC or qualified business unit.[126] An activity qualifies under this rule if the activity is performed by employees of the related person and if the related person is an eligible CFC, the home country of which is the same as the home country of the related CFC or qualified business unit; the activity is performed in the home country of the related person; and the related person receives arm's-length compensation that is treated as earned in the home country. Income from an activity qualifying under this rule is excepted from subpart F income so long as the other active financing requirements are satisfied.

Other exclusions from foreign personal holding company income include exceptions for dividends and interest received by a CFC from a related corporation organized and operating in the same foreign country in which the CFC is organized and for rents and royalties received by a CFC from a related corporation for the use of property within the country in which the CFC is organized.[127] These exclusions do not apply to the extent the payments reduce the subpart F income of the payor. There is an exception from foreign base company income and insurance income for any item of income received by a CFC if the taxpayer establishes that the income was subject to an effective foreign income tax rate greater than 90 percent of the maximum U.S. corporate income tax rate (that is, more than 90 percent of 35 percent, or 31.5 percent).[128]

Exclusion of previously taxed earnings and profits

A 10-percent U.S. shareholder of a CFC may exclude from its income actual distributions of earnings and profits from the CFC that were previously included in the 10-percent U.S. shareholder's income under subpart F.[129] Any income inclusion (under section 956) resulting from investments in U.S. property may also be excluded from the 10-percent U.S. shareholder's income when such earnings are ultimately distributed.[130] Ordering rules provide that distributions from a CFC are treated as coming first out of earnings and profits of the CFC that have been previously taxed under subpart F, then out of other earnings and profits.[131]

Basis adjustments

In general, a 10-percent U.S. shareholder of a CFC receives a basis increase with respect to its stock in the CFC equal to the amount of the CFC's earnings that are included in the 10-percent U.S. shareholder's income under subpart F.[132] Similarly, a 10-percent U.S. shareholder of a CFC generally reduces its basis in the CFC's stock in an amount equal to any distributions that the 10-percent U.S. shareholder receives from the CFC that are excluded from its income as previously taxed under subpart F.[133]

Passive foreign investment companies

The Tax Reform Act of 1986[134] established the PFIC anti-deferral regime. A PFIC is generally defined as any foreign corporation if 75 percent or more of its gross income for the taxable year consists of passive income, or 50 percent or more of its assets consists of assets that produce, or are held for the production of, passive income.[135] Alternative sets of income inclusion rules apply to U.S. persons that are shareholders in a PFIC, regardless of their percentage ownership in the company. One set of rules applies to PFICs that are qualified electing funds, under which electing U.S. shareholders currently include in gross income their respective shares of the company's earnings, with a separate election to defer payment of tax, subject to an interest charge, on income not currently received.[136] A second set of rules applies to PFICs that are not qualified electing funds, under which U.S. shareholders pay tax on certain income or gain realized through the company, plus an interest charge that is attributable to the value of deferral.[137] A third set of rules applies to PFIC stock that is marketable, under which electing U.S. shareholders currently take into account as income (or loss) the difference between the fair market value of the stock as of the close of the taxable year and their adjusted basis in such stock (subject to certain limitations), often referred to as "marking to market."[138]

Other anti-deferral rules

The subpart F and PFIC rules are not the only anti-deferral regimes. Other rules that impose current U.S. taxation on income earned through corporations include the accumulated earnings tax rules[139] and the personal holding company rules.[140] Until the enactment of AJCA, the Code included two other sets of anti-deferral rules, those applicable to foreign personal holding companies and those for foreign investment companies.[141] Because the overlap among the various anti-deferral regimes was seen as creating complexity, often with no ultimate tax consequences, AJCA repealed the foreign personal holding company and foreign investment company rules.[142]

Rules for coordination among the anti-deferral regimes are provided to prevent U.S. persons from being subject to U.S. tax on the same item of income under multiple regimes. For example, a corporation generally is not treated as a PFIC with respect to a particular shareholder if the corporation is also a CFC and the shareholder is a 10-percent U.S. shareholder. Thus, subpart F is allowed to trump the PFIC rules.

3. Foreign tax credit

Subject to certain limitations, U.S. citizens, resident individuals, and domestic corporations are allowed to claim credit for foreign income taxes they pay. A domestic corporation that owns at least 10 percent of the voting stock of a foreign corporation is allowed a "deemed-paid" credit for foreign income taxes paid by the foreign corporation that the domestic corporation is deemed to have paid when the related income is distributed as a dividend or is included in the domestic corporation's income under the anti-deferral rules.[143]

The foreign tax credit generally is limited to a taxpayer's U.S. tax liability on its foreign-source taxable income (as determined under U.S. tax accounting principles). This limit is intended to ensure that the credit serves its purpose of mitigating double taxation of foreign-source income without offsetting U.S. tax on U.S.-source income.[144] The limit is computed by multiplying a taxpayer's total U.S. tax liability for the year by the ratio of the taxpayer's foreign- source taxable income for the year to the taxpayer's total taxable income for the year. If the total amount of foreign income taxes paid and deemed paid for the year exceeds the taxpayer's foreign tax credit limitation for the year, the taxpayer may carry back the excess foreign taxes to the previous year or carry forward the excess taxes to one of the succeeding 10 years.[145]

The computation of the foreign tax credit limitation requires a taxpayer to determine the amount of its taxable income from foreign sources in each limitation category (described below) by allocating and apportioning deductions between U.S.-source gross income, on the one hand, and foreign-source gross income in each limitation category, on the other. In general, deductions are allocated and apportioned to the gross income to which the deductions factually relate.[146] However, subject to certain exceptions, deductions for interest expense and research and experimental expenses are apportioned based on taxpayer ratios.[147] In the case of interest expense, this ratio is the ratio of the corporation's foreign or domestic (as applicable) assets to its worldwide assets. In the case of research and experimental expenses, the apportionment ratio is based on either sales or gross income. All members of an affiliated group of corporations generally are treated as a single corporation for purposes of determining the apportionment ratios.[148]

The term "affiliated group" is determined generally by reference to the rules for determining whether corporations are eligible to file consolidated returns.[149] These rules exclude foreign corporations from an affiliated group.[150] AJCA modified the interest expense allocation rules for taxable years beginning after December 31, 2008.[151] The effective date of the modified rules has been delayed to January 1, 2021.[152] The new rules permit a U.S. affiliated group to apportion the interest expense of the members of the U.S. affiliated group on a worldwide-group basis (that is, as if all domestic and foreign affiliates are a single corporation). A result of this rule is that interest expense of foreign members of a U.S. affiliated group is taken into account in determining whether a portion of the interest expense of the domestic members of the group must be allocated to foreign-source income. An allocation to foreign-source income generally is required only if, in broad terms, the domestic members of the group are more highly leveraged than is the entire worldwide group. The new rules are generally expected to reduce the amount of the U.S. group's interest expense that is allocated to foreign-source income.

The foreign tax credit limitation is applied separately to passive category income and to general category income.[153] Passive category income includes passive income, such as portfolio interest and dividend income, and certain specified types of income. General category income includes all other income. Passive income is treated as general category income if it is earned by a qualifying financial services entity. Passive income is also treated as general category income if it is highly taxed (that is, if the foreign tax rate is determined to exceed the highest rate of tax specified in Code section 1 or 11, as applicable). Dividends (and subpart F inclusions), interest, rents, and royalties received by a 10-percent U.S. shareholder from a CFC are assigned to a separate limitation category by reference to the category of income out of which the dividends or other payments were made.[154] Dividends received by a 10-percent corporate shareholder of a foreign corporation that is not a CFC are also categorized on a look-through basis.[155]

In addition to the foreign tax credit limitation just described, a taxpayer's ability to claim a foreign tax credit may be further limited by a matching rule that prevents the separation of creditable foreign taxes from the associated foreign income. Under this rule, a foreign tax generally is not taken into account for U.S. tax purposes, and thus no foreign tax credit is available with respect to that foreign tax, until the taxable year in which the related income is taken into account for U.S. tax purposes.[156]

II. CURRENT POLICY CONCERNS RELATED TO THE TAXATION OF MULTINATIONAL CORPORATIONS

A. Promoting Domestic Investment and the Growth of Home-Country Multinationals

United States

Around the world, policymakers have been devoting significant attention to the design of tax rules that enhance the ability of home-country multinational firms to compete in the global economy. In the United States, this attention has produced a number of international tax reform proposals (described in Part IV of this document) that, despite having significant differences, are meant to address a set of common policy concerns.

Deferral and the choice between foreign and domestic investment

Some U.S. policymakers are concerned that the ability of U.S. corporations to defer U.S. tax on foreign earnings may discourage investment in the United States. As the following example illustrates, a U.S. corporation may prefer a foreign investment opportunity to a domestic investment opportunity if the returns on the domestic investment are subject to current taxation, even if both investments yield the same pre-tax rate of return.

Suppose that a U.S. taxpayer in the 35-percent tax bracket is considering whether to make an investment in an active enterprise in the United States or in an equivalent investment opportunity in a country in which the income tax rate is zero. Assume the U.S. taxpayer chooses to make the investment in the foreign country through a CFC that earns $100 of active income today, and the U.S. taxpayer defers tax on that income for five years by reinvesting the income in the CFC. Assume further that the CFC can invest the money and earn a 10-percent return per year, and the income earned is not subject to foreign tax or current U.S. taxation under subpart F. After five years, the taxpayer will have earned $161.05 of income and will pay tax of $56.37 on repatriation, for an after-tax income of $104.68.

If, instead, the U.S. taxpayer pursues the equivalent investment opportunity in the United States, income from such an investment will not be eligible for deferral. As a result, the taxpayer receives $100 in income today, pays tax of $35, and has only $65 to reinvest. The taxpayer invests that amount at an after-tax rate of 6.5 percent (this is a 10-percent pre-tax rate less 35 percent tax on the earnings each year). At the end of five years, this taxpayer has after-tax income of only $89.06, as compared to the foreign investment option which generates after-tax income of $104.68. The result is that the foreign investment option to defer tax on the income for five years leaves the taxpayer with $15.62 more in profits than the domestic investment option that requires the taxpayer to pay tax on the income immediately, even though the pre-tax rate of return (10 percent) is the same for both investments. As a result, the foreign investment is the preferred choice (all else being equal). In fact, the foreign investment in this example would be preferred even if it yielded a slightly lower pre-tax rate of return as the U.S. investment, which illustrates how deferral may lead companies to make less productive investment decisions.

However, some economic research suggests that, in the aggregate, deferral does not inefficiently subsidize foreign investment by U.S. companies.[157]

The "lockout effect"

Policymakers are also concerned that U.S. tax rules may create a "lockout effect," which is a colloquial reference to the possibility that the overseas earnings of U.S. corporations are being "locked out" and not reinvested in the United States because U.S. corporations prefer to defer payment of residual U.S. tax liability by not repatriating those earnings. This may occur because corporations can reduce the present value of their residual U.S. tax liability on overseas earnings by postponing repatriation of those earnings. This may also occur if corporations choose to make foreign investments, rather than domestic investments, because the ability to defer payment of residual U.S. tax liability on the returns to the foreign investments may make them more attractive on an after-tax basis, even if they yield the same pre-tax return as a domestic investment. The lockout effect disappears if repatriation of overseas earnings has no tax consequence, as would be the case if foreign earnings were exempt from U.S. tax or if those earnings were subject to current U.S. taxation.

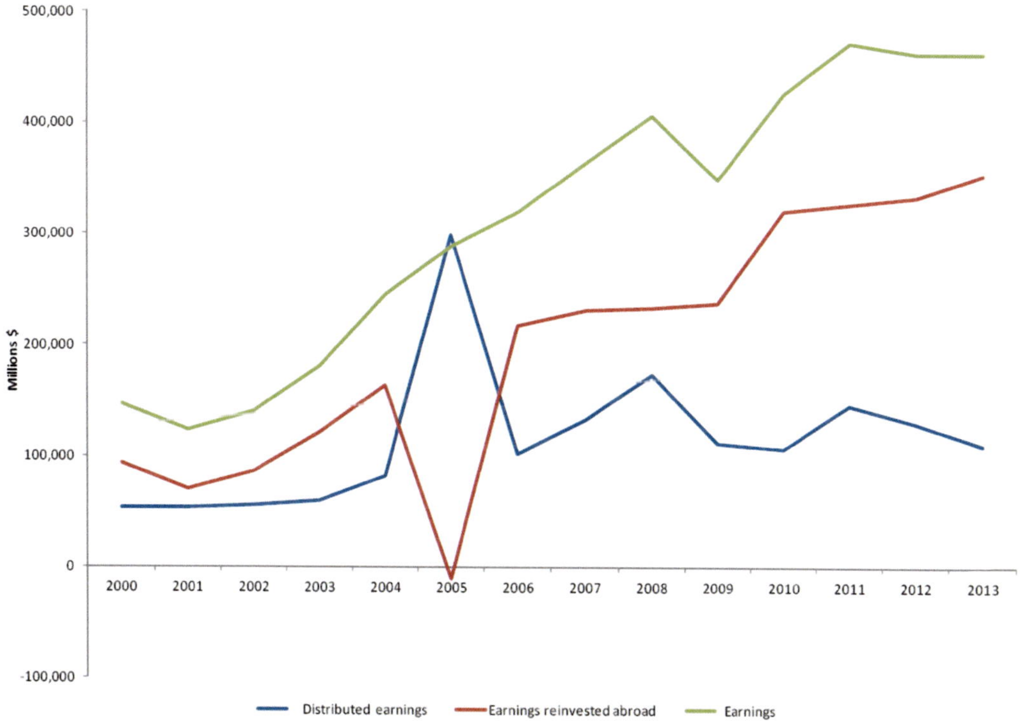

Source: Bureau of Economic Analysis.

Figure 1. Earnings from U.S. Direct Investment Abroad: 2000-2013.

Figure 1 illustrates the extent to which foreign earnings are being reinvested overseas. From 2000 to 2013, earnings from U.S. direct investment abroad grew from $151.8 billion to $470 billion, while the amount of those earnings that was reinvested overseas increased from $93.6 billion to $353.2 billion. The amount of earnings that was distributed rose from $52.9 billion in 2003 to $109 billion in 2013. Although a significant amount of foreign earnings was reinvested abroad and not distributed, that does not necessarily mean that the lockout effect is significant. Such reinvestment may be the most economically productive use of a corporation's funds if the pre-tax rate of return on its foreign investment exceeds the domestic investment opportunities available to it. Since most growth by U.S. multinational corporations is occurring in foreign markets, companies may be making productive investment decisions by reinvesting a large portion of their foreign earnings to support their expansion overseas.

However, a number of economists have found the burden of residual U.S. tax liability on repatriated earnings distorts a corporation's decision concerning how much to repatriate (and from which foreign subsidiaries), and that the economic cost of this distortion—which could cause U.S. corporations to incur more debt, or invest less in the United States, than they would if they had no residual U.S. tax liability on their foreign earnings—can be significant.[158] Some economists have found that the cost of this distortion increases as the accumulated stock of deferred income increases.[159] This may be of concern to policymakers because U.S. corporations defer paying taxes on a large portion of their worldwide earnings each year.[160] As Figure 2 shows, the amount of earnings on which U.S. tax liability has been deferred, as a percentage of the worldwide earnings of U.S. corporations, grew from 12 percent to 27.1 percent from 2000 to 2010.[161]

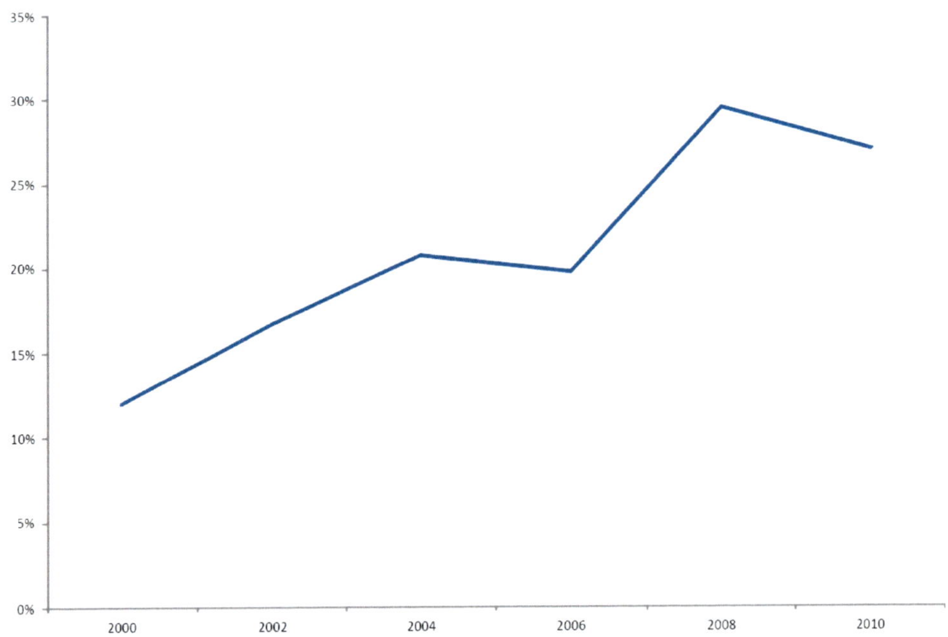

Source: Statistics of Income Division, IRS, and JCT staff calculations.

Figure 2. Deferral as a Share of U.S. Corporate Worldwide Income: 2000-2010.

Competition with foreign corporations

Although eliminating deferral and taxing the returns on foreign investment on a current basis would remove the tax distortion to the repatriation decisions of U.S. corporations, it would not address another concern that some policymakers have, which is that U.S. companies may not be able to compete effectively in foreign local markets with foreign companies who pay limited or no residual home-country tax on their overseas investments. This particular concern has grown over time as more countries have adopted some form of a territorial tax system: Of the 34 countries that make up the OECD, 28 have some form of a territorial tax system (compared to 13 at the start of 2000).

The competitive disadvantage that U.S. corporations may face could arise because their ability to grow in foreign local markets, relative to competing foreign corporations, may be more limited. For example, consider a U.S. corporation and foreign corporation that both require an after-tax rate of return of 10 percent on the investments they pursue in a given foreign local market with a tax rate of 20 percent. If the earnings of the foreign corporation are exempt from home-country tax, this means that it will pursue investment options that yield a required pre-tax rate of return of 12.5 percent. However, the U.S. corporation's required pre-tax rate of return may be greater than 12.5 percent, even though it can defer paying residual U.S. tax on its earnings, because it cannot reduce the present value of its U.S. residual tax liability below zero in the absence of cross-crediting.[162] Therefore, the U.S. corporation may forgo investments—such as expansion of its manufacturing facilities or acquisitions of local companies—that it would pursue if its returns were not subject to U.S. taxation. This may make it more difficult for the U.S. corporation to gain market share relative to the foreign corporation, and have an indirect, negative effect on employment and economic growth in the United States to the extent that a U.S. company's success overseas translates into increased domestic investment and sales. However, if the U.S. corporation is able to fully offset the residual U.S. tax liability on its earnings with credits allowed for income taxes paid in another jurisdiction, it would not be at a competitive tax disadvantage relative to the foreign corporation. Moreover, the ability of a U.S. corporation to defer paying residual U.S. tax on its earnings may limit its competitive tax disadvantage because its cash flow would not be immediately reduced by its U.S. tax liability.

Rest of the world

Decline in tax rates in the OECD

Over the past several years, a number of OECD countries have lowered their statutory corporate tax rates (sometimes accompanied by broadening of the corporate tax base or an increase in consumption taxes) and, as described earlier, have adopted systems that exempt active foreign income from home-country taxation. Although these developments have occurred for a variety of reasons, they may reflect strategic international competition over tax rates as countries attempt to support the growth of home-country multinationals and attract investment.[163]

The gradual decline in rates is illustrated in Table 1, which details the top combined statutory corporate income tax rates in the OECD from 2004 to 2014 and reflects tax rates set by central governments as well as sub-central governments.

Table 1. Top Combined Statutory Corporate Income Tax Rates in the OECD (Central and Sub-Central Governments): 2004-2014

	2004	2005	2006	2007	2008	2009	2010	2011	2012	2013	2014
Australia	30.0	30.0	30.0	30.0	30.0	30.0	30.0	30.0	30.0	30.0	30.0
Austria	34.0	25.0	25.0	25.0	25.0	25.0	25.0	25.0	25.0	25.0	25.0
Belgium	34.0	34.0	34.0	34.0	34.0	34.0	34.0	34.0	34.0	34.0	34.0
Canada	34.4	34.2	33.9	34.0	31.4	31.0	29.4	27.6	26.1	26.3	26.3
Chile	17.0	17.0	17.0	17.0	17.0	17.0	17.0	20.0	20.0	20.0	20.0
Czech Republic	28.0	26.0	24.0	24.0	21.0	20.0	19.0	19.0	19.0	19.0	19.0
Denmark	30.0	28.0	28.0	25.0	25.0	25.0	25.0	25.0	25.0	25.0	24.5
Estonia	26.0	24.0	23.0	22.0	21.0	21.0	21.0	21.0	21.0	21.0	21.0
Finland	29.0	26.0	26.0	26.0	26.0	26.0	26.0	26.0	24.5	24.5	20.0
France	35.4	35.0	34.4	34.4	34.4	34.4	34.4	34.4	34.4	34.4	34.4
Germany	38.9	38.9	38.9	38.9	30.2	30.2	30.2	30.2	30.2	30.2	30.2
Greece	35.0	32.0	29.0	25.0	25.0	25.0	24.0	20.0	20.0	26.0	26.0
Hungary	16.0	16.0	17.3	20.0	20.0	20.0	19.0	19.0	19.0	19.0	19.0
Iceland	18.0	18.0	18.0	18.0	15.0	15.0	18.0	20.0	20.0	20.0	20.0
Ireland	**12.5**	**12.5**	**12.5**	**12.5**	**12.5**	**12.5**	**12.5**	**12.5**	**12.5**	**12.5**	**12.5**
Israel	35.0	34.0	31.0	29.0	27.0	26.0	25.0	24.0	25.0	25.0	26.5
Italy	33.0	33.0	33.0	33.0	27.5	27.5	27.5	27.5	27.5	27.5	27.5
Japan	**39.5**	**39.5**	**39.5**	**39.5**	**39.5**	**39.5**	**39.5**	**39.5**	**39.5**	37.0	37.0
Korea	29.7	27.5	27.5	27.5	27.5	24.2	24.2	24.2	24.2	24.2	24.2
Luxembourg	30.4	30.4	29.6	29.6	29.6	28.6	28.6	28.8	28.8	29.2	29.2
Mexico	33.0	30.0	29.0	28.0	28.0	28.0	30.0	30.0	30.0	30.0	30.0
Netherlands	34.5	31.5	29.6	25.5	25.5	25.5	25.5	25.0	25.0	25.0	25.0
New Zealand	33.0	33.0	33.0	33.0	30.0	30.0	30.0	28.0	28.0	28.0	28.0
Norway	28.0	28.0	28.0	28.0	28.0	28.0	28.0	28.0	28.0	28.0	27.0
Poland	19.0	19.0	19.0	19.0	19.0	19.0	19.0	19.0	19.0	19.0	19.0
Portugal	27.5	27.5	27.5	26.5	26.5	26.5	26.5	28.5	31.5	31.5	31.5
Slovak Republic	19.0	19.0	19.0	19.0	19.0	19.0	19.0	19.0	19.0	23.0	22.0
Slovenia	25.0	25.0	25.0	23.0	22.0	21.0	20.0	20.0	20.0	17.0	17.0
Spain	35.0	35.0	35.0	32.5	30.0	30.0	30.0	30.0	30.0	30.0	30.0
Sweden	28.0	28.0	28.0	28.0	28.0	26.3	26.3	26.3	26.3	22.0	22.0
Switzerland	24.1	21.3	21.3	21.3	21.2	21.2	21.2	21.2	21.2	21.1	21.1
Turkey	33.0	30.0	20.0	20.0	20.0	20.0	20.0	20.0	20.0	20.0	20.0
United Kingdom	30.0	30.0	30.0	30.0	28.0	28.0	28.0	26.0	24.0	23.0	21.0
United States	39.3	39.3	39.3	39.3	39.3	39.1	39.2	39.2	39.1	**39.1**	**39.1**
OECD Median	30.0	29.0	28.0	27.0	26.8	26.0	25.8	25.5	25.0	25.0	25.0

Source: OECD Tax Database.

For each year, the cell corresponding to the country with the highest tax rate is shaded red, while the cell associated with the country with the lowest tax rate is shaded blue. From 2004 to 2014, the median combined statutory corporate income tax rate fell from 30 percent to 25 percent. As the table shows, the United States currently has the highest combined statutory corporate income tax rate (39.1 percent) among OECD countries, while Ireland has the lowest (12.5 percent). It is difficult to compare corporate income tax burdens across countries using data on top statutory tax rates alone. For example, countries may have different cost recovery systems and offer different tax incentives. However, to the extent that statutory tax rates are correlated with effective tax rates that take into account the base on which corporate income is being taxed, a comparison of statutory tax rates may provide information on relative tax burdens across countries. In fact, a number of studies have shown that the location of foreign direct investment is sensitive to statutory corporate income tax rates as well as effective tax rates.[164]

"Patent box" regimes

A number of countries have enacted "patent box" regimes under which income attributable to intellectual property is taxed at a lower, preferential rate. Policymakers have adopted patent boxes to (1) increase domestic investment in research and development and (2) encourage companies to locate intellectual property in their countries, among other goals. Some of these regimes are described in Part III of this document.

Patent boxes may promote domestic investment in research and development by lowering the tax burden on the returns to intellectual property, thereby increasing the after-tax returns to research and development activities. However, some of the patent box regimes adopted by countries do not require that the intellectual property benefiting from the patent box be the product of research and development undertaken in that country. As a result, the benefits of the patent box are not targeted to domestic investment in research and development, which limits the effectiveness of the patent box at promoting this type of investment.

Policymakers have also pursued patent boxes under the premise that the location where intellectual property is held also influences where companies make investments related to the intellectual property. For example, it may be the case that scientists who are making further developments to a piece of intellectual property are best located where the intellectual property is being held. Although there are a number of studies showing that innovation is spatially concentrated—research and development activities can cluster in particular geographic areas— there are few studies that examine whether investments related to a particular piece of intellectual property are also concentrated where its rights are being held.[165]

Given the lack of conclusive research supporting arguments that patent boxes have real economic effects, some policymakers are concerned that the economic benefits of these regimes may not outweigh possible reductions in tax revenue. For example, one study found that while patent box regimes are likely to attract patent-related income, they may lead to significant decreases in tax revenue.[166]

B. Addressing Difficulties with Taxing Corporations Engaged in Cross-Border Activities

United States

At the same time that U.S. policymakers are contemplating ways to make international tax rules more favorable to the growth of U.S. multinational corporations, they have also needed to address challenges associated with taxing corporations engaged in cross-border activities and their ability to shift income to low-tax jurisdictions.[167] Some of these challenges have been highlighted in recent hearings held by the U.S. Senate Permanent Subcommittee on Investigations on the cross-border tax planning techniques employed by U.S. corporations to manage their U.S. tax liability.[168] The Subcommittee's hearing on Apple, for example, showed how it was able to locate $74 billion of worldwide sales income in Ireland (at a negotiated tax rate below two percent) from 2009 to 2012 on intellectual property produced in the United States under cost-sharing arrangements with its Irish CFCs.[169]

Rest of the world

Policymakers outside the United States have shared similar concerns related to the difficulty of taxing corporations engaged in cross-border activities. At the Group of 20 ("G20") Leaders Summit in Mexico in June 2012, world leaders expressed the "need to prevent base erosion and profit shifting" and voiced support for the work being done in that area by the OECD.[170] At the request of the G20 Finance Ministers, the OECD issued an Action Plan on Base Erosion and Profit Shifting ("BEPS"), described in Part III of this document, that seeks to address the problem of double non-taxation on a multilateral basis.

Empirical studies

The taxation of income attributable to intangible property is a particularly difficult area for policymakers. A number of studies have shown that the location of intangible property—and the income derived from their exploitation—is highly sensitive to tax rates.[171] Some economists have found that income derived from intangible property accounts for a significant share of the income shifted from high-tax to low-tax jurisdictions by U.S. corporations.[172] One study found that income shifting, driven in large part by locating the ownership of intangible property in low- tax jurisdictions, can generate significant reductions in U.S. tax revenue.[173]

III. Recent Global Activity Related to the Taxation of Cross-Border Income

A. OECD Base Erosion and Profit Shifting Initiative

The following sections provide an overview of the OECD base erosion and profit shifting initiative. It includes a summary of reports published by the OECD as part of this initiative, including a summary of the 15 action items identified for further work by the OECD. Additionally, this section provides a summary of the discussion drafts released by the OECD related to four of the specific action items.

BEPS Report

In response to concerns raised by the G20, and the desire to provide an internationally coordinated approach, the OECD released a report on February 12, 2013, *Addressing Base Erosion and Profit Shifting*,[174] presenting an overview of data and global business models, and discussing some of the issues related to base erosion and profit shifting. The BEPS Report lists several key principles for the taxation of cross-border activities and the base erosion and profit shifting opportunities the principles may create.

Jurisdiction to tax

The right to tax is traditionally based on either the residence of the taxpayer or on activity or connection within a country. The treaty concept of permanent establishment refers not only to a substantial physical presence in the country, but also to a situation in which a non-resident carries on business through a dependent agent. According to the BEPS Report, "Nowadays it is possible to be heavily involved in the economic life of another country, *e.g.* by doing business with customers located in that country via the internet, without having a taxable presence therein (such as substantial physical presence or a dependent agent)."[175] The BEPS Report states that questions arise as to whether the current rules ensure a fair allocation of taxing right, especially where the profits from some transactions are not taxed anywhere.

Transfer pricing

The internationally accepted principle for establishing a fair price for transactions between related parties is the arm's-length principle. This requires that income is allocated between related parties as it would be if the transactions were carried on between third parties in the same or similar circumstances. According to the BEPS Report, "One of the underlying assumptions of the arm's length principle is that the more extensive the functions/assets/risks of one party to the transaction, the greater its expected remuneration will be and *vice versa*. This therefore creates an incentive to shift functions/assets/risks to where their returns are taxed more favorably."[176]

Leverage

Most countries have laws that distinguish between debt and equity for tax and other purposes. Interest payments on debt are generally deductible for tax purposes while dividend payments are generally not tax deductible. With respect to the income recipient, most countries require inclusion of interest income in the taxable base, whereas dividend income is excluded from taxable income in many jurisdictions. According to the BEPS Report, "This unsurprisingly may lead to a tax-induced bias toward debt finance as well as to attempts to characterise particular payments as deductible interest in the payer's jurisdiction and as dividends (that may not be taxed) in the jurisdiction of the recipient."[177]

Anti-avoidance

According to the BEPS Report, countries use a variety of anti-avoidance strategies to ensure fairness and effectiveness of their corporate tax system. These strategies include statutory general anti-avoidance rules, judicial doctrines limiting or denying the availability of undue tax benefits, CFC rules, thin-capitalization rules or other rules limiting interest deductions, anti- hybrid rules linking the domestic tax treatment with the tax treatment in the foreign country, and anti base-erosion rules imposing higher withholding taxes, or denying the deductibility of certain payments. A variety of strategies are used to avoid the application of anti-avoidance rules, including channeling the financing through an independent third party to avoid thin-capitalization rules, inversions, or the use of hybrid entities to make income "disappear" for purposes of avoiding application of the CFC rules.[178]

Conclusion

The BEPS Report concludes that it is often the interaction of various principles and practices of more than one taxing jurisdiction that allows base erosion and profit shifting to occur. For example, "[t]he interaction of withholding tax rules in one country, the territorial taxation system in another country, and the entity characterisation rules in a third country may combine to make it possible for certain transactions to occur in a way that gives rise to no current tax and have the effect of shifting income to a jurisdiction where, for various reasons, no tax is imposed."[179] The BEPS Report calls for a comprehensive action plan to provide countries with instruments for use which aim at a better alignment of taxing rights with economic activity.

BEPS Action Plan

On May 29, 2013, following the release of the BEPS Report, the 2013 Ministerial Council adopted its *Declaration on Base Erosion and Profit Shifting*.[180] The declaration recognized the need for national authorities to collaborate in addressing the issues and developing potential solutions to address the challenges raised by BEPS. In response, the OECD released its *Action Plan on Base Erosion and Profit Shifting* on July 19, 2013.[181] The BEPS Action Plan notes that pace of globalization and the integration of national economies and markets has substantially increased in recent years. Multinational enterprises represent a large proportion of the global economy and intra-firm trade represents a growing proportion of overall trade. The interaction of differing domestic tax rules in some cases leads to gaps and frictions, including potential double taxation and cases where income is not taxed at all. According to the BEPS Action Plan, one concern of the increase in base erosion and profit shifting is that the existing consensus-based international tax framework is at risk as governments seek to protect the corporate tax revenue base by replacing the current consensus-based framework by unilateral measures, possibly resulting in a re-emergence of double taxation. The BEPS Action Plan reiterates the need for new international standards and sets out 15 action items and a timeline for completion of the action items.

Action 1. Address the tax challenges of the digital economy

The BEPS Action Plan calls for a dedicated task force on the digital economy to analyze the business models, the business landscape, and to better understand the generation of value in the digital sector. Action 1 will identify the main difficulties that the digital economy poses for the application of existing international tax rules and develop detailed options to address these difficulties. The expected output for Action 1 is a report identifying issues raised by the digital economy and possible actions to address them to be delivered by September 2014. The OECD issued a public discussion draft on March 24, 2014 requesting comments no later than April 14, 2014.[182] It published comments on April 16, 2014 and April 18, 2014.[183]

Action 2. Neutralise the effects of hybrid mismatch arrangements

The BEPS Action Plan states that hybrid mismatch arrangements may be used to create double non-taxation or long-term deferral. It provides examples such as creating two deductions for a single borrowing, generating tax deductions without corresponding income inclusions, or misusing foreign tax credit or participation exemption regimes. Rules that allow taxpayers to choose the tax treatment may facilitate hybrid mismatch arrangements. The plan calls for development of model treaty provisions and recommendations regarding the design of domestic rules to neutralise the effect (*e.g.* double non-taxation, double deduction, long-term deferral) of hybrid instruments and entities. The expected output for Action 2 includes changes to the OECD Model Tax Convention and recommendations regarding the design of domestic hybrid rules, to be delivered by September 2014. The OECD issued a public discussion draft on the recommendation for domestic laws on March 19, 2014 requesting comments no later than May 2, 2014.[184] It published comments on May 7, 2014.[185]

Action 3. Strengthen CFC rules

The BEPS Action Plan recognizes that although CFC rules primarily lead to inclusions of income in the residence country, they may have positive spillover effects in source countries as the incentive to shift profits into third, low-tax jurisdictions is reduced. Action 3 calls for developing recommendations regarding the design of CFC rules. The work on CFC rules will be coordinated with other work as necessary. The deadline for these recommendations is September 2015.

Action 4. Limit base erosion via interest deductions and other financial payments

The deductibility of interest expense may have implications for both inbound and outbound investments. Inbound investors may use related parties in low-tax jurisdictions to create excessive interest deductions for the borrower without a corresponding interest income inclusion by the lender. Outbound investors may use debt to finance the production of exempt or deferred income. Action 4 provides that recommendations be developed regarding best practices in the design of rules to prevent base erosion through the use of interest expense. The work will evaluate the effectiveness of different types of limitations as well as providing transfer pricing guidance regarding the pricing of related party financial transactions. Recommendations regarding the design of domestic rules are expected to be completed by September 2015. The changes to the transfer pricing guidelines is targeted for a December 2015 deadline.

Action 5. Counter harmful tax practices more effectively, taking into account transparency and substance

The OECD issued a report in 1998 on harmful tax practices.[186] The BEPS Action Plan acknowledges that the policy concerns related to the mobile tax base and the "race to the bottom" is as much of a concern today as they were 15 years ago. Action 5 calls for the work on harmful tax practice to be revamped with a priority on improving transparency and on requiring substantial activity for any preferential regime. The plan contemplates a review of member country regimes to be conducted by September 2014, a strategy to expand participation to non- OECD members by September 2015, and a revision of existing criteria by December 2015.

Action 6. Prevent treaty abuse[187]

The BEPS Action Plan suggests that treaty rules be modified to address the interposition of third county entities in the bilateral framework of treaty partners. The plan calls for development of model treaty provisions and recommendations for the design of domestic rules to prevent treaty benefits in inappropriate circumstances. These actions are scheduled to be completed by September 2014. The OECD issued a public discussion draft on March 14, 2014 requesting comments no later than April 9, 2014.[188] It published comments on April 11, 2014.[189]

Action 7. Prevent the artificial avoidance of permanent establishment ("PE") status

The BEPS Action plan states that the interpretation of treaty rules on agency-PE allows arrangements such as "commissionaire arrangements" which result in a shifting of profits out of the country where the sales take place or arrangements by the multinational enterprise to artificially fragments their operations to qualify for the "preparatory and ancillary activities" exceptions to PE status. The plan calls for development of changes to the definition of PE to prevent the artificial avoidance of PE status in relation to base erosion and profit shifting. Changes to the OECD Model Tax Convention are targeted for September 2015.

Action 8. Assure that transfer pricing outcomes are in line with value creation: intangibles

According to the BEPS Action Plan, in many cases, the existing transfer pricing rules, based on the arm's-length principle, effectively and efficiently allocate the income of multinational enterprises among taxing jurisdictions; however, in other circumstances, multinational enterprises are able to use and/or misapply the rules to separate income from the economic activity producing the income. The BEPS Action plan includes several action items (action items 8, 9, and 10) to ensure that transfer pricing outcomes are in line with value creation (*i.e.*, the allocation of profit aligns with the activities that create value). Action 8 calls for developing rules to prevent base erosion and profit shifting resulting from the transfer of intangibles among group members. This includes adopting a broad and clearly delineated definition of intangibles; ensuring that profits associated with the transfer and use of intangibles are appropriately allocated in accordance with value creation; developing transfer pricing rules or special measures for transfers of hard-to-value intangibles; and updating the guidance on cost contribution arrangements. The output for Action 8 includes recommendations for changes to the OECD Transfer Pricing Guidelines and possibly to the OECD Model Tax Convention. These recommendations are scheduled for completion by September 2014.

Action 9. Assure that transfer pricing outcomes are in line with value creation: risks and capital

The plan calls for developing rules to prevent base erosion and profit shifting by transferring risks among, or allocating excessive capital to, group members. This includes adopting transfer pricing rules or special measures to ensure that inappropriate returns will not accrue to an entity solely because it has contractually assumed risks or has provided capital. The rules will require alignment of returns with value creation and the work will be coordinated with the work on interest expense deductions and other financial payments. Changes to the OECD Transfer Pricing Guidelines and possibly to the OECD Model Tax Convention are expected by September 2015.

Action 10. Assure that transfer pricing outcomes are in line with value creation: other high-risk transactions

The plan calls for developing rules to prevent base erosion and profit shifting by engaging in transactions which would not, or would only very rarely, occur between third parties. According to the BEPS Action plan, output on Action 10 could include adopting transfer pricing rules or special measures to clarify the circumstances in which transactions can be recharacterized; clarifying the application of transfer pricing methods, in particular profit splits, in the context of global value chains, and providing protection against common types of base eroding payments, such as management fees and head office expenses.

Action 11. Establish methodologies to collect and analyse data on base erosion and profit shifting and the actions to address it

While recognizing the progress on transparency made by the Global Forum on Transparency and Exchange of Information for Tax Purposes, the BEPS Action Plan states the need for more transparency on different fronts. Building on the BEPS Report's study of data indicating a disconnect between the location where value creating activities and investment take place and the location where tax profits are reported, the plan calls for developing recommendations regarding indicators of the scale and economic impact of base erosion and profit shifting and to ensure tools are available to monitor and evaluate the effectiveness and economic impact of the actions taken to address base erosion and profit shifting. Recommendations are expected by September 2015.

Action 12. Require taxpayers to disclose their aggressive tax planning arrangements

The BEPS Action plan highlights that tax audits are a key source of relevant information; however, they may not be the best tool for early detection of aggressive tax planning techniques. The plan calls for developing recommendations for the design of mandatory disclosure rules for aggressive or abusive transactions, arrangements, or structures. These recommendations should take into account the administrative costs for governments and businesses and should draw on experiences from a number of countries that have such rules in place. Recommendations regarding the design of domestic rules are due by September 2015.

Action 13. Re-examine transfer pricing documentation

The BEPS Action Plan notes that asymmetry of information between taxpayers and tax administrators is a key issue potentially undermining the administration of the arm's-length principle and enhancing opportunities for base erosion and profit shifting. The plan calls for developing transfer pricing documentation rules to enhance transparency for tax administrators while considering the compliance costs for business. The BEPS Action Plan specifies that the rules will include a requirement that multinational enterprises provide all relevant governments with needed information on their global allocation of the income, economic activity and taxes paid among countries in accordance with a common template. The changes to OECD Transfer Pricing Guidelines and recommendations regarding the design of domestic rules are due September 2014. The OECD released a discussion draft on transfer pricing documentation and country-by-country reporting on January 30, 2014 with comments due by February 23, 2014.[190] Comments on the discussion draft were released March 3, 2014.[191]

Action 14. Make dispute resolution mechanisms more effective

The BEPS Action Plan notes that the effectiveness of the mutual agreement procedure will be an important complement to the work on base erosion and profit shifting issues. The plan calls for developing solutions to address obstacles that prevent countries from solving treaty- related disputes under the mutual agreement procedure, including the absence of arbitration provisions. The plan calls for changes to the OECD Model Tax Convention to be completed by September 2015.

Action 15. Develop a multilateral instrument

The plan recognizes that there is a need to consider innovative ways to implement the measures resulting from the BEPS Action Plan. The plan requires analysis of the tax and public international law issues related to the development of a multilateral instrument for implementation of measures developed in the course of the OECD work on base erosion and profit shifting. On the basis of the analysis, interested parties will develop a multilateral instrument to provide an innovative approach to international tax matters. A report identifying the relevant public international law and tax issues is due for completion September 2015. The multilateral instrument will be completed December 2015.

OECD discussion drafts

Discussion drafts were issued by the OECD on several of the 15 action items listed in the BEPS Action Plan. These discussion drafts are briefly summarized below.

Action 1. Tax challenges of the digital economy

The discussion draft on the digital economy provides a description of some of the key features of the digital economy that are potentially relevant from a tax perspective. These features include mobility, reliance on "big data," network effects (the effect of user decisions on the benefit received by other users), use of multi-sided business models, tendency toward monopoly or oligopoly, and volatility. The draft provides some common features of tax planning structures which may contribute to base erosion and profit shifting including avoiding a taxable presence; minimizing functions, assets and risks in the market jurisdiction; and maximizing deductions in the market jurisdiction.

The draft states that the growth of the digital economy and the evolution of business models have resulted in operating models in market jurisdictions that are fundamentally different from the operating models that were in place when many of the international tax rules were designed. One example is the ability of a non-resident entity to sell into a jurisdiction without physical presence there. According to the draft, while this has always been possible, advances in digital technology have dramatically expanded the scale at which such activity is possible.

The draft also highlights potential options to address the tax challenges raised by the digital economy. The first three options address the concept of permanent establishment. One option modifies the exceptions from permanent establishment status provided in the OECD Model Tax Convention. For example, some of the activities included in the current OECD Model Tax Convention's exception for preparatory or auxiliary functions may constitute core functions of a business, and the task force will consider whether an exception from permanent establishment status for these activities should be available. The second option considers the establishment of an alternative test for nexus to address situations in which businesses are conducted wholly digitally. An entity engaged in certain "fully dematerialized digital activities" would have a permanent establishment if it maintains a "significant digital presence" in the economy of another country. The third option includes some broad alternatives, including a "virtual fixed place of business permanent establishment," which would create a permanent establishment when the enterprise maintains a website on a server of another enterprise and carries on a business through that website; extension of the existing dependent agent permanent establishment concept to a "virtual agency permanent establishment" where contracts are habitually concluded through technological means with persons located in the jurisdiction; and an "on-site business presence permanent establishment" which would look at the economic presence of an enterprise when the foreign enterprise provides on-site services or other business interface at the customer's location.

Other options include (1) imposing a final withholding tax on certain payments for digital goods or services provided by a foreign e-commerce provider, and (2) altering consumption tax rules where the rules result in no or an inappropriately low amount of value-added tax collection.

Action 2. Neutralise the effects of hybrid mismatch arrangements

The discussion draft defines a hybrid mismatch arrangement as "a profit shifting arrangement that utilises a hybrid element in the tax treatment of an entity or instrument to produce a mismatch in tax outcomes in respect of a payment that is made under that arrangement."[192] The draft only targets those instruments or entities that are hybrids for tax purposes. The draft specifies that the rules should target the mismatch rather than focus on establishing the jurisdiction in which the tax benefit arises. According to the draft, the rules, among other things, should be comprehensive, apply automatically, be coordinated to avoid double taxation, minimize disruption under existing domestic law, and be easily administered both by taxpayers and tax authorities.

The draft provides recommendations for domestic rules designed to neutralize the tax effects of three categories of hybrid mismatch arrangements. The first category includes hybrid financial instruments, where a deductible payment made under a financial instrument is not treated as taxable income under the laws of the payee's jurisdiction. The recommendations include denying a deduction for any payment made under a hybrid financial instrument to the extent that the payee does not include the payment as ordinary income under the laws of any jurisdiction; requiring payees to include any payment made under a hybrid financial instrument as ordinary income to the extent that the payer is entitled to claim a deduction for the payment (or equivalent tax relief) where the payer's jurisdiction does not apply a hybrid mismatch rule; and denying a dividend exemption to the extent that a dividend is a deductible payment.

The second category includes hybrid entity payments, where differences in the characterization of the hybrid payer results in a deductible payment in one jurisdiction and a disregarded payment or a second deduction in the other jurisdiction. Recommendations for this category include rules for double deduction structures (deductible hybrid payments) and for deduction/no inclusion structures (disregarded hybrid payments). The primary rule for the double deduction structures is to deny a deduction that arises in the investor jurisdiction to the extent it exceeds the taxpayer's dual-inclusion income for the same period. Any excess deduction can offset income in a subsequent period. The primary rule for a deduction/no inclusion structure is to limit the deduction granted by the payer jurisdiction such that it does not exceed a taxpayer's dual-inclusion income for the same period. For these purposes, an amount is dual-inclusion income in respect of a hybrid payment, if it is brought into account for tax purposes under the laws of both the subsidiary and the investor jurisdiction. An amount is dual- inclusion income in respect of a disregarded payment if it is taken into account for tax purposes under the laws of both the payer and the payee jurisdiction.

The third category includes reverse hybrid and imported mismatches, which cover payments made to an intermediary payee that are not taxable on receipt. The draft targets two kinds of arrangements, arrangements where differences in the characterization of the intermediary results in the payment being disregarded in both the intermediary jurisdiction and the investor's jurisdiction (reverse hybrid); and arrangements where the intermediary is a party to a separate hybrid mismatch arrangement and the payment is set-off against a deduction arising under that arrangement (imported mismatches). The draft's primary rule for these types of mismatch arrangements is for the investor jurisdiction to implement specific and targeted changes to its CFC or foreign investment fund rules, or to other areas of its domestic law, to tax on a current basis income of residents accrued through offshore investment structures. For payer jurisdictions, according to the draft, defensive rules should deny the deduction for a payment to an offshore non-inclusion structure (such as a reverse hybrid or imported mismatch arrangement) to the extent the payment results in a non-taxation outcome or is offset by an expenditure incurred under a hybrid mismatch arrangement and the taxpayer is part of the same controlled group as the parties to the mismatch or is a party to an avoidance arrangement.

Action 6. Prevent treaty abuse

The discussion draft on preventing treaty abuse distinguishes between cases where a person tries to circumvent limitations provided by the treaty itself and cases where a person tries to circumvent the provisions of domestic tax law using treaty benefits. The draft provides recommendations to address these intended circumventions of treaty limitations and domestic law.

Cases where a person tries to circumvent limitations provided by the treaty itself include treaty shopping. The draft recommends that tax treaties include in the title and preamble a clear statement that the treaty countries wish to prevent tax avoidance and its intent to avoid creating opportunities for treaty shopping. The draft also recommends that treaties include (1) a specific anti-abuse rule based on the limitation-on-benefits provisions included in recent United States treaties (without the "derivative benefits" test), and (2) a more general anti-abuse rule, incorporating principles reflected in the commentary to Article 1 of the OECD Model Income Tax Convention, limiting the benefits of a tax treaty where one of the main purposes of arrangements or transactions is to secure a benefit under the treaty and where obtaining the benefit would be contrary to the subject and purpose of the relevant provisions of the tax treaty.

Cases where a person tries to abuse the provisions of domestic tax law using treaty benefits include thin capitalization that use tax deductions to lower borrowing costs; dual-residence strategies; transfer mispricing; arbitrage transactions that take advantage of mismatches found in the domestic law of one state or both states related to the characterization of income, the treatment of taxpayers, or to timing differences; and transactions that abuse relief of double taxation mechanisms. Many of these cases will be addressed through the work on other aspects of the OECD Action Plan, and in current treaty practice. The discussion draft proposes treaty language to address some of these issues.[193]

Action 13. Transfer pricing documentation and country-by-country reporting

The discussion draft provides guidance for tax administrations to take into account in developing rules and/or procedures on transfer pricing documentation. It describes three objectives for transfer pricing documentation: 1) to provide tax administrations with the information necessary to conduct an informed transfer pricing risk assessment; 2) to ensure that taxpayers give appropriate consideration to transfer pricing requirements in establishing prices and other considerations for transactions between associated enterprises and in reporting income derived from such transactions in their tax returns; and 3) to provide tax administrations with the information that they require in order to conduct an appropriately thorough audit of the transfer pricing practices of entities subject to tax in their jurisdiction.

The draft recommends a two-tiered approach to transfer pricing documentation and encourages countries to adopt a standardized approach to documentation. The two tiers consist of a master file containing standardized information relevant for all multinational enterprise group members, and a local file referring specifically to material transactions of the local taxpayer. The master file would contain information in five categories: 1) the group's organizational structure; 2) a description of the business or businesses; 3) the group's intangibles; 4) the intercompany financial activities; and 5) the group's financial and tax positions. The master file section on the group's financial and tax positions would include country-by-country reporting of certain information relating to the allocation of profits, the taxes paid, and indicators of the location of economic activity (assets, employees, and total employee expense). The local file supplements the master file and helps to meet the objective of assuring that the taxpayer has complied with the arm's-length principle in its material transfer pricing positions affecting a specific jurisdiction. The draft report also includes recommendations on contemporaneous documentation, the timing of the preparation of documentation, materiality, document retention, frequency of documentation updates, language, penalties, confidentiality, and other issues. The draft suggests that the implementation of transfer pricing documentation requirements should continue to be features of local law.

B. Other Global Activity

Several countries have enacted legislation either to promote economic activity within their jurisdictions or to prevent base erosion and profit shifting. Two areas of activity may be of particular interest to the Committee and are discussed below. The first section discusses various favorable intellectual property regimes in several countries, and the second section discusses legislation to limit the benefits of using hybrid payments to facilitate base erosion and profit shifting.

Intellectual property or "patent box" regimes

A number of countries have enacted regimes providing low tax rates on profits derived from intellectual property. These countries include Belgium, France, Hungary, Luxembourg, the Netherlands, Spain and the United Kingdom. As discussed above, these regimes are intended to increase domestic investment in research and development and encourage companies to locate intellectual property within the country. Additionally regimes are intended to promote investment in new technology and provide incentives to encourage innovation. These regimes are briefly described below.[194]

The European Commission and the OECD are investigating whether certain of these regimes constitute harmful tax competition or facilitate base erosion and profit shifting. The European Commission launched its investigation to examine various patent box regimes on the grounds that these regimes may represent harmful tax competition. In a June 20, 2014 news conference, the European Taxation Commissioner, Algirdas Semeta, said, "Member states' tax incentives should never be used to lure profits away from where they should rightfully be taxed. We must verify that the principles of fair play are not being undermined. We will begin our assessment immediately and expand it further as member states clarify the criteria for certain elements. I remain hopeful that a full evaluation will be delivered by the end of this year."[195]

Belgium

Belgium introduced the "patent income deduction" in 2007, allowing a Belgian company or a Belgian permanent establishment to deduct 80 percent of qualifying gross patent income (an effective tax rate of 6.8 percent on qualifying income). The regime applies to qualifying patents and excludes rights such as know-how (unless closely associated with patents or supplementary protection certificates), trademarks, designs, models, secret recipes or process, and information concerning experience with respect to trade or science. The patent must have been developed either in whole or in part by the Belgian company or permanent establishment. In order for income from an acquired qualified patent to qualify for the regime, the Belgian company or permanent establishment must have further improved the patented products or processes. The research and development must have been completed by a research center owned by the Belgian legal entity, but not necessarily located in Belgium.

France

The French patent box regime was first introduced in 2000 and was amended in 2005 and 2010. France allows revenue or gain deriving from the license, sublicense, sale or transfer of qualified intellectual property to be taxed at 15 percent if it meets certain conditions. The regime applies to income from patents which have been granted in France, the United Kingdom, and by the European Patent Office or specified European countries. Other foreign patents are included if the invention would have been patentable in France. Intellectual property rights such as trademarks, design rights and copyrights are not included. To qualify, the intellectual property rights must be owned by the French company, or the French company must have full ownership of rights received under license agreements. License agreements can be exclusive or non- exclusive and can apply to all or a portion of the qualifying intellectual property. The regime does not include any restrictions on the location of research and development conducted for the development of intellectual property;

however, if a company acquires intellectual property rights, the company must own the rights for at least two years before income from these acquired rights qualify for the regime. Only royalty income and capital gains on the transfer or sale of the intellectual property are eligible for the regime (*i.e.*, embedded royalties are not included).

Hungary

Hungary allows a deduction of 50 percent of the royalties received (effective tax rate of 9.5 percent) from related or third parties for the use of intellectual property owned by the Hungarian company. The regime was enacted in 2003 and applies to royalties received for patents, know-how, trademarks, business names, business secrets and copyrights. It applies to developed and acquired intellectual property.

Luxembourg

Luxembourg provides an 80 percent tax exemption (resulting in an effective tax rate of 5.76 percent) for the net income derived from the use or right to use qualified intellectual property rights acquired or self-developed after December 31, 2007. The regime applies to patents, trademarks, designs, domain names, models and software copyrights. Know-how, copyrights not related to software, formulas and client lists do not qualify. The Luxembourg company must be the economic owner of the intellectual property rights, and the rights must give the company exclusive exploitation rights in the territory covered. Intellectual property acquired from a related company is not included in the regime. The property can be developed or acquired and there is no requirement that an acquired right is further developed by the Luxembourg company.

Netherlands

The Netherlands introduced a patent box regime in 2007 with a 10 percent tax rate. In 2010, the regime was expanded, the headline rate was reduced to five percent, and the regime's name was changed to "Innovation Box." The regime is available to Dutch resident companies and Dutch permanent establishments that are taxpayers in the Netherlands. The five-percent rate applies to the income from a qualifying intangible to the extent the income exceeds certain expenses, including related research and development and amortization expenses. The innovation box covers income from all worldwide patents, as well as from any intellectual property arising from research and development activities for which the taxpayer has obtained a declaration from the Dutch government. Trademarks, non-technical design rights and literary copyrights do not qualify. The Dutch company must be the economic owner of the intellectual property and bear the risks associated with that ownership. In order to qualify, the patent or intellectual property must be conducted at the risk of the Dutch company, but research activities can occur either in the Netherlands or elsewhere. For non-patented intellectual property, generally at least 50 percent of the research and development must be performed in the Netherlands and the Dutch company must play a key role in coordinating the development. In order to qualify for profits embedded in the sales prices of goods or services, more than 30 percent of the derived income must be attributable to the patent. Losses from qualified intangible property are deductible at the full corporate tax rate, but must be recovered in future years before the lower rate applies.

Spain

Spain adopted a patent box regime in 2007 that reduces the rate of corporate income tax on income derived from licensing the right to exploit intangible assets. The Entrepreneur Law[196] changed the patent box regime by extending the regime to transfers as well as licensing activity, computing the amount of intangible property income exempt from corporate income tax based on net income rather than gross revenues and eliminating the maximum amount income that may be exempted.[197] Instead of exempting 50 percent of the gross revenues from licensing qualified property, the exemption is now 60 percent of the net income derived from the license or transfer of the right to use qualifying intellectual property (an effective tax rate of 12 percent on qualifying income). Intellectual property rights included in the incentive regime include patents, drawings or models, plans, secret formulas or procedures, and rights on information related to industrial, commercial, or scientific experiments. The patent box regime does not distinguish between intellectual property income from foreign and domestic sources.

In order to qualify for the reduced tax: (1) the intellectual property must have been created by the company transferring the right; (2) the recipient of the right must actually use the intellectual property for business activities; (3) if the recipient is a related company, the intellectual property cannot be used to generate a deductible expense for the transferring company; (4) the recipient company must not be located in a listed tax haven jurisdiction;[198] (5) in the case where one intellectual property contract includes other services, the consideration related to the intellectual property must be clearly differentiated within the contract; and (6) the transferring taxpaying company must keep records of income and expenses pertinent to the intellectual property rights subject to the transfer.

United Kingdom

The U.K.'s patent box regime was initially proposed in 2009 and applies to profits of a U.K. company or a U.K. permanent establishment after April 1, 2013. The applicable tax rate is 10 percent on income from patented inventions and certain other innovations. The relevant patents must be granted by the United Kingdom Intellectual Property Office or European Patent Office. Certain know-how, trade secrets and some software copyrights that are closely associated with a qualifying patent may also be included in the regime. Trademarks and registered designs are specifically excluded. To qualify, a company must have legal ownership of the patent or qualifying intellectual property right outright, acquire an exclusive license to the intellectual property (including a limited geographical area or particular field of use right), have a beneficial ownership of all rights relating to the intellectual property (rights to protect, license and assign rights may be retained by another related company), or acquire rights over qualifying intellectual property by participating in a qualifying cost contribution arrangements (where the U.K. company contributes to the development of the intellectual property). To qualify, the patent or product which incorporates the patent must have been developed by a company in the worldwide corporate group, but there is no requirement for the research and development to be incurred in the United Kingdom or by the U.K. company; however, for acquired rights to qualify, the U.K. company must make a significant contribution to developing a product using the intellectual property, or the method of applying the intellectual property.

Restrictions on hybrid payments

In addition to the OECD work on hybrid mismatch arrangements, the European Commission and some countries, including Austria, France, Germany, and Mexico, have adopted legislation aimed at limiting the availability of these types of arrangements that could result in double non-taxation or in double deductions. This work is discussed below.

European Commission

In November 2013, the European Commission released an amendment to the Parent-Subsidiary Directive in order to address hybrid loan arrangements.[199] In general, the Parent-Subsidiary Directive was designed to eliminate tax obstacles for distributions between parent companies and subsidiaries based in different European Union member states.[200] The directive provides a tax exemption for dividends or other profit distributions paid by a subsidiary company in one member state to a parent company in another member state.

The European Commission was concerned that the directive was being used for a particular tax planning arrangement, the hybrid loan arrangement. Additionally, the European Commission wanted to introduce a general anti-abuse rule to the directive. According to the European Commission, hybrid loan arrangements have characteristics of both debt and equity which could give rise to different tax treatment by different member states. One member state might treat the payment as an interest payment on debt and allow a tax deduction while the other member state might treat the payment as a tax-exempt dividend. The proposed amendments would update the anti-abuse provision and require member states to adopt a common anti-abuse rule. This rule would allow member states to ignore artificial arrangements used for tax avoidance purpose to ensure taxation takes place on the basis of real economic substance. Additionally, under the proposal, the directive would require a member state where the parent company is established to tax a hybrid loan payment if the payment is tax deductible in the subsidiary's member state.

The Council of the European Union formally adopted the amendment requiring taxation at the parent level of a payment that is tax deductible at the subsidiary level on July 8, 2014.[201] Member states have until December 31, 2015 to incorporate the amendment into national law. No agreement was reached regarding adoption of a common anti-abuse rule.

Austria[202]

Austrian companies are generally eligible for a 100-percent participation exemption for dividends received from foreign subsidiaries. Austria's dividend exemption is not available to the Austrian parent if the dividend may be deducted by the foreign subsidiary. Additionally, effective for payments on or after March 1, 2014, royalty and interest payments are not deductible in Austria if the income derived from the interest and royalties is not taxed in the recipient's country or is subject to a tax rate of less than 15 percent. If the tax rate of the recipient is at least 10 percent, 50 percent of the interest and royalties are deductible.

France[203]

Beginning with tax years ending on or after September 25, 2013, interest on related party loans is deductible in France only if the French borrower can show that such interest is taxable to the lender at a rate equal to at least 25 percent of the French corporate income tax rate. Specific rules are provided where the lender is a flow-through entity such as an investment fund or partnership.

Germany[204]

Corporate shareholders resident in Germany are generally provided a 95-percent exemption for dividends. Germany recently enacted an anti-hybrid rule effective for dividends received in tax years beginning after December 31, 2013. This new rule provides that the dividend exemption is not available if the dividend payment is tax deductible to the dividend- paying subsidiary.

Mexico[205]

Effective January 14, 2014, payments for interest, royalties, or technical assistance will not be deductible if the payment is made to a foreign related party that either controls or is controlled, directly or indirectly, by the payer, and either (1) the payee is regarded as transparent under Mexican law (not applicable if the income of the recipient is taxed at the partner level and is an arm's-length payment), the payment is disregarded in the country of the payee, or (3) the foreign entity does not regard the payment as taxable income.

IV. Recent U.S. Proposals Related to the Taxation of Cross-Border Income

In response to the concerns described in Parts II and III regarding competitiveness, base erosion and shifting of profits out of a country's tax base, and recent developments in the international community, several possible legislative responses have been proposed to reform the U.S. international tax system. These proposals vary significantly in both form and substance. Five such proposals offered by the Administration, Senators Wyden and Enzi and former Senator Baucus, of the Senate Finance Committee, and by House Ways and Means Committee Chairman Camp are discussed below. These proposals reform the U.S. international tax rules by moving further toward either a full inclusion system (all foreign-source income is currently taxed without regard to whether the income is from business or investment) or a territorial system (foreign business income is exempt from U.S. taxation). The following discussion provides a general overview of each of the five proposals, and focuses on the extent to which the proposal is a departure from the present law U.S. hybrid system, whether it reforms the anti-deferral regimes, how it ensures elimination of double taxation (either through use of foreign tax credits or exemptions), whether and how it may implement anti-base-erosion mechanisms, and how transition to the reformed international tax system is addressed.

A. The Administration's Proposal to Reform the U.S. International Tax System[206]

In its budget proposal for fiscal year 2015, the Administration calls for work to begin on comprehensive tax reform, including business tax reform on a revenue neutral basis and includes as one of the five elements in the framework for such reform the strengthening of the international tax system. That framework and the 16 specific proposals under the rubric "Reform U.S. International Tax System" together comprise the Administration's proposal. Accordingly, the proposal remains inchoate as to the extent to which it will retain the fundamental nature of the present hybrid system in the U.S. international tax system in asserting worldwide taxing jurisdiction over domestic companies and whether a transitional rule will be provided. Although there is no specific proposal for a transitional rule, the description of the framework for reform alludes to the possibility that comprehensive reform would need to address the deferred earnings that are reported as permanently reinvested offshore. The remainder of this overview is limited to the specific proposals and their intended reform of the scope of U.S. taxation of cross-border business activity, foreign tax credit reforms, and the use of limitations on expenses to counter base-erosion.

1. Reform of subpart F and related reforms

The structure of subpart F is retained, albeit with several reforms that broaden the scope of income covered by the anti-deferral regime. Other reforms also address potential profit shifting.

Subpart F reforms

The Administration proposes two new categories of income required to be included in foreign base company income. Certain excess income from transactions connected with or benefiting from a covered intangible are treated as a new category of subpart F income.A covered intangible is an intangible that was transferred, directly or indirectly, from the United States to a related CFC, whether by sale, lease, license, or through any shared risk or development agreement (including any cost sharing arrangement). Excess income is gross income from transactions connected with or benefitting from a covered intangible in excess of the costs (excluding interest and taxes) properly allocated and apportioned to this income increased by a percentage mark-up, but is within the new subpart F category only if it was subject to a low foreign effective tax rate. If the foreign effective tax rate is 10 percent or less, all excess income is treated as subpart F income. The amount of excess income treated as subpart F income is phased out ratably for income that was subject to a foreign tax with an effective tax rate between 10 percent and 15 percent. This new category of subpart F income is also a new separate category of income for purposes of determining the taxpayer's foreign tax credit limitation under section 904.

The second new category of subpart F income is foreign base company digital income. Foreign base company digital income generally includes income of a CFC from the lease or sale of a digital copyrighted article or from the provision of a digital service, in cases where the CFC uses intangible property developed by a related party (including property developed pursuant to a cost sharing arrangement) to produce the income and the CFC does not, through its own employees, make a substantial contribution to the development of the property or services that give rise to the income. An exception applies where the CFC earns income directly from customers located in the CFC's country of incorporation that use or consume the digital copyrighted article or digital service in such country.

The proposal also expands the category of foreign base company sales income to include income of a CFC from the sale of property manufactured on behalf of the CFC by a related person. The existing exceptions to foreign base company sales income would continue to apply.

Finally, the same-country and CFC look-through treatment exceptions under subpart F are denied with respect to applicable payments that a foreign reverse hybrid receives from a foreign related person if the hybrid is held directly by a U.S. owner and the payments are deductible by the foreign payor.

Related reforms

The Administration's budget proposal also includes reforms to protect the tax base other than via the anti-deferral regime. These reforms include measures that clarify definitions and methodologies in administration of transfer pricing; limit the extent to which leveraged distributions may be used to avoid dividend treatment; and ensure that gain attributable to a

U.S. trade or business of a foreign partnership is recognized upon disposition of an interest held by a foreign partner. With respect to the latter proposal, because the reform deals with inbound rather than outbound investment, a new withholding tax modeled on the FIRPTA provisions requires that the transferee of a partnership interest withhold 10 percent of the amount realized on the sale or exchange of a partnership interest unless the transferor certifies that the transferor is not a nonresident alien individual or foreign corporation.

2. Foreign tax credit changes

With respect to direct credits, the Administration budget proposal makes several changes. First, it broadens the application of the section 338(h)(16) rules to all covered asset acquisitions within the meaning of section 901(m) for foreign tax credit computations. Thus, foreign taxes are not creditable to the extent they are paid with respect to an acquisition of an interest in a partnership that has an optional basis adjustment election in effect, or with respect to a hybrid transaction in which the transaction is treated as an asset acquisition under the Code but is disregarded or treated as a stock acquisition for purposes of income tax in the foreign jurisdiction. Second, it permits a dual-capacity taxpayer to treat as a creditable tax only the portion of a foreign levy that does not exceed the foreign levy that the taxpayer would pay if it were not a dual-capacity taxpayer, thus replacing the current regulatory safe harbor. It also converts the special foreign tax credit limitation rules of section 907 into a separate category within section 904 for foreign oil and gas income.

Two changes are also made with respect to indirect foreign tax credits. First, the limitation on the deemed-paid foreign credit is required to be computed on a pooling basis, under which a U.S. corporate taxpayer would take into account the aggregate foreign taxes and earnings and profits of all of the foreign subsidiaries with respect to which the U.S. taxpayer may claim a deemed-paid foreign tax credit (including lower-tier subsidiaries described in section 902(b)). After determining the U.S. corporate taxpayer's pro rata share of the consolidated earnings and profits of the foreign subsidiaries repatriated to the U.S. taxpayer and subject to U.S. tax in that year, a proportionate amount of deemed-paid foreign tax credit for a taxable year is determined. Amounts in excess of that proportionate amount are deferred, but may be creditable in a subsequent taxable year to the extent that the deemed paid foreign taxes in that subsequent year are less than the annual foreign tax credit limitation for that year.

Second, if a transaction results in the elimination of an uncontrolled section 902 foreign corporation's earnings and profits, foreign taxes associated with the eliminated earnings and profits are removed from the foreign corporation's pool of creditable taxes. The proposal does not apply to a reduction of earnings and profits by reason of a dividend or deemed dividend or by reason of a restructuring transaction in which income or loss is not recognized and in which, under section 381, the acquiring corporation succeeds to certain items of the distributing or transferring corporation, including that latter corporation's earnings and profits.

3. Limitations on expenses as anti-base-erosion measure

Any deduction to covered insurance companies for the full amount of reinsurance premiums paid to foreign affiliated insurance companies is disallowed unless the premium is subject to U.S. income taxation. A corresponding exclusion from income is provided for reinsurance recovered with respect to a reinsurance arrangement for which the premium deduction has been disallowed. The proposal also provides an exclusion from income for ceding commissions received with respect to a reinsurance arrangement for which the premium deduction has been disallowed. The exclusions are intended to apply only to the extent the corresponding premium deduction is disallowed.[207]

The proposal denies a deduction for interest and royalty payments made to related parties in certain circumstances described as "hybrid arrangements," in which asymmetrical treatment of a payment is provided under the laws of the jurisdictions of the related parties to the transaction. For example, a deduction may be denied if a taxpayer makes an interest or royalty payment to a related party, and either (1) as a result of the hybrid arrangement, there is no corresponding inclusion to the recipient in the foreign country or (2) the hybrid arrangement permits an additional deduction for the same payment in a third country.

In addition to the above-described rule on interest expenses related to hybrid arrangements, the Administration budget proposal also includes two other limitations on the deductibility of interest. First, it limits the deductibility of U.S. interest expenses of members of a group that prepares consolidated financial statements ("financial reporting group"). A member's U.S. interest expense deduction would generally be limited to either 10 percent of the member's adjusted taxable income (as defined under section 163(j)) or to an amount equal to the member's interest income plus the member's proportionate share of the net interest expense of the financial reporting group. The member's proportionate share of the financial reporting group's net interest expense computed under U.S. income tax principles, based on the member's proportionate share of the group's earnings (computed by adding back net interest expense, taxes, depreciation, and amortization) reflected in the group's financial statements. Regardless of whether a taxpayer computes the interest limitation under the proportionate share approach or using the 10-percent alternative, disallowed interest would be carried forward indefinitely and any excess limitation for a tax year would be carried forward to the three subsequent tax years. A member of a financial reporting group that is subject to the proposal would be exempt from the application of section 163(j).

Second, the deduction of interest expense that is properly allocated and apportioned to stock of a foreign corporation that exceeds an amount proportionate to the taxpayer's pro-rata share of income from such subsidiaries that is currently subject to U.S. tax is deferred. For purposes of the proposal, foreign-source income earned by a taxpayer through a branch is considered currently subject to U.S. tax; thus, the proposal does not apply to interest expense properly allocated and apportioned to such income. Other directly earned foreign-source income (for example, royalty income) is similarly treated. Interest expense that is deferred under the proposal is deductible in a subsequent tax year to the extent that the amount of interest expense allocated and apportioned to stock of foreign subsidiaries in such subsequent year is less than the annual limitation for that year.

B. Chairman Wyden's "Bipartisan Tax Fairness and Simplification Act of 2011"[208]

Chairman Wyden's proposal is a comprehensive plan to reform the tax system for both individuals and businesses. The international tax reforms are found in Title II of Chairman Wyden's proposal, "Corporate and Business Income Tax Reforms," which imposes a corporate income tax at the flat rate of 24 percent on all taxable income and terminates a variety of tax rules identified as "preferential treatment" including the deferral of taxation on foreign income. The legislation requires that a U.S. shareholder include as a deemed dividend its share of the current foreign earnings of the foreign corporation. Thus, although the architecture of subpart F is retained, the distinction under current law between subpart F and non-subpart F income is eliminated, and all foreign income is taxed currently. The proposal does not specify whether losses of a CFC flow through to U.S. shareholders.

Elimination of double taxation is retained by use of the foreign tax credit. The foreign tax credit rules are reformed by reinstituting the requirement that the limitation be computed on a country-by-country basis, and limiting the creditability of amounts paid by dual-capacity large integrated oil companies, similar to the Administration's proposal described above. U.S. corporate shareholders owning a 10-percent interest in a CFC would continue to claim indirect credits for their share of the foreign taxes paid by the CFC.

The legislation provides several specific provisions to address potentially abusive transactions. First, it removes the exception to the sourcing rules for inventory that permits place of sale to control the source of income. It also provides that certain past transactions will be subject to two aspects of present law for future years: First, the anti-inversion rules of section 7874 would apply to transactions that occurred one year earlier than under present law, that is, to transactions that occurred after March 12, 2002, rather than March 12, 2003.[209] Second, the legislation provides that the rules limiting deductions on leases of property to governments or other tax-exempt entities applies to property leased to a foreign tax-exempt entity for tax years beginning after December 31, 2011, under leases entered into on or before March 12, 2004.[210]

No transition rule is included in the proposal. The proposal is silent with respect to the treatment of previously deferred earnings, although a summary of the proposal refers to a one- time low-tax repatriation of foreign earnings.[211]

C. Senator Enzi's "United States Jobs Creation and International Tax Reform Act of 2012"[212]

The centerpiece of Senator Enzi's proposal is the establishment of a participation exemption system[213] under which a deduction is permitted for 95-percent of the qualified foreign-source portion of dividends a domestic corporation receives from CFCs of which they are U.S. shareholders. Other significant features are a reformed anti-deferral regime of subpart F, a deduction for U.S. corporations that earn foreign income from exploitation of those intangibles in a U.S. trade or business, reforms limiting the availability of credits for foreign taxes and a transition rule that allows a one-time election to deduct 70-percent of eligible amounts received from a CFC. The new dividends-received deduction for the qualified foreign- source portion, the new deduction for domestic corporations with qualified foreign intangible income, the transition rule, the reform of subpart F, and the related changes to foreign tax credit rules are described below.

1. Deduction for qualified foreign-source portion of dividends received

A deduction of 95 percent of qualified foreign income is available, provided that a one-year holding period requirement is satisfied and that the dividends are not hybrid dividends, which are described below. The proposal permits a taxpayer to elect to treat a noncontrolled section 902 corporation[214] as a CFC for all purposes of the Code, but neither allows nor requires foreign branches of U.S. corporations to be treated as CFCs. Consequently, as under present law, income of a foreign branch of a U.S. corporation is taxable by the United States, losses of a foreign branch generally are deductible in the United States, and a credit against U.S. tax is available for foreign income taxes imposed on branch income.

Qualified foreign-source portion of dividends

The participation exemption system is intended to apply only to foreign business income and not to U.S.-source income. The foreign-source portion of a dividend that qualifies for the 95-percent deduction represents the portion of the dividend that relates to the CFC's undistributed qualified foreign earnings. Specifically, the qualified foreign-source portion of any dividend is an amount which bears the same ratio to such dividend as the CFC's post-effective date undistributed qualified foreign earnings bears to its total post-effective date undistributed earnings.

A CFC's post-effective date undistributed earnings are the earnings and profits accumulated by the CFC in taxable years beginning after the first year that the provision is in effect, as of the close of the taxable year of the CFC, without diminution from dividends distributed during that taxable year. A CFC's post-effective date undistributed qualified earnings are the portion of its post-effective date undistributed earnings that are not attributable to income effectively connected with the conduct of trade or business in the United States[215] or dividends received from a domestic corporation of which the CFC holds at least 80 percent of the stock (by vote or value).[216] Distributions are treated as first made out of a CFC's earnings and profits which are not post-effective date undistributed earnings, and then out of post-effective date undistributed earnings.

The restriction of the 95-percent dividends-received deduction to the foreign-source portion of a dividend complements the present law section 245 rule allowing a deduction for the U.S.-source portion of a dividend received from a qualified 10-percent owned foreign corporation. As a result of this coordination with section 245, the proposal provides the 95-percent deduction for a dividend received by a U.S. shareholder from a CFC only to the extent the dividend is not deductible under present law section 245.

Hybrid dividends are not eligible for the 95-percent dividends-received deduction under the proposal. A hybrid dividend is a payment that is treated as a dividend for purposes of the Code but for which the CFC making the payment receives a deduction (or similar tax benefit) under the laws of the country in which the CFC was organized. Additionally, hybrid dividends of tiered CFCs are treated as subpart F income of the recipient CFC for the taxable year in which the dividend was received. This rule applies to hybrid dividends between CFCs with respect to which the same domestic corporation is a 10-percent shareholder. The 10-percent U.S. shareholder includes in gross income an amount equal to the shareholder's pro rata share (determined in the same manner as under section 951(a)(2)) of that subpart F income.

Rules governing the recognition of gain from disposition of stock in a CFC are provided that parallel the treatment of dividends received. When a domestic corporation recognizes a gain on the sale or exchange stock of a foreign corporation held for at least one year, any amount treated as a dividend under section 1248 is also treated as a dividend for purposes of applying the 95-percent dividends-received deduction rules. No deduction is allowed for any loss recognized by a domestic corporation from the sale or exchange of stock of a foreign corporation if (under section 1248(a)(2)) the domestic corporation owned at least 10 percent of the voting power of the foreign corporation at any time during the five years preceding the sale when the foreign corporation was a CFC. Special rules for determining treatment of sales or exchanges by an upper-tier CFC of stock in a lower-tier CFC are also provided.

One-year holding period requirement

A domestic corporation is allowed the 95-percent deduction for a dividend it receives on stock of a CFC only if the domestic corporation satisfies a one-year holding period requirement in respect of the stock on which the dividend is paid. No deduction is allowed in respect of any dividend on any share of CFC stock that is held by a domestic corporation for 365 days or less during the 731-day period beginning on the date that is 365 days before the date on which the share becomes ex-dividend with respect to the dividend. A deduction also is not permitted in respect of any dividend on any share of CFC stock to the extent that the domestic corporation owning the share is under an obligation (under a short sale or otherwise) to make related payments with respect to positions in substantially similar or related property.[217]

At all times during the requisite holding period, the CFC must be a CFC, and the domestic corporation must be a 10-percent U.S. shareholder of the CFC. A noncontrolled section 902 corporation that a domestic corporation has elected to treat as a CFC may count a continuous period ending one day prior to the election toward satisfying this requirement, if during that period the domestic corporation met the ownership requirements for determining that the foreign corporation was a noncontrolled section 902 corporation with respect to the domestic corporation.

2. Deduction for qualified foreign intangible income from a U.S. trade or business

This proposal allows for a deduction equal to 50 percent of the qualified foreign intangible income of a domestic corporation. Qualified foreign intangible income means, with respect to any domestic corporation, foreign intangible income derived by the domestic corporation from the active conduct of a trade or business within the United States with respect to the intangible property[218] giving rise to the income.

Foreign intangible income is any intangible income derived in connection with (1) property which is sold, leased, licensed, or otherwise disposed of for use, consumption or disposition outside the United States, or (2) services provided with respect to persons or property located outside the United States.[219] To be considered qualified foreign intangible income, the foreign intangible income must be derived from the active conduct of a U.S. trade or business with respect to the intangible property giving rise to the income. Foreign intangible income is considered derived from a domestic corporation's active conduct of a U.S. trade or business only if the domestic corporation developed, created, or produced in the United States the intangible property giving rise to the income or, in the case of acquired intangible property, added substantial value to it through the active conduct of the trade or business within the United States. Intangible income is gross income from the sale, lease, license, or other disposition of property in which intangible property is used directly or indirectly or from the provision of services in which intangible property is used directly or indirectly, reduced by deductions properly allocable to the income.

3. Modifications of subpart F

The anti-deferral regime of subpart F of the Code is retained with two modifications. Senator Enzi's proposal adds a new category of subpart F income for low-taxed income (explained below) and narrows the scope of subpart F income by removing sales and services income from foreign base company income. The remaining category of income from business operations included in foreign base company income for certain oil-related income is not modified. As a result, in combination with the other provisions in this proposal,[220] subpart F income is generally limited to passive income and low-taxed intangible income.

With respect to the new category of subpart F income, all gross income of a CFC is low-taxed income unless the 10-percent U.S. shareholder establishes that the income was subject to foreign tax at an effective rate greater than one-half of the maximum rate of income tax applicable to U.S. corporations for the relevant taxable period (that is, 17.5 percent, one-half of the current maximum U.S. corporate rate of 35 percent). The effective rate at which foreign income was taxed is determined by applying U.S. principles similar to those used in determining the high-tax exception of section 954(b)(4) on a country-by-country basis, for each country in which a CFC conducts any trade or business. Neither current losses nor losses carried to the taxable year are taken into account in determining the effective rate of tax imposed on income from a particular country, but properly allocable deductions are taken into account.

Income that was not subject to an effective rate of at least 17.5 percent may be excluded if it is qualified business income as described in the statute, other than intangible income. "Qualified business income" is income of the CFC that is derived in a foreign country and attributable to the active conduct of a trade or business in that foreign country by the CFC, through its office or fixed place of business in such country and by its officers and employees who are physically located in the country. The activities performed by the employees and officers physically located in the country must be substantial and contribute significantly to the conduct of the business in that country, when viewed in relation to all functions required for the conduct of the trade or business to which the income is attributed.

4. Modifications related to foreign tax credit

The proposal retains the use of foreign tax credits to eliminate double taxation with several changes. It also modifies the rules for availability of the section 902 deemed-paid credit, and changes limitations on computation of the foreign tax credit by adding a new separate income category for taxes paid with respect to intangible income and providing that the rule for determining the source of income from sales of inventory sales is changed for purposes of the limitations.

First, the proposal disallows any credit or deduction for taxes (including withholding taxes) paid or accrued with respect to dividends for which the 95-percent deduction or the transitional 70-percent deduction is available as well as with respect to hybrid dividends. The foreign tax credit disallowance and deduction denial apply to foreign tax with respect to the entire amount of any deductible dividend even though a deduction is available for only part of the dividend. For purposes of applying the section 904(a) foreign tax credit limitation, the non- deductible portion of a dividend is treated as U.S. source income.

Deemed-paid credits

The proposal repeals the deemed paid credit for any dividend or portion of any dividend paid by a foreign corporation to the extent paid out of the corporation's post-effective date earnings and profits (computed in accordance with sections 964(a) and 986). This rule disallows a deemed-paid credit in respect of dividends from foreign corporations regardless of whether the 95-percent dividends received deduction is available. The section 902 deemed-paid credit remains available in respect of dividends paid out of earnings and profits accumulated in taxable years beginning before the effective date of Senator Enzi's proposals. Any distribution in a subsequent taxable year is treated as made first out of earnings and profits accumulated in taxable years beginning before the effective date. Consequently, the proposal allows the section 902 deemed-paid credit to remain in effect for dividends received from a foreign corporation until the corporation's pre-effective date earnings and profits have been exhausted (including by reason of imposition of the transition tax, described below). In computing the amount of foreign income tax that a domestic corporation is deemed to have paid under section 902 in respect of dividends attributable to a foreign corporation's pre-effective date earnings, the term "post-1986 earnings" does not include the corporation's post-effective date earnings and profits.

The proposal amends the deemed paid credit rules applicable to subpart F inclusions. If a domestic corporation has subpart F income with respect to any CFC in which the domestic corporation is a 10-percent U.S. shareholder, and the subpart F income is attributable to earnings and profits of the CFC (computed in accordance with sections 964(a) and 986) accumulated in taxable years beginning after the effective date, the domestic corporation is deemed to have paid the portion of the CFC's foreign income tax that is properly attributable to the subpart F income. Under the deemed-paid foreign tax credit rule for foreign income taxes attributable to subpart F income, the term "foreign income taxes" has the same meaning as under present law: any income, war profits, or excess profits taxes paid or accrued by a CFC to any foreign country or U.S. possession. As under present law, in-lieu-of income taxes under section 903, such as foreign withholding taxes, are considered foreign income taxes.

Limitations

A new separate income category (basket) in the computation of the foreign tax credit limitation under section 904 is added for foreign intangible income as defined in Senator Enzi's legislation. The proposal retains the present law separate limitation categories for passive and active income for income that is not included in the new category of foreign intangible income. It also provides that foreign tax carried over from pre-effective date years continues to be treated as belonging to the separate limitation category applicable under present law. In the case of a carryback of foreign tax related to an item of foreign intangible income from a taxable year beginning after the effective date or later to a taxable year beginning before the effective date, the foreign tax is allocated to general category income.

The proposal overrides certain inventory sales source rules for purposes of computing the foreign tax credit limitation. Amounts treated as foreign source by reason of the application of the special inventory sourcing rules of section 862(a)(6) and section 863(b)(2), and the regulations promulgated thereunder,[221] are treated as U.S.-source for purposes of computing the foreign tax credit limitation under the provision.

5. Transition rule

A corporate 10-percent U.S. shareholder may elect a one-time 70-percent deduction for eligible amounts received from a CFC from pre-effective date earnings. The eligible amounts include both cash repatriated in the form of dividends and amounts that a taxpayer elects to treat as subpart F income ("deemed repatriation"). The deduction is available only for the taxable year of the U.S. shareholder with or within which the first taxable year of the CFC beginning after the effective date ends. As a result of claiming the deduction, the taxpayer is not entitled to any credit or deduction for foreign taxes paid that would otherwise be available with respect to any portion of the dividends or deemed repatriations. In the absence of an election, foreign taxes paid with respect to pre-effective date earnings are creditable or deductible when the earnings are distributed, subject to relevant limitations. The 70-percent deduction election is not available for earnings of noncontrolled section 902 corporations that the U.S. shareholder elects to treat as CFCs. An election to apply any of the benefits of this proposal (including the deduction, the deemed repatriation, and the election to pay the tax attributable to deemed repatriation in installments) is due no later than the due date (including any extensions) of the return on which the deduction is claimed.

The eligible amount with respect to which the deduction may be claimed comprises both cash dividends and deemed repatriations. It is the lesser of (1) the 10-percent U.S. shareholder's pro rata share of the pre-effective date earnings of the CFC as of the close of the taxable year immediately preceding the first taxable year beginning after the effective date, or (2) the sum of cash dividends paid out of pre-effective date earnings plus any portion of the taxpayer's pro rata share of CFC's pre-effective date earnings that the taxpayer elects to deem to be subpart F income. It does not include amounts included as a dividend by reason of a section 78 gross-up for taxes paid with respect to subpart F income or dividends that are not subject to the election under this proposal. An ordering rule for purposes of determining the eligible amount requires that cash dividends are treated as first paid from the pre-effective date earnings, to the extent thereof.

D. Former Chairman Baucus's Staff Discussion Drafts for International Tax Reform[222]

Former Chairman Baucus's discussion drafts depart from the current U.S. hybrid international tax system in each of the two proposals for taxing foreign business income, with Option Y adopting a participation exemption system and Option Z moving toward full inclusion and a minimum tax. Regardless of which alternative is considered, subpart F is retained but modified. In addition to subpart F changes that are tailored to the specific option in question, the Common provisions include additional changes to subpart F and significant modifications to the PFIC rules. A number of specific provisions that reduce opportunity for income shifting or base erosion are also included in the Common draft, as well as several reforms that address inbound issues. Finally, a transition rule that requires inclusion of all previously deferred earnings at an effective tax rate of 20-percent is included in the Common draft.

1. Dividend exemption or full inclusion system: Options Y and Z

Option Y

Under Option Y, a dividend exemption system is effectuated by means of a 100-percent deduction for the foreign-source portion of dividends received from CFCs by domestic corporations that are 10-percent U.S. shareholders of those CFCs and that have satisfied a one- year holding period requirement. The dividend exemption is not available with respect to dividends received from an uncontrolled section 902 company, nor does it apply to hybrid dividends. A hybrid dividend is a payment that is treated as a dividend for purposes of the Code but for which the CFC making the payment receives a deduction (or similar tax benefit) under the laws of any country in which the CFC is a resident for purposes of the country's income tax law. Option Y does not change the taxation of foreign branches of U.S. corporations.

The dividend exemption system is intended to apply only to foreign business income and not to U.S-source income. Some CFCs, however, may have U.S.-source income. Consequently, the 100-percent dividends-received deduction is available only for the foreign-source portion of a dividend. The foreign-source portion of a dividend for which the 100-percent deduction is allowed represents the portion of the dividend that relates to the CFC's undistributed foreign earnings. The foreign-source portion of any dividend is, therefore, the amount that bears the same ratio to the dividend as the CFC's undistributed foreign earnings bears to the CFC's undistributed earnings.[223]

This rule complements the present law section 245 rule allowing a deduction for the U.S.-source portion of a dividend received from a qualified 10-percent owned foreign corporation. Present law section 245 is intended to prevent a second imposition of U.S. corporate tax when a domestic corporation receives a dividend from a foreign corporation attributable to the foreign corporation's U.S.-source effectively connected income, whereas Option Y is intended to provide an exemption from U.S. corporate tax when a domestic corporation receives a dividend from a CFC attributable to the CFC's foreign-source business income (so long as that foreign- source business income is not low-tax income or U.S.-related income). Rules to provide parallel treatment for gains from disposition of stock in CFCs are provided.

In order to meet the one-year holding period, the share of CFC stock with respect to which the dividend is paid must be held by the domestic corporation for 365 days or less during the 731-day period beginning on the date that is 365 days before the date on which the share becomes ex-dividend with respect to the dividend. No deduction is permitted in respect of any dividend on any share of CFC stock to the extent the domestic corporation that owns the share is under an obligation (under a short sale or otherwise) to make related payments with respect to positions in substantially similar or related property.

Option Z

In contrast to the Option Y dividend exemption, Option Z is styled as full inclusion of all subpart F income, requiring that U.S. shareholders of CFCs include in income their pro rata share of all CFC income. Although it retains the structure of subpart F, Option Z repeals the existing definitions of subpart F income, insurance income, foreign base company income, shipping, and investment in US property. In their place, Option Z introduces as a new category of subpart F income the concept of active foreign market income, described below, for which a 40-percent exclusion is permitted. The result of the nominal full-inclusion and the

40-percent exclusion is that all reported income is treated as previously taxed income although only 60 percent was subject to tax.

Option Z also repeals the present law section 1248 rules that treat certain gains recognized by U.S. persons on the sale or exchange of stock of a CFC as dividends to the extent of the undistributed, non-previously-taxed earnings of the CFC attributable to that stock and replaces it with a rule excluding the "applicable portion" from the gross income of a U.S. 10- percent shareholder. The applicable portion for which an exclusion from gross income is allowed is generally the portion of the CFC's historic earnings that represents active foreign market income.

2. *Modifications of anti-deferral regimes*

Common provisions

The provisions applicable to both Option Y and Option Z make significant changes to the anti-deferral regime governing income from PFICs as well as several definitional changes to subpart F. With respect to the latter, the Baucus discussion draft eliminates the 30 day requirement, thereby broadening the scope of subpart F so that its rules apply to foreign corporations that are CFCs at any point during the taxable year. It also expands the definition of U.S. shareholder under subpart F to include any U.S. person who owns 10 percent or more of the total value of shares of all classes of stock of a foreign corporation.

The common provisions of the discussion draft repeals the PFIC rules that impose an interest charge when a U.S. person who owns stock of a PFIC receives an excess distribution in respect of that stock as well as the rules relating to elective annual taxation in respect of qualified elective funds in sections 1293, 1294, and 1295. In their place, Chairman Baucus's discussion draft requires a U.S. person who owns non-publicly-traded PFIC stock to include in income annually a deemed return, or interest accrual amount, on the PFIC stock equal to the Federal short-term rate plus five percent.[224] With respect to marketable stock, the mark-to-market regime is made mandatory in all circumstances in which a U.S. person owns PFIC stock that is marketable. The proposal also modifies the definition of marketable stock to add stock in any foreign corporation that is subject to governmental regulation comparable to Federal regulation of regulated investment companies (mutual funds), and that is redeemable or otherwise disposable at its net asset value or at any other price determined under an independent valuation method fixed at the time of purchase. A transition rule is provided for U.S. persons who owned marketable PFIC stock prior to the effective date of these reforms and who are required to recognize gain attributable to a deemed disposition of stock.

Option Y

Although the foreign-source portion of a dividend generally is 100-percent deductible when received by a 10-percent U.S. shareholder from a CFC, the 10-percent U.S. shareholder remains taxable in the United States on a current basis under the discussion draft on its pro rata share of certain items of passive, low-tax, or U.S.-related income of the CFC. The modified subpart F rules are intended to ensure that the dividend exemption applies only to income from the conduct of an active foreign business and to limit shifting of income from the United States to low-tax foreign countries. The inclusion of other foreign base company income (foreign base company sales income, foreign base company services income, and foreign base company oil related income) in subpart F is repealed. The rule exempting de minimis amounts from foreign personal holding company income and insurance income is repealed.

Two new categories of subpart F income are added by Option Y: United States related income and low-taxed income. The first new category, United States related income, is the sum of the CFC's imported property income and its United States services income. United States related income does not include income of a CFC that is (1) insurance income, (2) foreign personal holding company income, (3) international boycott income, (4) illegal bribes, etc., or (4) income derived from countries to which section 901(j) applies.

Imported property income is income derived from the manufacturing, producing, growing, extracting, the sale, exchange or other disposition, or the lease, rental, or licensing of imported property. Imported property is property which is imported into the United States by the CFC or a related person.[225] If property is ultimately imported into the United States and all sales, exchanges, or dispositions of the property (or property used in the manufacture of, or as a component part in the property), before the sale for use, consumption, or disposition in the United States are between related persons, the CFC is deemed to have had a reasonable expectation that the property would be imported into the United States.

United States services income is income derived in connection with services (including insurance, reinsurance, annuity contracts, banking, financing, or a similar business) provided with respect to persons or property located in the United States. It does not include imported property income.

The second new category, low-taxed income, is any item of income, other than certain other subpart F categories of income,[226] if the effective rate of income tax on such item of income is less than 80 percent of the maximum U.S. corporate tax rate. It does not include any dividend received or accrued from another CFC which is a member of the same applicable expanded affiliated group. The subpart F inclusion is reduced for items of income with effective income tax rates greater than 60 percent and less than 80 percent of the maximum U.S. corporate tax rate. The reduction is computed as a ratio (not greater than 100 percent) of the number of percentage points by which the effective rate of income tax exceeds 60 percent of the maximum U.S. corporate tax rate over 20 percent of the maximum U.S. corporate tax rate.

Option Y also modifies the definition of foreign personal holding company income. The rule exempting de minimis amounts from foreign personal holding company income and insurance income is repealed. It narrows the foreign currency gains business needs exception, repeals the export financing interest exception, and broadens and makes permanent the exception for regular dealers of property giving rise to certain properties. It does not revive and extend the CFC look-through rules, but does modify the same-country exception for dividends, interest, rents and royalties.

Option Y also makes permanent the active financing and active insurance income exceptions, with modifications to clarify the activities that qualify for each exception. Any CFC that is either a regulated financial institution or that derives 80-percent of its gross income from the active and regular conduct of a lending, finance, or financial services business from transactions with unrelated persons located outside the United States qualifies. The proposal codifies a list of activities to define the term, "lending, finance, or financial services business," and provides a definition of regulated financial institution that includes entities that are subject to the regulatory standards of the Basel Committee on Banking Supervision.

Option Z

The new definition of subpart F income eliminates deferral of income by a CFC and permits an exclusion of 40 percent of the active foreign market income of the CFC. As in present law, subpart F income does not include income effectively connected with a U.S. trade or business. Both subpart F income and active foreign market income are reduced by deductions, for expenses that are properly allocable to items of income taken into account in the determination of either subpart F income or active foreign market income. Once in effect, Option Z would provide that losses from non-active foreign market operations in a taxable year are carried forward and reduce non-active foreign market income in future years. Such a loss is measured as the amount by which a shareholder's pro rata share of deductions attributable to subpart F income exceeds subpart F income, determined without regard to active foreign market income, and thus do not include active foreign market losses. Similarly, active foreign market losses are carried forward to reduce active foreign market income in future years.

Active foreign market income is income attributable to economically significant contributions of a qualified trade or business derived in connection with property sold or exchanged for use outside the United States or services performed outside the United States with respect to persons or property located outside the United States. Economically significant contributions must be performed outside the United States by officers or employees of the controlled foreign corporation and must make a substantial contribution to the production of income. Active foreign market income does not include passive income, generally, but income that would otherwise be characterized as passive income qualifies as active foreign market income, and is thus eligible for the exclusion, if the item of income satisfies the exceptions for active banking, finance, or insurance income, or is certain rent and royalty income, as explained below. Similarly, Option Z provides rules for determining the extent to which gains or losses from sales of CFC stock are taken into account in determining active foreign market income.

In determining active foreign market income, a special rule generally excludes any income derived from any transactions if it was reasonable for a CFC or related person to anticipate that the property would be used, consumed, or disposed of in the United States or would be incorporated into another item that would be used, consumed or disposed of in the United States. For purposes of this rule, related persons includes any person that controls or is controlled by the CFC, or is controlled by common owners that control the CFC.

Passive income is excluded from the definition of active foreign market income. In addition, Option Z defines passive income for purposes of the passive foreign investment company rules of section 1291 *et seq.*, subject to certain limited exceptions. Similar to foreign personal holding company income under present law, passive income includes dividends, interest, rents, royalties, and annuities, the excess of gains over losses from the sale or exchange of certain property, the excess of gains over losses from transactions in commodities, the excess of foreign currency gains over foreign currency losses, certain interest and dividend equivalent payments, net income from notional principal contracts, and amounts received under a personal services contract or from the sale or other disposition of such contract.

The active financing exception exempts certain income from the passive income category. An item of income eligible for the active financing exception is active foreign market income under section 953. Under Option Z, the active financing exception is permanent.

3. Anti-base-erosion measures and inbound tax reform

Under both options, the Chairman's staff discussion drafts require the following measures intended to limit earnings stripping, or other transactions with tax avoidance potential:

- Repeal the regulatory rules that enable certain entities owned by CFCs to select their own entity classification;
- Repeal the statutory exemption from withholding tax for portfolio interest on corporate debt obligations, without overriding treaty obligations to the contrary, so that a portfolio interest exemption remains available for residents of other countries only when reciprocal exemptions are available to U.S. residents under U.S. income tax treaties;
- Repeal the DISC rules, and provide that deemed distributions or actual distributions
- as a result of the DISC election termination do not result in qualified dividend income eligible for the preferential tax rate allowed under section 1(h)(11);
- Deny deductions for related party indebtedness that arise from a base erosion arrangement;
- Disallow deductions for nontaxed reinsurance premiums paid and determine income without taking into account any return premium, ceding commission, reinsurance recovered or other amount received, or additional amount paid, with respect to the reinsurance for which the nontaxed reinsurance premium is paid to the extent the items are properly allocable to the premium;
- Reform the sourcing rules, specifically repealing the title passage rules for determining source of income from sale of inventory and the use of fair market valuation as a method of determining interest expense apportionment;
- Require recognition of gain or loss on disposition by a foreign partner of an interest in a foreign partnership that has income effectively connected with a U.S. trade or business and impose withholding tax with respect to amounts received on such disposition;
- Reform FIRPTA; and
- Disallow deductions as U.S.-source dividends those dividends from foreign corporations that are attributable to dividends from RICs and REITs.

Option Y also disallows deductions for interest expenses allocable to exempt income of a CFC.

Option Z disallows a deduction for a portion of the interest expense of a 10-percent U.S. shareholder of a CFC. In broad terms the portion of the interest expense for which a deduction is disallowed represents the interest that is apportioned to income of a CFC that is exempt from taxation by the United States (because it is the excludable portion of the CFC's active foreign market income). The interest disallowance rule applies before any other provision of the Code that limits the deductibility of any allocable CFC interest. The interest expense disallowance rule is applied separately with respect to the separate foreign tax credit limitation categories.

4. Modifications related to foreign tax credit

Chairman Baucus's staff discussion draft provides several reforms to the foreign tax credits that apply regardless of whether Option Y or Option Z is implemented. These reforms include the repeal of the section 902 indirect credit for foreign taxes deemed paid by 10-percent U.S. corporate shareholders of 10/50 companies by reason of dividends received from those 10/50 companies and the repeal of the splitter rules in section 909. In addition, a general rule is provided with respect to the transition rule that no credit is allowed for taxes attributable to the applicable percentage of previously deferred foreign income that is deducted from gross income. It also denies a deduction for any foreign tax for which a credit is disallowed. The income of the U.S. shareholder is not increased under section 78 by the amount of tax for which a foreign tax credit is not allowed.

Option Y

The proposal modifies the foreign tax credit limitation categories. Under the proposal, the foreign tax credit limitation is applied separately for six separate categories of income: (1) passive income; (2) subpart F income attributable to United States related income (as defined in amended section 955); (3) subpart F income attributable to low-taxed income (as defined in amended section 956); (4) foreign branch income, (5) subpart F income attributable to insurance income (as defined in section 953), and (6) all other income. This proposal relies on the new subpart F provisions to categorize CFC subpart F income for foreign tax credit purposes. By definition within the subpart F provisions, CFC subpart F income is either passive income (if it is attributable to foreign personal holding company income), United States related income, insurance income, or low-taxed income. Look-through rules apply to subpart F income inclusions to characterize such inclusions based on CFC's income to which it is attributable. Passive income earned by a branch is included in the passive income category and not as branch income under this proposal.

No foreign tax credit is allowed for any taxes (including withholding taxes) paid or accrued, or treated as paid or accrued, with respect to any dividend for which the 100-percent dividends-received deduction is allowed. A deduction for any foreign tax paid or accrued in respect of a deductible dividend also is denied. By contrast, a foreign tax credit is allowed for foreign tax imposed on income included under subpart F and for foreign tax paid directly by a domestic corporation on foreign-source income (on, for example, income from foreign sales). Likewise, a foreign tax credit generally is available for foreign withholding tax imposed on payments such as royalties and interest. A foreign tax credit is not, however, available for foreign withholding tax imposed on dividends for which the 100-percent deduction is permitted.

Option Z

The proposal modifies the foreign tax credit category limitations. Under the proposal, the foreign tax credit limitation is applied separately for three separate categories of income: (1) subpart F income from active foreign market income; (2) passive income; and (3) all other income. Financial services income, other than financial services income that is active foreign market income, is included in the all other income category in the case of a member of a financial services group and any other person which is predominantly engaged in the active conduct of a banking, insurance, financing, or similar business.

If income would be treated as derived from sources in the United States, but is treated as foreign source by the taxpayer in accordance with a treaty provision, the foreign tax credit limitation applies separately with respect to such income.

Finally, Option Z permits a taxpayer to select the separate income category to which it allocates taxes carried from taxable years prior to the effective date of Option Z to subsequent taxable years.

5. Transition rule

Regardless of which reform option for taxation of foreign income of CFCs is adopted, a transition rule for taxation of previously deferred foreign income is included. The proposal requires that a domestic corporation that is a U.S. shareholder of a CFC include its pro rata share of the accumulated deferred foreign income in gross income. A deduction of an applicable percentage of the mandatory inclusion is permitted, resulting in a 20-percent effective tax rate. A foreign tax credit is available only for taxes paid with respect of the taxable portion of the included income. The increase in the U.S. tax liability of the U.S. shareholder as a result of the mandatory inclusion is generally payable in installments over a period of up to eight years.

The mechanism for the mandatory inclusion of pre-effective date foreign earnings is subpart F. As of the close of the last taxable year of a CFC that ends before the revised subpart F regime takes effect, the subpart F income of the foreign corporation is increased by the accumulated deferred foreign income of the corporation. Consistent with the general operation of subpart F, each corporate U.S. shareholder of a CFC must include in income its pro rata share of the foreign corporation's subpart F income attributable to its accumulated deferred foreign income.

A new ordering rule for distributions out of previously taxed income is added to section 959. Under the new rule, distributions are made first out of the deductible portion of the subpart F inclusion for previously deferred foreign income. Absent this rule distributions would be considered made only partly out of this deductible portion and partly out of other previously taxed subpart F earnings (to the extent of those other previously taxed earnings). Because no foreign tax credits are allowed for foreign taxes related to the deductible portion of this subpart F income, absent this rule, additional foreign taxes imposed on previously taxed income that is distributed to a U.S. shareholder would be partly allowed and partly disallowed. To address the complexity and administrability concerns this raises, the proposal first sources distributions out of earnings attributable to the deductible portion of the subpart F inclusion for previously deferred foreign income. This has the effect of accelerating the distribution of historical earnings with a corresponding disallowance of credits for foreign taxes imposed on such earnings.

E. Chairman Camp's Tax Reform Act of 2014[227]

Chairman Camp's discussion draft is a comprehensive reform of individual and business income tax law. As part of its business reform proposals, it reduces the maximum corporate tax rate to 25 percent. The reforms to the U.S. international tax system are located in Title IV of Chairman Camp's discussion draft.

1. Participation exemption system

Chairman Camp's discussion draft establishes a participation exemption system for foreign income. This exemption is effectuated by means of a 95-percent deduction for the foreign-source portion of dividends received from certain foreign corporations ("specified 10-percent owned foreign corporations") by domestic corporations that are United States shareholders of those foreign corporations within the meaning of section 951(b).[228] The remaining five percent of an otherwise deductible dividend from a foreign corporation remains taxable. A specified 10-percent owned foreign corporation is any foreign corporation if any domestic corporation owns directly, or indirectly through a chain of ownership described under section 958(a), 10 percent or more of the voting stock of that foreign corporation. Thus, the deduction is available with respect to income received from either CFCs or uncontrolled section 902 corporations. This participation exemption does not change present law with respect to taxation of foreign branches of domestic companies.

The 95-percent dividends-received deduction is available only for the foreign-source portion of a dividend. The foreign-source portion of a dividend from a specified 10-percent owned foreign corporation for which the 95-percent deduction is allowed represents the portion of the dividend that relates to the foreign corporation's post-1986 undistributed foreign earnings.[229] The foreign-source portion of any dividend is, therefore, the amount that bears the same ratio to the dividend as the foreign corporation's post-1986 undistributed foreign earnings bears to the corporation's total post-1986 undistributed earnings. This rule complements the present law section 245 rule allowing a deduction for the U.S.-source portion of a dividend received from a qualified 10-percent owned foreign corporation.

The stock with respect to which the dividend is paid must have been held for a six-month period. No deduction is allowed in respect of any dividend on any share of stock that is held by the domestic corporation for 180 days or less during the 361-day period beginning on the date that is 180 days before the date on which the share becomes ex-dividend with respect to the dividend. A deduction also is not permitted in respect of any dividend on any share of stock to the extent the domestic corporation that owns the share is under an obligation (under a short sale or otherwise) to make related payments with respect to positions in substantially similar or related property. The 180-out-of-361-days test described above is satisfied only if the specified 10-percent owned foreign corporation is a specified 10-percent owned foreign corporation at all times during the period and the domestic corporation is a United States shareholder of the foreign corporation at all times during the period.

Under the proposal, solely for the purpose of determining a loss, a domestic corporate shareholder's adjusted basis in the stock of a specified 10-percent owned foreign corporation is reduced by an amount equal to the portion of any dividend received with respect to such stock from such foreign corporation that was not taxed by reason of a dividends received deduction allowable in any taxable year of such domestic corporation.

2. Modifications of anti-deferral regimes

Chairman Camp's discussion draft addresses base erosion through its modifications to subpart F with two of its provisions, one regarding passive and mobile income and another that addresses income from exploitation of intangibles. With respect to the first, the scope of what is considered subpart F passive or mobile income is modified to include only low-taxed foreign income. Chairman Camp's proposal provides that foreign base company income and insurance income do not include items of income received by a controlled foreign corporation which are subject to an effective tax rate imposed by a foreign country which is greater than or equal to the maximum U.S. corporate rate in effect (or half the maximum U.S. corporate tax rate in the case of foreign base company sales income). Foreign base company income does not include the "foreign percentage" (as defined under the proposal) of foreign base company intangible income if such foreign base company intangible income is subject to an effective tax rate imposed by a foreign country which is greater than the applicable percentage.[230] When fully implemented, the proposal results in requiring an effective tax rate of 15 percent for foreign base company intangible income. All foreign personal holding company intangible income is treated as a single item of income for purposes of the tax rate test.

In addition to the above, Chairman Camp's discussion draft also includes the following changes to the subpart F regime:

- makes permanent the CFC look-through rule;
- modifies and extends for five years (for taxable years beginning before January 1, 2020) the present-law temporary exceptions from subpart F foreign personal holding company income, foreign base company services income, and insurance income for certain income that is derived in the active conduct of a banking, financing, or similar business, or in the conduct of an insurance business;
- indexes for inflation the $1,000,000 de minimis amount for foreign base company income; and
- excludes from foreign base company sales income any income subject to a foreign tax rate of at least 50 percent of the maximum U.S. corporate tax rate and permits an exclusion of 50 percent of all other foreign base company sales income, increased to 100 percent if the foreign corporation is eligible for benefits as a qualified resident under a comprehensive income tax treaty[231] with the United States, and allows related deemed paid taxes to remain creditable notwithstanding the exclusion.

3. Anti-base-erosion measures

Chairman Camp's discussion draft includes two proposals that specifically are intended to target base erosion and inappropriate shifting of profits offshore.

Intangible income

The first of the two proposals that specifically address erosion of the U.S. tax base through shifting intangible income creates a new category of subpart F income requiring inclusion of certain intangible income derived by CFCs while also providing a phased-in deduction for a domestic corporation that directly earns income from its foreign exploitation of intangibles. The fully phased-in deduction from the gross income of the domestic corporation results in a reduced tax rate of 15 percent for income from the foreign exploitation of intangible property. As a result, Chairman Camp's discussion draft both increases the current U.S. taxation of income derived from intangibles owned or licensed by a CFC by requiring an effective tax rate of 15 percent and decreases the U.S. tax on the income of a U.S. corporation from its use of intangibles in foreign markets to a rate of 15 percent.[232]

The new subpart F category, foreign base company intangible income, is the excess of the corporation's adjusted gross income over 10 percent of the corporation's qualified business asset investment. This amount is reduced by the applicable percentage of the corporation's foreign personal holding company income, foreign base company sales income, foreign base company services income, and foreign base company oil related income. The applicable percentage is the excess of the corporation's adjusted gross income over 10 percent of the corporation's qualified business asset investment divided by the total adjusted gross income of the corporation. Adjusted gross income means the gross income of the corporation reduced by commodities gross income. Foreign base company intangible income is only subpart F income under the proposal to the extent that the income is subject to a foreign effective tax rate lower than the effective U.S. tax rate imposed after taking into account the deduction for foreign intangible income discussed below.

The deduction for the domestic corporation that has income from its foreign exploitation of intangibles is equal to the applicable percentage of the lesser of (1) the sum of the domestic corporation's foreign percentage of its net intangible income and the domestic corporation's share of a CFC's foreign base company intangible income multiplied by the CFC's foreign percentage, and (2) the taxable income of the domestic corporation.

Under the proposal, foreign-derived adjusted gross income is gross income derived in connection with property which is sold for use, consumption, or disposition outside the United States, or services provided with respect to persons or property located outside the United States. Property is not treated as sold for use, consumption, or disposition outside the United States if the taxpayer knew, or had reason to know, that the property would ultimately be sold for use, consumption, or disposition in the United States. Property sold to a related party will not be treated as sold for use, consumption, or disposition outside the United States unless the property is ultimately sold by a related party for use, consumption, or disposition outside the United States, or if the property is resold to an unrelated party outside the United States and no related party knew or had reason to know that the property would ultimately be sold for use, consumption, or disposition in the United States. Similar rules apply with respect to services.

Limitation on excessive interest expense deductions

Chairman Camp's discussion draft also addresses base erosion that results from excessive and disproportionate borrowing in the United States by limiting the deductibility of net interest expense[233] of a U.S. corporation that is a U.S. shareholder with respect to any CFC if both the CFC and the U.S. corporation are part of a worldwide affiliated group. Such a rule, commonly referred to as a thin-capitalization rule, is based in part on a relative leverage test. Under the proposal, a portion of otherwise deductible interest is disallowed if the U.S. group fails to meet both a relative-leverage test and a percentage-of-adjusted taxable income test. The lesser of the two amounts determined under these tests is the amount by which deductible interest is reduced. The proposal does not apply to a wholly domestic group.

In the relative leverage test, all U.S. members of the worldwide affiliated group are treated as one member in order to determine whether the group has excess domestic indebtedness as a result of a debt-to-equity differential. Excess domestic indebtedness is the amount by which the total indebtedness of the U.S. members exceeds 110 percent of the debt those members would hold if their aggregate debt-to-equity ratio were proportionate to the ratio of debt-to- equity in the worldwide group. The percentage of aggregate domestic debt represented by excess domestic indebtedness is the debt-to-equity differential by which net interest expense is multiplied to determine the amount of interest that would be disallowed under the relative leverage test. Intragroup debt and equity interests are disregarded for purposes of this computation.

The percentage of adjusted taxable income test computes the amount by which the net interest expense of a U.S. shareholder exceeds 40 percent of adjusted taxable income. The proposal requires that the U.S. shareholder first compute adjusted taxable income as defined in section 163(j)(6)(A), that is, taxable income increased by deductible losses, interest, depreciation and amortization, qualified production expenses and as prescribed under regulations. The net interest expense is the amount of interest paid or accrued in the taxable year in excess of the amount of interest includible in gross income for the same taxable year, as defined in section 163(j)(6)(B).

Several changes to section 163(j) conform its operation to the new subsection. Interest disallowed under either this rule or under section 163(j) may be carried forward to subsequent taxable years.

4. Modifications related to foreign tax credit

No foreign tax credit is allowed for any taxes (including withholding taxes) paid or accrued with respect to any dividend for which the 95-percent dividends-received deduction is allowed. A deduction for any foreign tax paid or accrued in respect of a deductible dividend also is denied. This foreign tax credit disallowance and deduction denial applies to foreign tax with respect to the entire amount of any deductible dividend even though a deduction is available for only 95 percent of the dividend. By contrast, a foreign tax credit is allowed for foreign tax imposed on income included under subpart F and for foreign tax paid directly by a domestic corporation on foreign-source income (on, for example, income from foreign sales). Likewise, a foreign tax credit generally is available for foreign withholding tax imposed on payments such as royalties and interest. A foreign tax credit is not, however, available for foreign withholding tax imposed on dividends for which the 95-percent deduction is permitted. Similar disallowance of foreign tax credits or deductions apply to the transitional mandatory repatriation.

With respect to indirect credits, the deemed-paid credit is repealed with respect to dividends received by a domestic corporation which owns 10-percent or more of the voting stock of a foreign corporation. A deemed-paid credit is provided with respect to any income inclusion under subpart F, limited to the amount of foreign income taxes properly attributable to the subpart F inclusion. Foreign income taxes under the proposal include income, war profits, or excess profits taxes paid or accrued by the CFC to any foreign country or possession of the United States. The proposal eliminates the need for computing and tracking cumulative tax pools.

Chairman Camp's discussion draft makes several changes to the limitations on foreign tax credits. It generally retains the separate category rules (that is, general category and passive category) for determining the foreign tax credit limitation. It renames the passive category as mobile category income and expands it to include a shareholder's foreign base company sales income and foreign base company intangible income. For purposes of computing the limitation, only directly allocable deductions are subtracted from gross foreign-source income to compute foreign-source taxable income. Taxpayers are not required under the proposal to allocate other deductions against foreign-source income for purposes of determining the foreign tax credit limitation. Directly allocable deductions are deductions that are directly incurred as a result of the activities that produce the related foreign-source income, such as salaries of sales personnel, supplies, and shipping expenses directly related to the production of foreign-source income, but not stewardship or interest expenses.

The proposal overrides certain inventory sales source rules for purposes of computing the foreign tax credit limitation. Amounts treated as foreign source by reason of the application of the special inventory sourcing rules of section 862(a)(6) and section 863(b)(2), and the regulations promulgated thereunder,[234] are treated as U.S.-source for purposes of computing the foreign tax credit limitation under the proposal.

5. Transition rule

The proposal generally requires that, for the last taxable year beginning before the participation exemption takes effect, any 10-percent U.S. shareholder of a CFC or other 10-percent owned foreign corporation must include in income its pro rata share of the undistributed, non-previously-taxed post-1986 foreign earnings of the corporation. Up to 90 percent of the amount so included in income is deductible by the U.S. shareholder, depending on whether the deferred earnings are in cash or other assets. The noncash portion is eligible for a deduction of 90 percent; the U.S. shareholder aggregate foreign cash position is eligible for a deduction of 75 percent. An amount equivalent to the taxes collected under this proposal is appropriated to the Highway Trust Fund.

The deduction results in a reduced rate of tax with respect to income from the required inclusion of pre-effective date earnings. A corresponding portion of the credit for foreign taxes is disallowed, thus limiting the credit to the taxable portion of the included income. In determining the increase in a 10-percent U.S. shareholder's U.S. tax liability as a result of the mandatory inclusion, the Code is applied as in effect before enactment of the discussion draft. For example, the corporate tax rate remains unchanged and the separate foreign tax credit limitation rules of present law section 904 apply.

The mechanism for the mandatory inclusion of pre-effective date foreign earnings is subpart F. In the last taxable year of a specified foreign corporation before the participation exemption system begins, the subpart F income of the foreign corporation is increased by the accumulated deferred foreign income of the corporation determined as of the close of that taxable year. The income inclusion required of a U.S. shareholder under this transition rule is reduced by the portion of aggregate foreign earnings and profits deficit allocated to that person by reason of that person's interest in one or more earnings and profits deficit foreign corporations. An earnings and profits deficit foreign corporation is defined as any specified foreign corporation owned by the U.S. shareholder as of February 26, 2014 and which also has a deficit in post-1986 earnings and profits as of that date. The U.S. shareholder aggregates its pro rata share in the foreign earnings and profits deficits of each such company and allocates it among the deferred foreign income corporations in which the shareholder is a U.S. shareholder. The aggregate foreign earnings and profits deficit allocable to a specified foreign corporation is in same ratio as the U.S. shareholder's pro rata share of post-1986 deferred income in that corporation bears to the U.S. shareholder's pro rata share of accumulated post-1986 deferred foreign income from all deferred income companies of such shareholder.

In contrast to the participation exemption deduction available only to domestic corporations that are U.S. shareholders under subpart F, the transition rule applies to all U.S. shareholders[235] of a specified foreign corporation, which includes any foreign corporation in which a U.S. person owns 10 percent of the voting stock. Consistent with the general operation of subpart F, each 10-percent U.S. shareholder of a specified foreign corporation must include in income its pro rata share of the foreign corporation's subpart F income attributable to its accumulated deferred foreign income.[236]

A taxpayer may elect to pay the increased tax liability over an eight-year period, without interest, in the following amounts: installments one through five in an amount equal to eight percent of the net tax liability; a sixth installment of 15 percent of the net tax liability; the seventh is 20 percent and the eighth, 25 percent. In addition, a special rule permits election to defer the transition net tax liability for shareholders of a 10-percent U.S. shareholder that is a flow-through entity known as an S corporation until a triggering event occurs, such as transfer of shares in the S corporation, liquidation, or change in status of the company. When such an event occurs, the shareholder of an S corporation that elected deferral under the special rule for S corporation shareholders may be eligible to elect to pay the net tax liability in installments, subject to rules similar to those generally applicable absent deferral.

V. Recent U.S. International Tax Proposals Compared

A. Introduction

To varying degrees, the proposals described above to change the U.S. international tax rules alter the timing and scope of U.S. taxation of foreign income of U.S. multinational companies. The Administration's budget proposals provide discrete, though significant, modifications within the existing U.S. international tax framework. Chairman Wyden's legislation, Senator Enzi's legislation, Chairman Baucus's staff discussion draft, and Chairman Camp's discussion draft represent more thoroughgoing reform of the existing framework. Among the proposals, only the Administration's budget proposals largely leave in place the existing U.S. system's mixed timing of U.S. taxation of income of foreign subsidiaries of U.S. companies. Under this system of mixed timing, some income is taxed when it is earned ("current U.S. taxation"), and other income is taxed when, if ever, it is repatriated ("deferred U.S. taxation"). The other recent proposals, by contrast, change the timing of U.S. taxation of income derived by foreign subsidiaries. All of these other proposals largely or entirely eliminate deferred U.S. taxation of foreign subsidiary income. In place of deferred U.S. taxation, Wyden's legislation and Option Z of Chairman Baucus's staff discussion draft provide current U.S. taxation of all foreign subsidiary income. Senator Enzi's legislation, Option Y of Chairman Baucus's staff discussion draft, and Chairman Camp's discussion draft replace deferred U.S. taxation with current U.S. taxation of some foreign subsidiary income and exemption from U.S. taxation of other foreign subsidiary income.

The proposals also alter the scope of U.S. taxation of foreign income of U.S. multinational companies. The Administration's budget proposals, Chairman Wyden's legislation, and Option Z of Chairman Baucus's staff discussion draft expand the scope of current U.S. taxation of foreign income. Senator Enzi's legislation, Option Y of Chairman Baucus's staff discussion draft, and Chairman Camp's discussion draft expand the scope of current U.S. taxation of foreign income in significant ways but also include elements that relax current U.S. taxation. All the proposals other than the Administration's budget proposals include rate-lowering features, either generally applicable rate lowering or targeted rate reductions.

Some of the recent proposals include special rules related to the taxation of foreign intangible income, passive income, income from a banking, financing, or insurance business, income from related party sales and services, and income from sales or services to U.S. customers.

The recent proposals are more directed at the U.S. taxation of foreign income of U.S. multinational companies ("outbound") than they are at the U.S. taxation of U.S. income of foreign multinational companies ("inbound"), but some proposals include provisions addressed to inbound issues.

B. Timing and Scope of U.S. Taxation of Foreign Income

The U.S. international tax rules provide a mix of current U.S. taxation and deferred U.S. taxation of income of foreign subsidiaries of U.S. companies. Most business income of foreign subsidiaries is subject to deferred U.S. taxation only when the income is distributed as a dividend to U.S. parent companies. By contrast, subpart F imposes on a U.S. parent company current U.S. taxation of its share of a foreign subsidiary's passive investment income and income from certain related party sales and services.

Maintain mixed timing of taxation of foreign income

The Administration's budget proposals largely leave in place this mixed system of timing. Individually and in the aggregate, however, the proposals shift timing toward current U.S. taxation and away from deferred U.S. taxation. Some proposals – such as those to tax currently excess returns associated with transfers of intangibles offshore; to create a new category of subpart F income for transactions involving digital goods or services; to prevent avoidance of foreign base company sales income through manufacturing services arrangements; and to limit the application of exceptions under subpart F for transactions that use reverse hybrids to create so-called stateless income – provide this shift toward current taxation by expanding, or by eliminating exceptions from, subpart F. Other proposals – including those to defer a deduction for interest expense related to deferred foreign income of foreign subsidiaries; to limit shifting of income through intangible property transfers; to disallow a deduction for excessive non-taxed reinsurance premiums paid to affiliates; to restrict deductions for excessive interest of members of financial reporting groups; and to restrict the use of hybrid arrangements to create stateless income – shift the U.S. mixed timing system toward current U.S. taxation by increasing U.S. parent companies' taxable income outside subpart F, chiefly by restricting deductions that under present law reduce the U.S. tax base. Although the Administration's budget proposals shift the U.S. system toward current U.S. taxation, they leave in place deferred U.S. taxation of much routine business income of foreign subsidiaries of U.S. companies. Consequently, the Administration's budget proposals are discrete responses to profit shifting and base erosion in particular contexts – for example, in relation to valuable intellectual property – rather than a systematic overhaul of the mixed timing system. Consequently, the proposals address in discrete contexts one fundamental criticism of the mixed timing system, that deferred U.S. taxation provides an incentive to locate profits or to invest outside the United States rather than within the United States. The Administration's budget proposals largely leave unaddressed a second fundamental criticism of the mixed timing system, that deferred U.S. taxation discourages repatriation of foreign earnings.

Impose current taxation on all foreign income

Two recent proposals, Chairman Wyden's legislation and Option Z of Chairman Baucus's staff discussion draft, replace the mixed timing features of the current U.S. international tax rules with current U.S. taxation of all the income of foreign subsidiaries of U.S. companies. Chairman Wyden's legislation treats all income of a CFC as subpart F income, thereby subjecting the income to full U.S. taxation in the hands of the CFC's shareholders at the time the CFC derives the income. Chairman Baucus's Option Z similarly imposes tax on a CFC shareholder for its share of all items of income of the CFC. Because both proposals impose current U.S. taxation on all CFC earnings (to the extent the CFC is owned by 10-percent U.S. shareholders), both proposals exempt from U.S. tax subsequent distributions of those earnings. Accordingly, these proposals eliminate present law's tax disincentive to repatriate earnings and respond to the criticism that present law favors foreign investment over U.S. investment. On the other hand, by increasing the present value of some U.S. companies' U.S. tax liabilities associated with foreign income compared with their U.S. tax liabilities under present law, the proposals might create or increase a tax disadvantage for U.S. companies when those companies compete in foreign markets with foreign companies that face no home country taxation on foreign investment. Chairman Wyden's legislation attempts to address competitiveness concerns by reducing the generally applicable corporate tax rate to a flat 24 percent. Option Z of Chairman Baucus's staff discussion draft attempts to address competitiveness concerns by providing a preferential tax rate, by means of a 40-percent exclusion, for a CFC's active foreign market income.[237]

Eliminate deferred taxation of foreign income

Senator Enzi's legislation, Option Y of Chairman Baucus's staff discussion draft, and Chairman Camp's discussion draft eliminate deferred U.S. taxation of income of foreign subsidiaries of U.S. companies. By contrast with Chairman Wyden's legislation and Chairman Baucus's Option Z, Senator Enzi's legislation, Chairman Baucus's Option Y, and Chairman Camp's discussion draft do not impose (through subpart F) current U.S. taxation on all earnings of CFCs. Instead, these latter proposals, like some of the Administration's budget proposals, expand subpart F to new categories of income such as intangible income and low-taxed foreign income, but they also reform the taxation of foreign income in certain taxpayer favorable ways, such as by repealing (Senator Enzi's legislation and Option Y) or narrowing (Chairman Camp's discussion draft) the foreign base company sales and services income rules; by providing a preferential tax rate for some intangible income derived directly by U.S. companies (Senator Enzi's legislation and Chairman Camp's discussion draft); and by liberalizing the treatment of certain cross-border income under the active finance and active insurance exceptions (Option Y). The broad timing and scope consequences of Senator Enzi's legislation, Option Y, and Chairman Camp's discussion draft are to replace present law's mix of current U.S. taxation and deferred U.S. taxation of CFC earnings with a mix of current U.S. taxation – broadened in certain ways and narrowed in other ways – and U.S. tax exemption of CFC earnings. [238]

A chart at the end of section V.C., immediately below, gives an overview of the timing and scope of U.S. taxation of the earnings of foreign subsidiaries under present law and the recent proposals.

C. Special Rules for the Taxation of Certain Kinds of Income

The recent proposals to modify the U.S. international tax rules include various special rules for, among other concerns, the taxation of intangible income, passive income, income from a banking, financing, or insurance business, income from related party sales and services, and income from sales or services to U.S. customers. Some of the recent proposals also include provisions addressed at inbound issues.

Intangible income

Three of the recent proposals – Chairman Wyden's legislation and Options Y and Z of Chairman Baucus's staff discussion draft – include no special rules for the taxation of intangible income. Chairman Wyden's legislation provides current U.S. taxation of all CFC earnings at the generally prevailing U.S. tax rate (24 percent for income of corporate shareholders); it does not distinguish among different items of income based on the character of each item. Chairman Baucus's Option Z similarly provides current U.S. taxation of all CFC earnings. This proposal includes one distinction, that between active foreign market income, for which the proposal allows a 40-percent exclusion, and all other CFC income, for which the proposal provides current U.S. taxation at the generally prevailing U.S. tax rate. Chairman Baucus's Option Y provides current U.S. taxation of some CFC earnings and exemption from U.S. taxation of other CFC earnings. Current U.S. taxation or exemption from U.S. taxation under the proposal depends on the character of the income as, for example, passive income or low-taxed income. But the proposal introduces no new distinctions between intangible income and all other income of a CFC.

The other three recent proposals – the Administration's budget proposals, Senator Enzi's legislation, and Chairman Camp's discussion draft – provide special rules for the taxation of intangible income. Some of the special rules may broaden U.S. taxation significantly. For example, the Administration's budget proposals (1) tax a U.S. person on excess income from transactions connected with intangibles transferred by the U.S. person to a related CFC and (2) provide a new category of subpart F income (called foreign base company digital income) for some income of a CFC related to the CFC's use of intangible property developed by a related party. Chairman Camp's discussion draft provides current U.S. taxation (at a preferential tax rate) of CFC earnings in excess of a 10 percent return on the CFC's investment in tangible, depreciable property. Senator Enzi's legislation disadvantages intangible income not by directly expanding current taxation, but instead by providing that intangible income may not benefit from the legislation's exception from current taxation of a CFC's low-taxed foreign income for qualified business income.

Two special sets of rules for intangible income in the recent proposals provide taxpayer-favorable incentives. Chairman Camp's discussion draft provides a preferential tax rate for intangible income derived in connection with sales or services to non-U.S. customers through a CFC or directly by a domestic corporation. The preferential tax is allowed by means of a deduction that phases down from 55 percent in 2015 to 40 percent in 2019 and thereafter (with a resulting 15 percent U.S. tax rate based on the legislation's maximum U.S. tax rate of 25 percent). Senator Enzi's legislation provides a preferential tax rate for intangible income derived directly by a domestic corporation – and not also, as in Chairman Camp's discussion draft, indirectly through a CFC – from the active conduct of a U.S. trade or business in connection with intangible property giving rise to the income. The preferential tax rate is allowed by means of a 50 percent deduction.

Passive income; income from a banking, financing, or insurance business

The recent proposals to modify the U.S. international tax rules include a number of changes to the present law treatment of passive income and income from a banking, financing, or insurance business. For passive income, the changes include taxpayer-favorable provisions such as (1) the provisions in Senator Enzi's legislation and Chairman Camp's discussion draft to make the exclusion from foreign personal holding company income for payments by a CFC to a related CFC of dividends, interest, rents, and royalties (the CFC look-through rule) permanent and (2) the similar exclusion in Option Y of Chairman Baucus's staff discussion draft for dividends paid by a CFC to a related CFC. The changes to passive income in the recent proposals also include restrictions that prevent some passive income from benefiting from preferential treatment. For example, Senator Enzi's legislation and Chairman Baucus's Option Y deny the dividends received deduction for payments that are considered dividends for U.S. tax purposes but that are deductible under foreign law.[239] Option Z of Chairman Baucus's staff discussion draft provides that active foreign market income, for which a 40-percent exclusion is permitted, may not include passive income. One Administration budget proposal denies the section 954(c)(6) CFC look-through and section 954(c)(3) same-country exclusions for payments made to related foreign reverse hybrid entities held directly by a U.S. owner when the payments are deductible under foreign law.

Options Y and Z of Chairman Baucus's staff discussion draft also modify the present law definition of foreign personal holding company income (considered "passive income" under Option Z). For example, Options Y and Z broaden the present law exception for regular dealers in property that gives rise to dividends, interest, rents, royalties, and annuities, and other categories of property. Under Options Y and Z, any item of income, gain, deduction, or loss (including dividends, interest, rents, royalties, annuities, and certain equivalent amounts) from any transaction entered into in the ordinary course of the CFC's trade or business as a dealer is not taken into account in computing passive income.[240]

The recent proposals include rules related to the exempt insurance exception from subpart F insurance income and to the expired temporary exceptions from foreign personal holding company income for income from the active conduct of a banking, financing, or insurance business. Senator Enzi's legislation and Options Y and Z of Chairman Baucus's staff discussion draft makes permanent the exempt insurance, active finance, and active insurance exceptions.[241] Chairman Camp's discussion draft extends those exceptions for five years but, in the case of active finance and active insurance income that is subject to a foreign tax rate of less than 50 percent of the legislation's 25-percent maximum corporate tax rate, limits the exceptions to a 50- percent, rather than complete, exclusion.

Option Y and Option Z of Chairman Baucus's staff discussion draft also modify exempt insurance, active finance, and active insurance exceptions. Among the more significant modifications, Options Y and Z liberalize the exceptions when CFCs derive banking, financing, or insurance income in the context of cross-border activities.[242]

Chairman Wyden's legislation imposes current U.S. taxation on all CFC earnings. As a consequence, the present law special rules for passive income and banking, financing, and insurance income have no significance (and, as a technical matter, are repealed).

Related party sales and services income

The recent proposals modify or repeal the present law foreign base company sales and services income rules. These rules treat some income from related-party sales and services as subpart F income. Chairman Wyden's legislation, Senator Enzi's legislation, and Options Y and Z of Chairman Baucus's staff discussion draft repeal the foreign base company sales and services income rules. In their place, Chairman Wyden's legislation and Option Z impose current U.S. taxation of all CFC earnings, and Senator Enzi's legislation and Option Y create new categories of subpart F income for low-taxed CFC income. An Administration budget proposal and Chairman Camp's discussion draft modify the foreign base company sales rules. One Administration budget proposal broadens subpart F treatment for related-party sales by including within the definition income derived by a CFC from the sale of property manufactured on behalf of the CFC by a related party. Chairman Camp's discussion draft provides a 50-percent exclusion for foreign base company sales income, and excludes entirely from foreign base company sales income (1) any item of income that is subject to foreign tax at a rate at least half the 25-percent maximum corporate tax rate provided by the legislation and (2) any income of a CFC if the CFC is eligible for the benefits of a U.S. income tax treaty.

Income from U.S. sales and services

Senator Enzi's legislation, Options Y and Z of Chairman Baucus's staff discussion draft, and Chairman Camp's discussion draft include special rules imposing current U.S. taxation, at the generally applicable tax rates under those proposals, on certain items of income derived in connection with sales and services to U.S. customers. Senator Enzi's legislation allows a 50-percent deduction for intangible income from the active conduct of a U.S. trade or business with respect to the intangible property giving rise to the income, but it permits the deduction only for income derived in connection with sales for use outside the United States or with services for persons or properties outside the United States. Option Y creates a new category of subpart F income for United States related income, generally defined as income from sales or services for the U.S. market. Chairman Camp's discussion draft denies the preferential U.S. tax rate for intangible income derived by a CFC or a U.S. corporation to the extent the income is, in broad terms, derived from sales or services for the U.S. market.

On the following page is a summary, in chart form, of the preceding comparison in section V.B. and V.C. of the recent proposals to alter the current U.S. international tax rules.

D. Inbound Provisions

Some of the recent proposals include provisions to address the U.S. taxation of the U.S. income of foreign multinational businesses with U.S. operations. For example, an Administration's budget proposal limits the U.S. net interest deduction of a member of a foreign- parented group to the member's proportionate share of the group's net interest expense. Another Administration proposal and a provision in Chairman Baucus's staff discussion draft treat a non- U.S. person's gain or loss from the sale of a partnership interest as effectively connected with the conduct of a U.S. trade or business to the extent the gain or loss is attributable to the person's distributive share of the partnership's unrealized gain or loss attributable to property used in the U.S. trade or business. A third Administration proposal and a provision in Chairman Baucus's staff discussion draft deny a deduction for related-party payments involving, among other things, hybrid payments, hybrid transfers, or hybrid entities. The Administration's budget proposals, Chairman Baucus's staff discussion draft, and Chairman Camp's discussion draft include rules denying an insurance company a deduction for certain reinsurance premiums paid to an affiliated foreign company to the extent the company is not subject to U.S. income tax on the premiums.

Table 1. Timing and Scope of U.S. Taxation of CFC Income Under Present Law and Recent Proposals

	Current U.S. Taxation	Deferred U.S. Taxation	Exempt from U.S. Taxation
Present Law	Investment income; related party sales and services income	Business income (except for left-column items taxed currently)	None
Administration's budget proposals	Investment income; related party sales and services income; high-return, low-tax intangible income; digital income	Business income (except for left-column items taxed currently)	None
Chairman Wyden's legislation	All income[1]	None[2]	None
Senator Enzi's legislation	Investment income; low-tax income (including low-tax intangible income)	Minimal[3]	Business income (except for left-column items taxed currently)
Chairman Baucus's Option Y	Investment income (modified); low-tax income; U.S.-related income	None	Foreign market business income (except for left-column items taxed currently)
Chairman Baucus's Option Z	All income[4]	None	None
Chairman Camp's discussion draft	Investment income;[5] low-taxed intangible income;[6] related-party services income; low-taxed, related party sales income[7]	Minimal[8]	Business income (except for left-column items taxed currently)

Notes:

[1] But the legislation reduces the corporate tax rate to 24 percent.

[2] The legislation does not, however, provide a rule for the taxation of untaxed CFC earnings derived before the effective date of the legislation.

[3] The legislation imposes a 1.75-percent tax (by means of a 95-percent dividends received deduction against income taxed at the 35-percent corporate tax rate) when taxpayers receive distributions of previously untaxed CFC earnings. The legislation also preserves present law's deferred U.S. taxation of CFC earnings to the extent taxpayers do not elect the preferential transition tax for those earnings.

[4] But the legislation allows taxpayers to exclude 40 percent of active foreign market income.

[5] Chairman Camp's discussion draft reduces the generally prevailing U.S. corporate tax rate (applicable to income of the U.S. parent corporation and also to, among other items, investment income of a CFC) to 25 percent.

[6] When fully phased in, Chairman Camp's discussion draft allows a 40-percent deduction for intangible income from serving foreign markets. Against a generally prevailing corporate tax rate of 25 percent, the 40-percent deduction produces U.S. taxation of foreign intangible income at a 15 percent rate.

[7] Chairman Camp's discussion draft allows a 50-percent exclusion for low-tax related party sales income and a 100-percent exclusion if the CFC that derives the income is eligible for the benefits of a U.S. income tax treaty.

[8] The legislation imposes a 1.25-percent tax (by means of a 95-percent dividends received deduction against income taxed at the legislation's reduced 25-percent corporate tax rate) when taxpayers receive distributions of previously untaxed CFC earnings.

End Notes

[1] This document may be cited as follows: Joint Committee on Taxation, *Present Law and Background Related to Proposals to Reform the Taxation of Income of Multinational Enterprises* (JCX-90-14), July 21, 2014.

[2] Department of the Treasury, *General Explanations of the Administration's Fiscal Year 2015 Revenue Proposals* ("Administration's budget proposal" or "Administration's proposal"), March 2014, p. 9 and pp. 42-65.

[3] The proposals described in this document are the following: Bipartisan Tax Fairness and Simplification Act of 2011, S. 727 (112th Cong., 1st Sess., April 5, 2011) ("Chairman Wyden's proposal" or "Chairman Wyden's legislation"); United States Jobs Creation and International Tax Reform Act of 2012, S. 2091 (112th Cong., 2d Sess., Feb. 9, 2012), ("Senator Enzi's proposal" or "Senator Enzi's legislation"); Chairman Baucus's staff discussion draft, Nov. 19, 2013 ("Chairman Baucus's staff discussion draft" (or Option Y and/or Option Z thereof) or "Chairman Baucus's discussion draft"); Chairman Camp's discussion draft, Tax Reform Act of 2014, Feb. 21, 2014 ("Chairman Camp's discussion draft" or "Chairman Camp's proposal").

[4] Senator Enzi's legislation and Chairman Camp's discussion draft preserve a minimal amount of deferred U.S. taxation of foreign subsidiary earnings because they permit a 95-percent deduction for dividends received from foreign subsidiaries out of foreign income, not a 100-percent deduction.

[5] Restatement (Third) of Foreign Relations Law of the United States, secs. 402 and 403, (1987).

[6] American Law Institute, *Federal Income Tax Project: International Aspects of United States Income Taxation, Proposals on U.S. Taxation of Foreign Persons and of the Foreign Income of U.S. Persons*, 4-8 (1987).

[7] Unless otherwise indicated, all section references are to the Internal Revenue Code of 1986, as amended (the "Code"). Section 7701(a)(30) defines U.S. person to include all U.S. citizens and residents as well as domestic entities such as partnerships, corporations, estates, and certain trusts. Whether a noncitizen is a resident is determined under rules in section 7701(b).

[8] A U.S. citizen or resident living abroad may be eligible to exclude from U.S. taxable income certain foreign earned income and foreign housing costs under section 911. For a description of this exclusion, see *Present Law and Issues in U.S. Taxation of Cross-Border Income* (JCX-42-11), September 6, 2011, p. 52.

[9] Secs. 951-964.

[10] Secs. 1291-1298.

[11] In lieu of the foreign tax credit, foreign income, war profits, and excess profits taxes are allowed as deductions under section 164(a)(3).

[12] Secs. 901, 902, 960, 1291(g).

[13] See sec. 7874. For a description of provisions designed to curtail inversion transactions, see Joint Committee on Taxation, *Present Law and Issues in U.S. Taxation of Cross-Border Income* (JCX-42-11), September 6, 2011, p. 50.

[14] For a detailed description of the U.S. transfer pricing rules, see Joint Committee on Taxation, *Present Law and Background Related to Possible Income Shifting and Transfer Pricing* (JCX-37-10), July 20, 2010, pp. 18- 50.

[15] The term "related" as used herein refers to relationships described in section 482, which refers to "two or more organizations, trades or businesses (whether or not incorporated, whether or not organized in the United States, and whether or not affiliated) owned or controlled directly or indirectly by the same interests."

[16] Section 1059A buttresses section 482 by limiting the extent to which costs used to determine custom valuation can also be used to determine basis in property imported from a related party. A taxpayer that imports property from a related party may not assign a value to the property for cost purposes that exceeds its customs value.

[17] H.R. Rep. No. 99-426, p. 423.

[18] Treas. Reg. sec. 301.7701-1, *et seq.*

[19] The check-the-box regulations replaced Treas. Reg. sec. 301.7701-2, as in effect prior to 1997, (the "Kintner regulations") under which the classification of unincorporated entities for Federal tax purposes was determined on the basis of four characteristics indicative of status as a corporation: continuity of life, centralization of management, limited liability, and free transferability of interests. An entity that possessed three or more of these characteristics was treated as a corporation; if it possessed two or fewer, then it was treated as a partnership. Thus, to achieve characterization as a partnership under this system, taxpayers needed to arrange the governing instruments of an entity in such a way as to eliminate two of these corporate characteristics. The advent and proliferation of limited liability companies ("LLCs") under State laws allowed business owners to create customized entities that possessed a critical common feature—limited liability for investors—as well as other corporate characteristics the owners found desirable. As a consequence, classification was effectively elective for well- advised taxpayers.

[20] For domestic entities, the State corporation statute must describe the entity as a corporation, joint-stock company, or in similar terms. The regulations also treat insurance companies, organizations that conduct certain banking activities, organizations wholly owned by a State, and organizations that are taxable as corporations under other Code provisions as *per se* corporations.

[21] See, *e.g.*, *Hunt v. Commissioner*, 90 T.C. 1289 (1988).

[22] Sec. 861(a)(1); Treas. Reg. sec. 1.861-2(a)(1).

[23] Secs. 861(a)(1) and 862(a)(1). For purposes of certain reporting and withholding obligations the source rule in section 861(a)(1)(B) does not apply to interest paid by the foreign branch of a domestic financial institution. This results in the payment being treated as a withholdable payment. Sec. 1473(1)(C).

[24] Sec. 884(f)(1).

[25] Secs. 861(a)(2), 862(a)(2).

[26] Sec. 861(a)(2)(B).

[27] Sec. 861(a)(4).

[28] *Ibid.*

[29] Sec. 865(a).

[30] Sec. 865(g)(1)(B).

[31] Sec. 865(g)(1)(A).

[32] Sec. 865(g).

[33] Secs. 865(b), 861(a)(6), 862(a)(6); Treas. Reg. sec. 1.861-7(c).

[34] Sec. 865(e)(2).

[35] Sec. 863(b). A taxpayer may elect one of three methods for allocating and apportioning income as U.S.- or foreign-source: (1) 50-50 method under which 50 percent of the income from the sale of inventory property in such a situation is attributable to the production activities and 50 percent to the sales activities, with the income sourced based on the location of those activities; (2) IFP method under which, in certain circumstances, an independent factory price ("IFP") may be established by the taxpayer to determine income from production activities; (3) books and records method under which, with advance permission, the taxpayer may use books of account to detail the allocation of receipts and expenditures between production and sales activities. Treas. Reg. sec. 1.863-3(b), (c). If production activity occurs only within the United States, or only within foreign countries, then all income is sourced to where the production activity occurs; when production activities occur in both the United States and one or more foreign countries, the income attributable to production activities must be split between U.S. and foreign sources. Treas. Reg. sec. 1.863-3(c)(1). The sales activity is generally sourced based on where title to the property passes. Treas. Reg. secs. 1.863-3(c)(2), 1.861-7(c).

[36] Rev. Rul. 91-32, 1991-1 C.B. 107.

[37] Sec. 865(c).

[38] Sec. 865(d).

[39] Sec. 861(a)(3). Gross income of a nonresident alien individual, who is present in the United States as a member of the regular crew of a foreign vessel, from the performance of personal services in connection with the international operation of a ship is generally treated as foreign-source income.

[40] Treas. Reg. sec. 1.861-4(b).

[41] Sec. 861(a)(7).

[42] Sec. 863(c).
[43] Sec. 863(d).
[44] Sec. 863(e).
[45] Sec. 861(a)(9). This provision effects a legislative override of the opinion in *Container Corp. v. Commissioner*, 134 T.C. 122 (February 17, 2010), aff'd 2011 WL1664358, 107 A.F.T.R.2d 2011-1831 (5th Cir. May 2, 2011), in which the Tax Court held that fees paid by a domestic corporation to its foreign parent with respect to guarantees issued by the parent for the debts of the domestic corporation were more closely analogous to compensation for services than to interest, and determined that the source of the fees should be determined by reference to the residence of the foreign parent-guarantor. As a result, the income was treated as income from foreign sources.
[46] For purposes of U.S. tax law, a corporation is treated as domestic if it is incorporated under the laws of the United States or of any State; all other corporations are foreign. Secs. 7701(a)(4) and 7701(a)(5).
[47] A lesser set of sanctions is provided with respect to a transaction that would meet the definition of an inversion transaction described above, except that the 80 percent ownership threshold is not met. In such a case, if at least a 60 percent ownership threshold is met, then a second set of rules applies to the inversion. Under these rules, the inversion transaction is respected (that is, the foreign corporation is treated as foreign), but any applicable corporate-level "toll charges" for establishing the inverted structure are not offset by tax attributes such as net operating losses or foreign tax credits. Certain partnership transactions are also subject to the inversion rules.
[48] *E.g.*, the portfolio interest exception in section 871(h) (discussed below).
[49] The United States has set forth its negotiating position on withholding rates and other provisions in the United States Model Income Tax Convention of November 15, 2006 (the "U.S. Model Treaty"). Because each treaty reflects considerations unique to the relationship between the two treaty countries, treaty withholding tax rates on each category of income are not uniform across treaties.
[50] Secs. 871(a), 881. If the FDAP income is also ECI, it is taxed on a net basis, at graduated rates.
[51] *Commissioner v. Wodehouse,* 337 U.S. 369, 388-89 (1949). After reviewing legislative history of the Revenue Act of 1936, the Supreme Court noted that Congress expressly intended to limit taxes on nonresident aliens to taxes that could be readily collectible, i.e., subject to withholding, in response to "a theoretical system impractical of administration in a great number of cases. H.R. Rep. No. 2475, 74th Cong., 2d Sess. 9-10 (1936)." In doing so, the Court rejected P.G. Wodehouse's arguments that an advance royalty payment was not within the purview of the statutory definition of FDAP income.
[52] *Commissioner v. Wodehouse,* 337 U.S. 369, 393 (1949).
[53] Although technically insurance premiums paid to a foreign insurer or reinsurer are FDAP income, they are exempt from withholding under Treas. Reg. sec. 1.1441-2(a)(7) if the insurance contract is subject to the excise tax under section 4371. Treas. Reg. sec. 1.1441-2(b)(1)(i), -2(b)(2).
[54] For purposes of this rule, whether a person is considered a resident in the United States is determined by application of the rules under section 7701(b).
[55] Sec. 871(a)(2). In addition, certain capital gains from sales of U.S. real property interests are subject to tax as effectively connected income (or in some instances as dividend income) under the Foreign Investment in Real Property Tax Act of 1980, discussed *infra* at part II.B.4.
[56] Secs. 871(a)(1)(D), 881(a)(4).
[57] Secs. 871(i)(2)(A), 881(d); Treas. Reg. sec. 1.1441-1(b)(4)(ii).
[58] Sec. 861(a)(1)(B); Treas. Reg. sec. 1.1441-1(b)(4)(iii).
[59] Secs. 871(g)(1)(B), 881(a)(3); Treas. Reg. sec. 1.1441-1(b)(4)(iv).
[60] Treas. Reg. sec. 1.1461-1(c)(2)(ii)(A), (B). Regulations require a bank to report interest if the recipient is a nonresident alien who resides in a country with which the United States has a satisfactory exchange of information program under a bilateral agreement and the deposit is maintained at an office in the United States. Treas. Reg. secs. 1.6049-4(b)(5) and 1.6049-8. The IRS has published a list of the 78 countries whose residents are subject to the reporting requirements, and a list of countries with respect to which the reported information will be automatically exchanged naming only one country, Canada. Rev. Proc. 2012-24, I.R. B. 2012-20 (May 14, 2012), available at http://www.irs.gov/irb/2012-20_IRB/ar11.html.
[61] Sec. 871(h)(2).
[62] Sec. 163(f)(2)(B). The exception to the registration requirements for foreign targeted securities was repealed in 2010, effective for obligations issued two years after enactment, thus narrowing the portfolio interest exemption for obligations issued after March 18, 2012. See Hiring Incentives to Restore Employment Law of 2010, Pub. L. No. 111-147, sec. 502(b).
[63] Sec. 871(h)(3).
[64] Sec. 871(h)(4).
[65] Sec. 881(c)(3)(C).
[66] Sec. 881(c)(3)(A).
[67] Secs. 1441, 1442.

[68] Withholding agent is defined broadly to include any U.S. or foreign person that has the control, receipt, custody, disposal, or payment of an item of income of a foreign person subject to withholding. Treas. Reg. sec. 1.1441-7(a).
[69] Secs. 871, 881, 1441, 1442; Treas. Reg. sec. 1.1441-1(b).
[70] A reduced rate of withholding of 14 percent applies to certain scholarships and fellowships paid to individuals temporarily present in the United States. Sec. 1441(b). In addition to statutory exemptions, the 30- percent withholding tax with respect to interest, dividends or royalties may be reduced or eliminated by a tax treaty between the United States and the country in which the recipient of income otherwise subject to withholding is resident.
[71] Treas. Reg. sec. 1.1461-1(b), (c).
[72] See Treas. Reg. secs. 1.1441-7(a) (definition of withholding agent includes foreign persons).
[73] Sec. 1462.
[74] Secs. 4371-4374.
[75] Generally, when a foreign person qualifies for benefits under such a treaty, the United States is not permitted to collect the insurance premiums excise tax from that person.
[76] In Rev. Rul. 2008-15, 2008-1 C.B. 633, the IRS provided guidance to the effect that the excise tax is imposed separately on each reinsurance policy covering a U.S. risk. Thus, if a U.S. insurer or reinsurer reinsures a U.S. risk with a foreign reinsurer, and that foreign reinsurer in turn reinsures the risk with a second foreign reinsurer, the excise tax applies to both the premium to the first foreign reinsurer and the premium to the second foreign reinsurer. In addition, if the first foreign reinsurer is resident in a jurisdiction with a tax treaty containing an excise tax exemption, the revenue ruling provides that the excise tax still applies to both payments to the extent that the transaction violates an anti-conduit rule in the applicable tax treaty. Even if no violation of an anti-conduit rule occurs, under the revenue ruling, the excise tax still applies to the premiums paid to the second foreign reinsurer, unless the second foreign reinsurer is itself entitled to an excise tax exemption.
[77] Secs. 871(b), 882.
[78] Secs. 871(b)(2), 882(a)(2).
[79] Sec. 875.
[80] Sec. 864(b).
[81] Sec. 864(b)(1).
[82] Sec. 864(b)(2).
[83] Sec. 864(c).
[84] Sec. 864(c)(2).
[85] Sec. 864(c)(3).
[86] This income is subject to net-basis U.S. taxation after allowance of a credit for any foreign income tax imposed on the income. Sec. 906.
[87] Sec. 864(c)(4)(B).
[88] Sec. 864(c)(4)(D)(i).
[89] Sec. 864(c)(5)(A).
[90] Sec. 864(c)(5)(B).
[91] Sec. 864(c)(4)(C).
[92] Sec. 864(c)(1)(B).
[93] Sec. 864(c)(6).
[94] Sec. 864(c)(7).
[95] Pub. L. No. 96-499. The rules governing the imposition and collection of tax under FIRPTA are contained in a series of provisions enacted in 1980 and subsequently amended. See secs. 897, 1445, 6039C, 6652(f).
[96] Sec. 897(a). In addition, section 6039C authorizes regulations that would require a return reporting foreign direct investments in U.S. real property interests. No such regulations have been issued, however.
[97] Sec. 1445 and Treasury regulations thereunder. The Treasury Department is authorized to issue regulations that reduce the 35-percent withholding on distributions to 20-percent withholding during the time that the maximum income tax rate on dividends and capital gains of U.S. persons is 20 percent.
[98] See Treas. Reg. sec. 1.884-1(g), -5.
[99] Sec. 884(a).
[100] Sec. 884(b).
[101] See sec. 884(d)(2) (excluding, for example, earnings and profits attributable to gain from the sale of U.S. real property interests described in section 897 (discussed below)).
[102] Sec. 884(b).
[103] Sec. 884(f)(1)(A).
[104] Sec. 884(f)(1)(B).
[105] U.S. multinational companies also may engage in earnings stripping, but the subpart F rules limit earnings stripping opportunities (by, for example, treating a loan from a controlled foreign corporation to its U.S. parent

corporation as an investment in U.S. property subject to inclusion under section 956 (described below) and by treating interest paid to a CFC as subpart F income (barring availability of an exception from subpart F).
[106] Sec. 163(j).
[107] If a tax treaty reduces the rate of tax on interest paid or accrued by the taxpayer, the interest is treated as interest on which no Federal income tax is imposed to the extent of the same proportion of such interest as the rate of tax imposed without regard to the treaty, reduced by the rate of tax imposed under the treaty, bears to the rate of tax imposed without regard to the treaty. Sec. 163(j)(5)(B).
[108] Secs. 951-964.
[109] Secs. 1291-1298.
[110] Secs. 901, 902, 960, 1293(f).
[111] Secs. 951-964.
[112] Secs. 951(b), 957, 958.
[113] Sec. 951(a).
[114] Sec. 954.
[115] Sec. 953.
[116] Sec. 952(a)(3)-(5).
[117] Sec. 954. Prior to 2005, subpart F income also included foreign base company shipping income derived from the use of an aircraft or vessel in foreign commerce, the performance of services directly related to the use of any such aircraft or vessel, the sale or other disposition of any such aircraft or vessel, and certain space or ocean activities. However, for taxable years beginning after 1975 and before 1987, subpart F income did not include foreign base company shipping income to the extent that such shipping income was reinvested during the taxable year in certain qualified shipping investments.[117] To the extent that, in a subsequent year, a net decrease in qualified shipping investments occurred, however, the amount of previously excluded subpart F income equal to such decrease is itself considered subpart F income under section 955. Therefore, withdrawal of previously excluded subpart F income from qualified shipping investments triggers an equivalent increase in the subpart F income of the CFC.
[118] Sec. 953(c).
[119] Joint Committee on Taxation, *General Explanation of the Tax Reform Act of 1986* (JCS-10-87), May 4, 1987, p. 968.
[120] Secs. 951(a)(1)(B), 956.
[121] Sec. 956(c)(1).
[122] Sec. 956(c)(2).
[123] Sec. 954(c)(6).
[124] Sec. 954(c)(6)(C). Tax Relief, Unemployment Insurance Reauthorization, and Job Creation Act of 2010, Pub. L. No. 111-312, sec. 751(a).
[125] Congress has extended the application of section 954(h) several times, most recently in 2013. Sec. 954(h). American Taxpayer Relief Act of 2012, Pub. L. No. 112-240, sec. 322(b); Pub. L. No. 111-312, sec. 750(a), 2010; Pub. L. No. 110-343, div. C, sec. 303(b), 2008; Pub. L. No. 109-222, sec. 103(a)(2), 2006; Pub. L. No. 107-147, sec. 614, 2002; Pub. L. No. 106-170, sec. 503, 1999; Pub. L. No. 105-277, 1998.
[126] Sec. 954(h)(3)(E).
[127] Sec. 954(c)(3).
[128] Sec. 954(b)(4).
[129] Sec. 959(a)(1).
[130] Sec. 959(a)(2).
[131] Sec. 959(c).
[132] Sec. 961(a).
[133] Sec. 961(b).
[134] Pub. L. No. 99-514.
[135] Sec. 1297.
[136] Secs. 1293-1295.
[137] Sec. 1291.
[138] Sec. 1296.
[139] Secs. 531-537.
[140] Secs. 541-547. The accumulated earnings tax rules and the personal holding company rules apply in respect of both U.S.-source and foreign-source income.
[141] Secs. 551-558, 1246-1247.
[142] AJCA, sec. 413.
[143] Secs. 901, 902, 960, 1291(g).
[144] Secs. 901, 904.
[145] Sec. 904(c).
[146] Treas. Reg. sec. 1.861-8(b), Temp. Treas. Reg. sec. 1.861-8T(c).
[147] Temp. Treas. Reg. sec. 1.861-9T, Treas. Reg. sec. 1.861-17.

[148] Sec. 864(e)(1), (6); Temp. Treas. Reg. sec. 1.861-14T(e)(2).

[149] Secs. 864(e)(5), 1504.

[150] Sec. 1504(b)(3).

[151] AJCA sec. 401.

[152] Hiring Incentives to Restore Employment Act, Pub. L. No. 111-147, sec. 551(a).

[153] Sec. 904(d). AJCA generally reduced the number of income categories from nine to two, effective for tax years beginning in 2006. Before AJCA, the foreign tax credit limitation was applied separately to the following categories of income: (1) passive income, (2) high withholding tax interest, (3) financial services income, (4) shipping income, (5) certain dividends received from noncontrolled section 902 foreign corporations (also known as "10/50 companies"), (6) certain dividends from a domestic international sales corporation or former domestic international sales corporation, (7) taxable income attributable to certain foreign trade income, (8) certain distributions from a foreign sales corporation or former foreign sales corporation, and (9) any other income not described in items (1) through (8) (so-called "general basket" income). A number of other provisions of the Code, including several enacted in 2010 as part of Pub. L. No. 111-226, create additional separate categories in specific circumstances or limit the availability of the foreign tax credit in other ways. See, *e.g.*, secs. 865(h), 901(j), 904(d)(6), 904(h)(10).

[154] Sec. 904(d)(3). The subpart F rules applicable to CFCs and their 10-percent U.S. shareholders are described below.

[155] Sec. 904(d)(4).

[156] Sec. 909.

[157] Mihir A. Desai, C. Fritz Foley, and James R. Hines, "Tax Policy and the Efficiency of U.S. Direct Investment Abroad," *National Tax Journal*, vol. 64, no. 4, December 2011, pp. 1055-1082.

[158] Mihir A. Desai, C. Fritz Foley, and James R. Hines Jr., "Repatriation Taxes and Dividend Distortions," *National Tax Journal*, vol. 54, no. 4, pp. 829-851.

[159] Harry Grubert and Rosanne Altshuler, "Fixing the System: An Analysis of Alternative Proposals for the Reform of International Tax," *National Tax Journal*, vol. 66, no. 3, September 2013, pp. 671-712.

[160] However, repatriation of foreign earnings by U.S. corporations each year reduces the total stock of foreign earnings on which U.S. tax liability has been deferred.

[161] This is a flow concept, showing the relative amount of corporate income deferred every two years from 2000 to 2010. Worldwide income is defined as total receipts minus deductions, plus constructive taxable income received from related foreign corporations, plus CFC deferred income. CFC data before 2004, included above, was from a restricted sample based on U.S. parent size. CFC data is for CFC's with net earnings and profits, and is before foreign (and U.S.) tax. Corporate income includes all U.S. subchapter C corporations with net income, before tax. There may be a time lag between the CFC and U.S. corporate income tax data because of fiscal year reporting differences.

[162] Some research has shown that investors discount their valuation of a firm's permanently reinvested earnings, on which no U.S. income tax expense has been recognized for financial accounting purposes, to reflect estimated future U.S. tax liability, and that the lower valuation is more pronounced for companies that have high levels of excess cash. See Lisa Bryan-Kutcher, Lisa Eiler, and David A. Guenther, "Taxes and Financial Assets: Valuing Permanently Reinvested Foreign Earnings," *National Tax Journal*, vol. 61, no. 4, December 2008, pp. 699-720.

[163] Michael P. Devereux, Ben Lockwood, and Michela Redoano, "Do Countries Compete Over Corporate Tax Rates?" *Journal of Public Economics*, vol. 92, no. 5-6, June 2008, pp. 1210-1235.

[164] This research is surveyed in Ruud A. De Mooij and Sjef Ederveen, "Taxation and Foreign Direct Investment: A Synthesis of Empirical Research," *International Tax and Public Finance*, vol. 10, no. 6, November 2003, pp. 673-693. Studies do, however, generally find that foreign direct investment is more responsive to effective tax rates than statutory tax rates.

[165] Maryann P. Feldman and Dieter F. Kogler, "Stylized Facts in the Geography of Innovation," in Bronwyn H. Hall and Nathan Rosenberg (eds.), *Handbook of the Economics of Innovation*, vol. 1, pp. 381-410, North-Holland Publishing Co., 1986.

[166] Rachel Griffith, Helen Miller, and Martin O'Connell, "Ownership of Intellectual Property and Corporate Taxation," *Journal of Public Economics*, vol. 112, April 2014, pp. 12-23.

[167] For case studies and analysis of how U.S. multinational enterprises may shift income to low-tax jurisdictions, see Joint Committee on Taxation, *Present Law and Background Related to Possible Income Shifting and Transfer Pricing* (JCX-37-10), July 20, 2010.

[168] The Subcommittee hearings included: "Offshore Profit Shifting and the U.S. Tax Code," held on September 20, 2012 which focused on certain tax strategies used by Microsoft and Hewlett-Packard (available to view at http://www.hsgac.senate.gov/subcommittees/investigations/hearings/offshore-profit-shifting-and-the-us-tax-code); "Offshore Profit Shifting and the U.S. Tax Code - Part 2 (Apple Inc.)," held on May 21, 2013 (available to view at http://www.hsgac.senate.gov/subcommittees/investigations/hearings/offshore-profit-shifting-and-the-us-tax- code_-part-2); and "Caterpillar's Offshore Tax Strategy," held on April 1, 2014 (available to view at http://www.hsgac.senate.gov/subcommittees/investigations/hearings/caterpillars-offshore-tax-strategy).

[169] See U.S. Senate Permanent Subcommittee on Investigations, "Memorandum: Offshore Profit Shifting and the U.S. Tax Code - Part 2 (Apple Inc.)," May 21, 2013, available at http://www.hsgac.senate.gov/download/?id=CDE3652B-DA4E-4EE1-B841-AEAD48177DC4.

[170] See http://www.consilium.europa.eu/uedocs/cms_Data/docs/pressdata/en/ec/131069.pdf.

[171] Matthias Dischinger and Nadine Riedel, "Corporate Taxes and the Location of Intangible Assets Within Multinational Firms," *Journal of Public Economics*, vol. 95, no. 7-8, August 2011, pp. 691-707.

[172] Harry Grubert, "Intangible Income, Intercompany Transactions, Income Shifting, and the Choice of Location," *National Tax Journal*, vol. 56, no. 1, March 2003, pp. 221-242.

[173] Kimberly Clausing, "Multinational Firm Tax Avoidance and Tax Policy," *National Tax Journal*, vol. 62, no. 4, December 2009, pp. 703-725.

[174] OECD Publishing, *Addressing Base Erosion and Profit Shifting*, 2013, available at http://dx.doi.org/10.1787/9789264192744-en ("BEPS Report").

[175] *Ibid.*, pp.35-36.

[176] *Ibid.*, p.42.

[177] *Ibid.*, p.37.

[178] *Ibid.*, p.44.

[179] *Ibid., p.44.*

[180] OECD, *Declaration on Base Erosion and Profit Shifting*, May 29, 2013, available at http://www.oecd.org/tax/C-MIN(2013)22-FINAL-ENG.pdf.

[181] OECD Publishing, *Action Plan on Base Erosion and Profit Shifting*, 2013, available at http://dx.doi.org/10.1787/9789264202719-en ("BEPS Action Plan").

[182] OECD, *Public Discussion Draft, BEPS Action 1: Address the Tax Challenges of the Digital Economy*, March 24, 2014, available at http://www.oecd.org/ctp/tax-challenges-digital-economy-discussion-draft-march- 2014.pdf, ("Digital Economy Discussion Draft").

[183] OECD, *Comments Received on Public Discussion Draft, BEPS Action 1: Address the Tax Challenges of the Digital Economy*, April 16, 2014, available at http://www.oecd.org/ctp/comments-action-1-tax-challenges-digital-economy.pdf; OECD, *Additional Comments Received on Public Discussion Draft, BEPS Action 1: Address the Tax Challenges of the Digital Economy*, April 18, 2014, available at http://www.oecd.org/ctp/additional- comments-action-1-tax-challenges-digital-economy.pdf.

[184] OECD, *Public Discussion Draft, BEPS Action 2: Neutralise the Effects of Hybrid Mismatch Arrangements (Recommendations for Domestic Laws)*, March 19, 2014, available at http://www.oecd.org/ctp/aggressive/hybrid-mismatch-arrangements-discussion-draft-domestic-laws- recommendations-march-2014.pdf, ("Hybrid Discussion Draft").

[185] OECD, *Comments Received on Public Discussion Drafts, BEPS Action 2: Neutralise the Effects of Hybrid Mismatch Arrangements*, May 1, 2014, available at http://www.oecd.org/tax/aggressive/comments-action-2-hybrid-mismatch-arrangements.pdf.

[186] OECD, *Harmful Tax Competition: an Emerging Global Issue*, 1998, available at http://www.oecd.org/tax/transparency/44430243.pdf. Since that time, the OECD has issued updates to this report including, OECD, *Towards Global Tax Co-operation*, 2000, available at http://www.oecd.org/tax/harmful/2090192.pdf; OECD, *The OECD's Project on Harmful Tax Practices: The 2001 Progress Report*, 2001, available at http://www.oecd.org/ctp/harmful/2664438.pdf; OECD, *The OECD's Project on Harmful Tax Practices: The 2004 Progress Report*, 2004, available at http://www.oecd.org/tax/harmful/30901115.pdf; OECD, *The OECD's Project on Harmful Tax Practices: 2006 Update on Progress in Member Countries*, 2006, available at http://www.oecd.org/tax/harmful/37446434.pdf.

[187] On July 15, 2014, the OECD approved an update to the OECD Model Tax Convention. According to the OECD announcement, the update does not include any results from the ongoing work on the BEPS Action Plan. See, OECD Announcement, *OECD Approves the 2014 Update to the OECD Model Tax Convention*, available at www.oecd.org/ctp/treaties/2014-update-model-tax-convention.htm.

[188] OECD, *Public Discussion Draft, BEPS Action 6: Preventing the Granting of Treaty Benefits in Inappropriate Circumstances*, March 14, 2014, available at http://www.oecd.org/ctp/treaties/treaty-abuse- discussion-draft-march-2014.pdf, ("Treaty Discussion Draft").

[189] OECD, *Comments Received on Public Discussion Draft, BEPS Action 6: Preventing the Granting of Treaty Benefits in Inappropriate* Circumstances, April 11, 2014, available at http://www.oecd.org/tax/treaties/comments-action-6-prevent-treaty-abuse.pdf.

[190] OECD, *Public Consultation, Discussion Draft on Transfer Pricing Documentation and CbC Reporting*, 30 January 2014, available at http://www.oecd.org/ctp/transfer-pricing/discussion-draft-transfer-pricing-documentation.pdf, ("Transfer Pricing Discussion Draft").

[191] Comments received on the discussion draft, volumes I through IV, are available at http://www.oecd.org/ctp/transfer-pricing/comments-discussion-draft-transfer-pricing-documentation.htm.

[192] Hybrid Discussion Draft, p.8.

[193] Treaty Discussion Draft, pp.24-31.

[194] The descriptions of various intellectual property regimes relies largely on secondary sources including: Lisa Evers, Helen Miller, and Christoph Spengel, Centre for European Economic Research, *Intellectual Property Box Regimes: Effective Tax Rates and Tax Policy Considerations*, (Discussion Paper No. 13-070), November 2013, available at http://ftp.zew.de/pub/zew-docs/dp/dp13070.pdf; Japan External Trade Organization, *European Patent Box Regimes*, April 2013, available at https://www.jetro.go.jp/world/europe/ip/pdf/european_patent_box_regimes_en.pdf; Peter Merrill, *et. al.*, "Time for the United States to Consider the Patent Box?," *Tax Notes*, March 26, 2012, p.1665; Robert Atkinson and Scott Andes, The Information Technology & Innovation Foundation, *Patent Boxes: Innovation in Tax Policy and Tax Policy for Innovation*, October 2011, available at http://www.itif.org/files/2011-patent-box-final.pdf; Ernst & Young, *Patent Income Deduction*, 2011, available at http://www.ey.com/Publication/vwLUAssets/Patent_Income_Deduction_2011/$FILE/PID%202011.pdf; and Garrigues, *International Tax Review*, April 2008, available at http://www.garrigues.com/es/Publicaciones/Articulos/Documents/Antonio_Matute_04042008135214.pdf.

[195] Bloomberg BNA, *Daily Tax Report*, "EU Ends Parent-Subsidiary Provision, Begins Probe of 'Patent Box' Tax Schemes," June 20, 2014, 120 DTR I-1.

[196] Transition rules provide that prior law remains applicable to licenses in effect prior to the effective date of the statute. This summary of the Entrepreneur Law is largely based on publications of KPMG Abogados S.L., "New Tax Measures introduced by law 14/2013 of 27 September 2013, on support for and the internationalization of entrepreneurs," available at http://www.catedraemprenedoria.udl.cat/sites/default/files/Novedades-2013-Ley-14- ingles.pdf, and KPMG, *flash International Executive Alert 2013-144* (October 23, 2013), available at http://www.kpmg.com/US/en/IssuesAndInsights/ArticlesPublications/flash-international-executive- alert/Documents/flash-international-executive-alert-2013-144-oct.pdf.

[197] For licenses subject to the law prior to the Entrepreneur Law, the availability of the exemption ends in the fiscal year when sales or revenues from exploitation of the intangible exceed six times the cost of developing the intangible.

[198] However, if the zero-tax jurisdiction is a member state in the European Union, the taxpayer may provide evidence that the entity is economically sound.

[199] European Commission Memo, *Questions and Answers on the Parent Subsidiary Directive*, November 25, 2013, available at http://europa.eu/rapid/press-release_MEMO-13-1040_en.htm.

[200] The member states are Austria, Belgium, Bulgaria, Croatia, Cyprus, Czech Republic, Denmark, Estonia, Finland, France, Germany, Greece, Hungary, Ireland, Italy, Latvia, Lithuania, Luxembourg, Malta, Netherlands, Poland, Portugal, Romania, Slovakia, Slovenia, Spain, Sweden, and the United Kingdom.

[201] Council of the European Union Press Release, *Council adopts amendment closing tax loophole for corporate groups*, July 8, 2014, available at www.consillium.eropa.eu/uedocs/cms_data/docs/pressdata/en/ecofin/143709.pdf. Council of the European Union, Interinstitutional File: 2013/0400 (CNS), June 27, 2014, available at register.consillium.europa.eu/doc/svr?l=EN&f=ST%2010996%202014%20INIT.

[202] See, Landwell & Associes Societe d'avocats, *Changes to Austrian Tax Law*, January 20, 2014, available at http://www.landwell.fr/proposed-changes-to-austrian-tax-law.html.

[203] See, Deloitte, *International Tax World Tax Advisor*, January 24, 2014, pp.1-2, available at http://www2.deloitte.com/content/dam/Deloitte/global/Documents/Tax/dtt_tax_worldtaxadvisor_140124.pdf.

[204] See, Deloitte, *International Tax Germany Tax Alert*, June 13, 2013, available at http://www2.deloitte.com/content/dam/Deloitte/global/Documents/Tax/dttl-tax-alert-germany-130613.pdf.

[205] Omar Zuniga, "The New Mexican BEPS Legislation," *Tax Notes International*, January 6, 2014, p.78.

[206] Department of the Treasury, *General Explanations of the Administration's Fiscal Year 2015 Revenue Proposals*, March 2014, p. 9 and pp. 42-65.

[207] The proposal states that the exclusions for reinsurance recovered and ceding commissions are allowed "in the same proportion that the premium deduction was denied." Department of the Treasury, *General Explanations of the Administration's Fiscal Year 2015 Revenue Proposals*, March 2014, p. 48.

[208] "Bipartisan Tax Fairness and Simplification Act of 2011," S. 727 (112th Congress 1st Sess. April 5, 2011), introduced by Chairman Wyden and Senators Coats and Begich.

[209] Chairman Wyden's proposal sec. 209.

[210] See Chairman Wyden's proposal sec. 206 (amending section 849(b) of the AJCA).

[211] See http://www.wyden.senate.gov/imo/media/doc/Wyden-Coats%20Two%20Pager%20FINAL1.pdf.

[212] Senator Enzi's legislation and a more detailed description of the legislation are available at http://www.enzi.senate.gov/public/index.cfm/files/serve?File_id=74f4e648-4a80-474e-a393-2f8fec36e6f4.

[213] The term "participation exemption," commonly used in describing similar systems in other countries, refers to the exemption granted to a domestic corporation for earnings of a foreign corporation by virtue of the present corporation's participation in the ownership of the subsidiary.

[214] A noncontrolled section 902 corporation is a foreign corporation in which a domestic corporation owns 10 percent or more of the voting stock and from which the domestic corporation receives dividends. Sec. 904(d)(2)(E)(i).

[215] Sec. 245(a)(5)(A).

[216] Sec. 245(a)(5)(B).

[217] These holding period requirements parallel the section 246(c)(1) requirements for the dividends- received deduction available under present law sections 243, 244, and 245.

[218] The proposal adopts the definition of intangible property found in section 936.

[219] It does not include amounts treated as received by the domestic corporation under section 367(d)(2) with respect to any intangible property, payments under a cost-sharing arrangement entered into under section 482, or amounts received from a CFC by a 10-percent U.S. shareholder of that CFC that is attributable or properly allocable to subpart F income or to effectively connected income subject to net-basis U.S. income tax. An amount otherwise not treated as subpart F is treated as such if the amount creates or increases a deficit that under section 952(c) may reduce the subpart F income of the payor or any other CFC.

[220] That is, the permanent extension of the look-through provision and active financing income exception, and the active business exception (other than for intangible income) in the new category of subpart F income.

[221] Under present law, section 862(a)(6) treats income from the sale outside the United States of inventory property purchased within the United States as foreign-source income and section 863(b)(2) treats income from the sale of inventory property produced (in whole or in part) by a taxpayer in the United States and sold outside the United States, or produced (in whole or in part) outside the United States and sold in the United States, as partly U.S.-source and partly foreign-source income.

[222] On November 19, 2013, former Senator Baucus released his proposed international tax reform in the form of three legislative discussion drafts while Chairman of the Senator Finance Committee: International Discussion Draft Common provisions, International Discussion Draft Option Y and International Discussion Draft Option X, collectively referred to interchangeably as Chairman Baucus's discussion drafts or Chairman Baucus's staff discussion drafts; if referred to separately, as Common Provisions, Option Y or Option Z. Links to the full text of the legislative language as well as staff summaries are available at http://www.finance.senate.gov/ newsroom/chairman/release/?id=f946a9f3-d296-42ad-bae4-bcf451b34b14. See also, Joint Committee on Taxation, *Technical Explanation of the Senate Committee on Finance Chairman's Staff Discussion Draft of Provisions to Reform International Business Taxation* (JCX-15-13), November 19, 2013.

[223] Under the proposal, a CFC's undistributed foreign earnings are undistributed earnings that are not attributable to income that is effectively connected with the conduct of a U.S. trade or business and subject to U.S. income tax or to any dividend received directly or indirectly from a U.S. corporation (including, for example, a corporation taxable under subchapter C of the Code, a regulated investment company, or a real estate investment trust).

[224] The interest accrual amount with respect to PFIC stock in any taxable year is the stock owner's adjusted basis in the stock at the beginning of the year (or, if the taxpayer acquires stock during the year, the adjusted basis at the time of acquisition) multiplied by the sum of five percentage points plus the monthly Federal short-term rate determined under section 1274(d) for the first month ending during that year.

[225] A related person for purposes of this proposal means a related person as defined in section 954(b).

[226] Low-taxed income does not include insurance income (as defined under section 953), foreign personal holding income (as determined under section 954), United States related income (as defined in section 955), certain income subject to the international boycott factor, illegal bribes, kickback, etc. included in subpart F, and income derived from any foreign country during any period to which section 901(j) applies to such foreign country.

[227] Complete legislative language of the Tax Reform Act of 2014, released by Chairman Camp is available at http://waysandmeans.house.gov/uploadedfiles/statutory_text_tax_reform_act_of_2014_discussion_draft 022614.pdf. For a complete description, see, Joint Committee on Taxation, *Technical Explanation of the Tax Reform Act of 2014, A Discussion Draft of the Chairman of the House Committee on Ways and Means to Reform the Internal Revenue Code: Title IV Participation Exemption System for the Taxation of Foreign Income* (JCX-15-14), February 26, 2014.

[228] Under section 951(b) a corporation is a United States shareholder of a foreign corporation if it owns (within the meaning of section 958(a)), or is considered as owning by applying the rules of section 958(b), 10 percent or more of the voting stock of the foreign corporation.

[229] Undistributed foreign earnings include both foreign income on which a U.S. taxpayer may be taxed under subpart F and other foreign income on which no U.S. taxpayer is taxed before receipt of the dividend.

[230] The applicable percentage corresponds to the phase-down of the corporate income tax rate under section 3001 of the discussion draft. For the purpose of the tax rate test, the applicable percentage for any taxable year beginning in 2015 is 45 percent, 2016 is 48 percent, 2017 is 52 percent, 2018 is 56 percent and 2019 and thereafter is 60 percent.

[231] The phrase "comprehensive income tax treaty" refers to any bilateral treaty for the elimination of double income taxation. By limiting the provision to companies that are eligible as qualified resident for all benefits of such a treaty, the scope of the provision is intended to be limited to those companies that satisfy the robust limitation-on-benefits provisions of income tax treaties that are included to prevent the inappropriate claims of treaty benefits by third-country residents.

[232] The applicable percentage phases in over time in accordance with the phase-in of the lower domestic corporate tax rate. The applicable percentage is 55 percent for 2015, 52 percent for 2016, 48 percent for 2017, 44 percent for 2018, and 40 percent for 2019 and thereafter.

[233] Net interest for these purposes is defined in section 163(j)(6)(B) as the excess of interest paid or accrued over the interest includible in gross income for the taxable year.

[234] Under present law, section 862(a)(6) treats income from the sale outside the United States of inventory property purchased within the United States as foreign-source income and section 863(b)(2) treats income from the sale of inventory property produced (in whole or in part) by a taxpayer in the United States and sold outside the United States, or produced (in whole or in part) outside the United States and sold in the United States, as partly U.S.-source and partly foreign-source income.

[235] Sec. 951(b), which defines United States shareholder as any U.S. person that owns 10 percent or more of the voting classes of stock of a foreign corporation.

[236] For purposes of taking into account its subpart F income under this rule, a noncontrolled 10/50 corporation is treated as a CFC.

[237] Active foreign market income is income that is "attributable to economically significant activities" in relation to a trade or business and that is derived in connection with sales to for use outside the United States or services for people or property outside the United States. The rules related to active foreign market income are described in more detail in Part IV.D.

[238] Senator Enzi's legislation and Chairman Camp's discussion draft leave a small remaining tax when CFCs repatriate previously untaxed earnings. Both proposals allow a 95-percent deduction for dividends received from CFCs out of foreign earnings. At the present law 35-percent maximum corporate tax rate, this 95-percent deduction in Senator Enzi's legislation provides deferred U.S. taxation of CFC earnings at a 1.75 percent rate (five percent of 35 percent). At the 25-percent corporate tax rate of Chairman Camp's discussion draft, the 95-percent deduction provides deferred U.S. taxation of CFC earnings at a 1.25 percent rate. Senator Enzi's legislation also leaves in place deferred U.S. taxation of pre-effective-date earnings at the full 35-percent rate under present law to the extent that taxpayers choose not to subject those pre-effective-date earnings to the optional 10.5 percent transition tax on actual and deemed repatriations in transition.

[239] In the case of payments between related CFCs that are treated as dividends for U.S. tax purposes but that are deductible under foreign law, Senator Enzi's legislation and Chairman Baucus's Option Y deny look- through treatment and instead treat the payments as subpart F income.

[240] For a description of other changes to the definition of foreign personal holding company income, see Joint Committee on Taxation, *Technical Explanation of the Senate Committee on Finance Chairman's Staff Discussion Draft of Provisions to Reform International Business Taxation* (JCX-15-13), November 19, 2013, pp. 33, 41-42.

[241] In Option Z, these exceptions have the consequence that exempt insurance, active financing, and active insurance income are considered active foreign market income for which the 40-percent exclusion is available.

[242] For detailed descriptions of these and other modifications, see Joint Committee on Taxation, *Technical Explanation of the Senate Committee on Finance Chairman's Staff Discussion Draft of Provisions to Reform International Business Taxation* (JCX-15-13), November 19, 2013, pp. 34-37, 43-46.

In: U.S. International Tax System
Editor: Holly Lanford
ISBN: 978-1-63321-976-2

Chapter 2

OPENING STATEMENT OF RON WYDEN, CHAIRMAN, SENATE COMMITTEE ON FINANCE. HEARING ON "THE U.S. TAX CODE: LOVE IT, LEAVE IT OR REFORM IT!"*

The U.S. tax code is infected with the chronic diseases of loopholes and inefficiency. These infections are hobbling America's drive to create more good-wage, red, white and blue jobs here at home. They are a significant drag on the economy and are harming U.S. competitiveness. The latest outbreak of this contagion is the growing wave of corporate inversions, where American companies move their headquarters out of the U.S. in pursuit of lower tax rates.

The inversion virus now seems to be multiplying every few days. Medtronic, Mylan, Mallinckrodt and many more deals have either occurred recently or are currently in the works. Medtronic's proposed $42 billion merger with Covidien was record-breaking when it was announced in June. But the ink in the record books had barely dried when AbbVie announced its intention on Friday to acquire Shire for almost $55 billion. According to the July 15th edition of Marketplace, "What's going on now is a feeding frenzy ... Every investment banker now has a slide deck that they're taking to any possible company and saying, 'you have to do a corporate inversion now, because if you don't, your competitors will.'"

Congress has been aware of the inversion virus for a long time. In fact, it passed legislation purporting to solve the problem a decade ago. But the underlying sickness continues to gnaw away at the American economy with increasing intensity. The American tax code is an anti-competitive mess. Accountants, lawyers, and fast-buck artists looking for tax shelters feed off it. This mess is driving American investment dollars overseas, and according to the Joint Committee on Taxation, it is costing American taxpayers billions.

On a bipartisan basis, the Finance Committee must respond now. First, let's work together to immediately cool down the inversion fever. The inversion loophole needs to be plugged now. Second, let's use the space created by these immediate steps to apply the indisputable, ultimate cure: comprehensive tax reform.

* This is an edited, reformatted and augmented version of a statement presented July 22, 2014 before the Senate Committee on Finance.

I've got nine long years of sweat equity in tax reform. With former Senator Gregg, and current Senators Begich and Coats, we have produced what still is the Senate's only bipartisan federal income tax overhaul in almost thirty years. Obviously Senators here have differing ideas about tax reform. Let's recognize that what really counts is that the Finance Committee isn't back here once again discussing inversions a decade from now.

Comprehensive tax reform needs to happen soon. The outbreak of inversions shows that without curing the disease once and for all, the illness will keep plaguing the American economy. It will get tougher to create those red, white and blue American jobs. Our tax base will keep eroding. Cash piles trapped overseas will grow. Investment will be driven elsewhere.

The Finance Committee invited a number of CEOs from the inverting companies to join our discussion today. None accepted our invitation. I hope these executives will soon change their minds and be willing to answer questions Finance Committee members have about this issue.

The fact is, without immediate, comprehensive tax reform, an antidote to the inversion virus is needed now to protect the American economy. This wave of inversions may be good for shareholders, investment bankers and private equity firms, yet it is bad for America. America's free enterprise system is at its best when there is a level playing field. And inversions bestow tax favors on some parties and further distort the free market.

Absent tax reform being enacted immediately, what happens if the inversion virus leads to 20 more inversions over the summer? Many inversions to this point have happened in the medical field, but the Wall Street Journal just reported that there is evidence of inversions spreading to manufacturing and retail. How many more infections can America's economic body endure?

Global markets are expanding. Stockpiles of cash sitting overseas are growing at record levels. Foreign competitors are getting more aggressive in chomping at the bit to get a deal on the backs of the American taxpayer. The time for action is now. This committee needs to move now, on a bipartisan basis, to close the loopholes that are fueling the growth of the inversion virus. Then the Finance Committee needs to cure the disease once and for all with comprehensive tax reform. Let's come together on a bipartisan basis to accomplish both tasks, and I will work with each member of the committee every step of the way.

In: U.S. International Tax System
Editor: Holly Lanford
ISBN: 978-1-63321-976-2

Chapter 3

TESTIMONY OF ROBERT B. STACK, DEPUTY ASSISTANT SECRETARY FOR INTERNATIONAL TAX AFFAIRS, U.S. DEPARTMENT OF THE TREASURY. HEARING ON "THE U.S. TAX CODE: LOVE IT, LEAVE IT OR REFORM IT!"*

Chairman Wyden, Ranking Member Hatch, and distinguished members of the Committee, I appreciate the opportunity to appear today to discuss some key international tax issues, including the G-20's Base Erosion and Profit Shifting (BEPS) project. We appreciate the Committee's interest in these issues and the great amount of attention and effort the Committee has devoted toward reforming the international tax system in a way that would improve its sustainability and improve the U.S. system of taxation.

I would like to begin by describing the work we are doing in the BEPS project and then link that discussion to a consideration of the need for general corporate and international tax reform, as well as measures to address U.S. base stripping and inversion transactions that are outlined in the Administration's FY2015 budget proposals.

In June 2012, at the G-20 Summit in Los Cabos, Mexico, the leaders of the world's largest economies identified the ability of multinational companies to reduce their tax bills in high-tax countries by shifting income into low- and no-tax jurisdictions as a significant concern. They instructed their governments to develop an action plan to address these issues, which was developed over the course of 2012-2013 and endorsed by G-20 leaders last September at the G-20 Summit in St. Petersburg. The Organization for Economic Cooperation and Development (OECD) has hosted this process, but G-20 governments, some of whom are not members of the OECD, are driving the process.

The BEPS Action Plan adopted last year outlines 15 specific areas where governments need to work to change the rules of the road that encourage companies to shift their income at the expense of the global tax base. The action items are generally aimed at developing recommendations to help countries combat BEPS. Ultimately, these recommendations will require changes to countries' domestic laws and changes to the OECD model income tax

---

* This is an edited, reformatted and augmented version of testimony presented July 22, 2014 before the Senate Committee on Finance.

convention, and there is even discussion of a multilateral treaty to address BEPS. The BEPS project is expected to release its first set of recommendations on policies related to transfer pricing documentation and country-by-country reporting, transfer pricing with respect to intangibles, treaty abuse, hybrid mismatch arrangements, harmful tax practices, and the digital economy this fall. The BEPS project is set to conclude at the end of 2015 with final recommendations under all of the action items.

To provide some context for the BEPS project, I would like to discuss a number of factors that gave rise to the need for the BEPS project. First, the interaction of various countries' rules for taxing cross-border income creates incentives for companies to let tax decisions drive corporate policy in order to pay very low rates of tax or even to entirely avoid paying tax anywhere on large portions of their income. Public frustration arises when companies that do business in one country pay low or no tax there or anywhere else. While it is national governments that write the tax laws, and companies should not be expected to pay more tax than they owe, much of the global interest nonetheless centers around the activities of U.S.- based multinational companies because, as global household names, their activities have received the most publicity perhaps and also because various government inquiries here and abroad have focused on them. This frustration on the part of the public and also national governments, in turn, is not surprisingly reflected in the political arena such that, as noted above, the G-20 leaders came together in an effort to rein in this activity through the G-20/OECD BEPS Project.

The United States has a great deal at stake in the BEPS project and a strong interest in its success. Our active participation is crucial to protecting our own tax base from stripping by multinational companies, much of which occurs as a result of exploiting differences in national regimes. A key goal of BEPS is to seek to identify those differences and write rules that plug the holes. Because the United States provides a foreign tax credit to companies for taxes they pay overseas, the United States also has a direct financial stake in rules that enjoy broad international consensus. In addition, as the home of some of the world's most successful and vibrant multinationals, we have a stake in ensuring that companies and countries play by tax rules that are clear and administrable and that companies can avoid unrelieved double taxation, as well as time-consuming, expensive tax disputes. Both the United States and our companies also have a strong interest in access to robust dispute resolution mechanisms around the world. In contrast, failure in the BEPS project could well result in countries taking unilateral, inconsistent actions thereby increasing double taxation, the cost to the U.S. Treasury, and the number of tax disputes.

The principal target of the BEPS project is so-called "stateless income," basically very low- or non-taxed income within a multinational group. Low and non-taxed income located in various jurisdictions around the world is an inviting fiscal target for other countries. The existence of large amounts of stateless income in a time of global austerity has put pressure on the longstanding, widely accepted international tax rules. This pressure is increased in a global economic environment in which superior returns can accrue to intangibles that can be easily located anywhere in the world and that are often the result, for example, of intensive research and development activities that a single multinational may conduct in many countries, or marketing intangibles can be exploited in one country but owned and financed from another, often low-tax, country. Some countries with large markets believe that some of these premium profits enjoyed by multinationals should be taxed in those market countries, whereas current international norms attribute those profits to the places where the functions, assets, and risks of the multinational firm are located – which are often not in the market countries.

The G-20/OECD BEPS project is made even more challenging by the reality that some of the gaps in the international tax rules are created by countries intentionally seeking to attract mobile income through various special tax regimes. Left unchecked, these regimes could result in an unproductive race-to-thebottom in tax competition. When otherwise legitimate practices, such as the desire to subsidize research and development, drop any pretense linking the tax break to activity in the country itself, these regimes become no more than open invitation to strip more highly taxed income from countries like the United States.

I am happy to report that the OECD BEPS project has had a promising beginning and there are areas where commendable work is being done to resolve gaps in existing international rules and where broad consensus should be possible. These areas include minimizing potential for hybrid mismatches (situations in which a multinational issues an instrument that gives rise to a tax deduction in one country without a corresponding inclusion in another); helping countries minimize abuse of their bilateral income tax treaties, including through so-called "treaty shopping"; requiring country-by-country reporting of profits and taxes by multinationals so that they can be made available to tax administrators for purposes of risk assessment; designing interest limitation rules that can be applied across borders; updating the transfer pricing rules on the application of the "arm's length" standard to intangibles and endorsing "special measures" when those rules produce stateless income; and updating the rules on permanent establishment to minimize the artificial avoidance of those rules.

As the work moves into 2015, there is more that can be achieved, and also several areas where we must guard against bad outcomes. One of the key 2015 action items will focus on making dispute resolution more efficient, which we hope will include a significant broadening of the use of mandatory arbitration to resolve tax disputes between the tax authorities of the two countries. When countries know that tax disputes will be settled by a neutral arbitrator, it improves the dispute resolution process from beginning to end. In 2015, we will also work closely with other countries to limit the base stripping that results from excessive interest deductions, a topic of strong interest to the United States and that, as discussed below, is also the subject of one of the President's FY2015 budget proposals.

We must also work hard in several areas to preserve our national interest in rules based on principles and not merely individual country revenue interests. Let me highlight just a few. In the area of transfer pricing, we must ensure that the currently-used arm's length standard is clearly articulated and that profits are attributable to the place of economic activity – that is, where the assets, functions, and risks of the multinational are located. We must further ensure that any "special measures" agreed at the OECD are firmly anchored in these principles, and that legal and contractual relationships are ignored in determining intercompany prices only in unusual circumstances. The arm's length standard has been a bedrock of international taxation for over 50 years, and while it is not perfect, it is the best tool available to deal with the difficult issue of pricing among affiliates of a multinational group. We must steadfastly avoid turning longstanding transfer pricing principles into a series of vague concepts easily manipulated by countries to serve their revenue needs at the expense of the U.S. tax base and our multinationals.

With respect to country-by-country reporting by multinationals of income and tax information, we must strongly support measures that ensure that the information is used by countries' tax administrators solely as a risk assessment tool. Country-by-country data is useful to tax administrators because it will permit them to identify companies that have shifted income into low- or no-tax jurisdictions. In those cases, countries may appropriately feel that such a company deserves a closer look on audit to determine whether income has been shifted out of their jurisdiction through non-arm's length pricing. Given the potentially sensitive nature of this information, we must ensure that information of U.S.-based multinationals is made available only through our treaty and information exchange networks so as to ensure its confidentiality and appropriate use by our treaty or information exchange partners. Finally, this work should contain a remedy in the event countries misuse the information to make tax adjustments that do not conform to agreed international standards.

In the area of digital businesses, we must guard against the desire of some countries to use new business models as a pretext for taxing income beyond that which arises from the functions, assets, and risks located in those countries. We continue to believe that long standing, widely accepted rules that require a physical presence in another country before that country receives the right to impose an income tax is the most administrable and appropriate rule even in a digital age, and we are very encouraged by the work at the OECD to further adapt the rules concerning value added taxes to the digital age – so that countries with a VAT can have a revenue source from the digital economy without resorting to new, exceedingly complex and difficult to administer income tax solutions. Finally, as a matter of U.S. tax treaty policy, the United States took the international lead in limiting treaty abuse by adopting "limitation of benefits" provisions in our treaties. We believe that they have worked fairly and effectively to limit treaty shopping. In the G-20/OECD BEPS project we will continue to propose the limitation on benefits provision as a solution to protect against treaty shopping and will oppose proposals to include a main purpose test (or principal purpose test) in our own treaties as this test is too vague and subjective and creates unacceptable uncertainty about how such rules will be administered. In short, the remainder of 2014 and 2015 will be a very challenging time in the G-20/OECD BEPS Project. The United States needs to remain deeply engaged in moving the project to a successful conclusion.

While the international negotiations over BEPS progress, it is worth acknowledging steps the United States could take today to reform our own tax system to improve competitiveness, secure our tax base, and reduce incentives for profit shifting by U.S. firms.

As the President has proposed, we should reform our business tax system by reducing the rate and broadening the base. It is frequently noted that the United States has a high statutory corporate rate, but much lower effective tax rates. High statutory rates encourage multinationals to find ways to shift profits, especially on intangible income, to other jurisdictions. So lowering our statutory rate while broadening the base could be a start toward reducing stripping of the U.S. base.

But it would only be a start, because even with lower rates U.S. multinationals would continue to aggressively seek ways to lower their tax bills by shifting income out of the United States. So what other tools do we have at our disposal? We can examine the ways multinationals lower their U.S. effective rates and take sensible protective measures.

First, in the international arena specifically, the President's framework for business tax reform proposes a minimum tax on foreign earnings. Other recent tax reform plans have included similar proposals, which would improve on the current complex and porous international tax rules by requiring that companies pay tax on all foreign earnings, but at a somewhat reduced rate.

Whether as part of tax reform or in the context of our current tax system, we should also take a close look at interest deductibility, noting that in this area our thin capitalization rules are inadequate and that our system actually gives an overall advantage to foreign-owned multinationals in this regard. Foreign-owned multinationals typically lend funds into the United States to benefit from interest deductions against income that would otherwise be subject to a 35 percent tax rate, while the related interest income is subject to significantly lower tax rates in the lending jurisdiction. It is especially disconcerting to observe that among the foreign multinationals that can most aggressively take advantage of the deficiencies in our thin capitalization rules are so-called "inverted" companies – that is, foreign-parented companies that were previously U.S.-parented. The Administration's FY 2015 budget contains a proposal that would strengthen our interest-stripping rules and level the playing field by limiting the ability of U.S. subsidiaries of a foreign multinational to deduct a disproportionate amount of the group's global interest expense in the United States. Specifically, this proposal would limit the U.S. group's share of global interest expense deductions by reference to the U.S. group's proportionate share of the multinational's worldwide consolidated earnings, as computed under Generally Accepted Accounting Principles (GAAP) or International Financial Reporting Standards (IFRS).

Another Administration FY 2015 budget proposal would limit the deduction of interest expense of U.S. multinationals related to deferred foreign subsidiary income. Our own multinationals typically do all of their borrowing in the United States to benefit from interest deductions against income that would otherwise be subject to a 35 percent tax rate, but they then use borrowed cash throughout the multinational group, financing operations generating income that may not be subject to current U.S. tax. Indeed, we have recently seen examples of U.S. multinationals borrowing in the United States – rather than bringing back cash from offshore – to pay dividends to their shareholders. By aligning the timing of interest expense deductions with the timing of the recognition of the income supported by the proceeds of borrowing, the Administration's proposal would address the mismatch under current law that allows companies to take current deductions for interest related to income that is not subject to current U.S. tax.

In addressing stripping of the U.S. base, it is also important to consider so-called "hybrid arrangements," which may allow taxpayers to claim U.S. deductions with respect to payments that do not result in a corresponding income item in the foreign jurisdiction. These arrangements serve little function other than to produce stateless income and could easily be reined in. To neutralize these arrangements, the Administration's FY 2015 budget proposal would deny deductions for interest and royalty payments made to related parties under certain circumstances involving hybrid arrangements. For example, the proposal would deny a U.S. deduction where a taxpayer makes an interest or royalty payment to a related person and there is no corresponding inclusion in the payee's jurisdiction, or where the taxpayer is able to claim a deduction with respect to the same payment in another jurisdiction.

Additionally, it has been well documented that shifting intangibles outside the United States is a key avenue through which U.S. base erosion occurs. The principal means of shifting intangible income is to undervalue intangible property transferred offshore or to take advantage of perceived loopholes in our definition of intangibles. Once this intellectual property is offshore, the income that it produces can accrue in low- or no-tax jurisdictions, outside the scope of U.S. taxation. The Administration's FY 2015 Budget contains a number of proposals that would discourage the corporate tax base erosion that occurs via intangibles transfers. One of those proposals would clarify the definition of intangible property to address taxpayer arguments that certain value does not fall within the current definition and therefore may be transferred offshore without any U.S. tax charge. Another proposal would modify our subpart F rules to tax currently certain excess returns of a controlled foreign corporation from intangibles transferred to it by a U.S. person, while yet another proposal would update subpart F to currently tax certain highly mobile income from digital goods and services where the controlled foreign corporation earning the income did not itself make a substantial contribution to the development of the relevant intangible property.

Finally, and as underscored by Secretary Lew's July 15th letter to Congress, I want to emphasize the serious need for the United States to once again directly address the potential loss of federal tax revenues from corporate inversion transactions. Letting our corporate tax base erode through inversions will worsen our fiscal challenges over the coming years. Once companies invert, there is a permanent loss to the U.S. income tax base since it is safe to assume these companies are not coming back to the United States.

An anti-inversion provision has been part of the Internal Revenue Code since 2004, but experience has shown that this provision insufficiently deters inversion given the large tax rate and other tax disparities between United States and the countries to which formerly U.S.-based multinationals have relocated. According to a recent Congressional Research Service report, forty-seven U.S. corporations have reincorporated overseas through corporate inversions in the last 10 years. This is an increase from only 29 inversions in the prior 20 years. And proposed inversions are being reported in the media on a much more frequent basis.

To reinforce the existing anti-inversion statute, the Administration, in the FY 2015 Budget, has proposed to broaden the scope of inversion transactions subject to the statute. As amended, where shareholder continuity in the inverted company after a transaction is more than 50 percent, or where the inverted company meets certain criteria demonstrating that it retains a close connection to the United States and does not have a close connection to the country to which it relocates, the statute would provide that the inverted company would continue to be treated as a domestic corporation for U.S. federal income tax purposes. Regardless of any other base stripping or tax reform legislation adopted, such strengthened anti-inversion legislation is necessary to prevent a permanent reduction in federal corporate income tax revenues. As the Secretary indicated in his June 15 letter, Congress should pass legislation immediately with an effective date of May 2014 to prevent companies from effectively renouncing their citizenship to get out of paying taxes.

In closing, I would like to acknowledge the tireless work and dedication of the office of the International Tax Counsel at the Treasury Department, which has been a leader in providing technical guidance on these issues in the G-20 and at the OECD.

Thank you for the opportunity to speak to you today. I look forward to answering your questions.

In: U.S. International Tax System
Editor: Holly Lanford
ISBN: 978-1-63321-976-2

Chapter 4

TESTIMONY OF PASCAL SAINT-AMANS, DIRECTOR, CENTRE FOR TAX POLICY AND ADMINISTRATION, ORGANISATION FOR ECONOMIC CO-OPERATION AND DEVELOPMENT (OECD). HEARING ON "THE U.S. TAX CODE: LOVE IT, LEAVE IT OR REFORM IT!"*

Chairman Wyden, Ranking Member Hatch, and Members of the Committee, thank you for inviting me to testify today regarding the work of the Organisation for Economic Co-operation and Development (OECD) on base erosion and profit shifting (BEPS).

The OECD is an international organization founded by the United States and other nations in the aftermath of World War II. The OECD includes 34 market economy democracies from North America, Europe, and Asia, and has five key partners (Brazil, China, India, Indonesia, and South Africa) among emerging economies. Officials from the levels of experts to Ministers meet at the OECD to address common problems, develop international standards, guidelines, principles, and best practices, and monitor performance through peer reviews. The common thread of our work is a shared commitment to market economies backed by democratic institutions and focused on the well-being of all citizens.

The work of the OECD is done by consensus. That is, measures cannot be adopted without the consensus of all member countries. Moreover, the results of the work at the OECD are generally tools that countries can use to address problems they themselves agreed to put on the OECD agenda. Each country ultimately must make its own policy choices. The OECD's goal is to produce better policies, in part by allowing countries to coordinate with one another, and in so doing improve the quality of people's lives.

In developing our polices, we consult with business, including through the Business and Industry Advisory Committee to the OECD, and with labor, including through the Trade Union Advisory Committee to the OECD. We also engage with civil society organizations and academic researchers.

Our commitment to external stakeholders is strong. For instance, the Committee on Fiscal Affairs (CFA), which is the forum at the OECD for addressing issues affecting taxation, has

* This is an edited, reformatted and augmented version of testimony presented July 22, 2014 before the Senate Committee on Finance.

provided numerous opportunities for comment on the various discussion drafts the OECD's member countries and partners agreed to release over the last twelve months. These discussion drafts have generated more than 3,500 pages of comments, and provoked a large number of participants from all constituencies commenting at 5 public consultations. The OECD's public webcasts of these consultations and our updates on the project have attracted over 10,000 viewers.

BACKGROUND

Taxation is at the core of countries' sovereignty and each country is free to set up its corporate tax system as it chooses. When independent sets of rules created by sovereign countries interact, however, it can lead to gaps where corporate income is not taxed at all, and to frictions where income is taxed by multiple countries. Since at least the 1920s, it has been recognized that the interaction of domestic tax systems can lead to overlaps in the exercise of taxing rights that in turn can result in double taxation. Countries have long worked and are strongly committed to eliminating such double taxation in order to minimize trade distortions and impediments to sustainable economic growth, while affirming their sovereign right to establish their own tax rules. However, there are gaps and frictions among different countries' tax systems that were not taken into account in designing the existing standards and which are not dealt with by bilateral tax treaties. Thus, the modern global economy requires countries to collaborate on tax matters in order to be able to protect their tax sovereignty.

Inheriting work initiated in the 1920s, the OECD countries have worked together to elaborate standards and instruments to eliminate double taxation. Adopted by consensus, these soft law instruments provide an international framework, and include a Model Tax Convention (which serves as the basis for over 3,000 bilateral tax treaties) and Transfer Pricing Guidelines (which provide common standards for allocating taxable income among members of a group of affiliated companies). These instruments have been critical in supporting the OECD agenda to promote cross border investments and competitive tax systems. In that vein, as illustrated in the report Tax Policy Reform and Economic Growth (http://dx.doi.org/10.1787/9789264091085-en), the OECD recommends that countries favor broad bases and lower rates for corporate income taxes.

NEED FOR INTERNATIONAL TAX REFORM

Over time, the current rules have failed to keep pace with economic developments, and have begun to show weaknesses. While the key international tax standards are intended to eliminate double taxation by providing for principles to allocate taxing rights on a bilateral basis between the countries involved, they are now facilitating double non-taxation in a significant number of instances. This results from changes in the international economic environment such as the globalization of businesses and economies of countries becoming increasingly intertwined.

In the global economy of the 21st century, multinational enterprises (MNEs) represent a large proportion of global GDP, and intra-firm trade represents a growing proportion of overall trade. Globalization has resulted in a shift from country-specific operating models and a bilateral paradigm for direct investment to global models based on matrix management organizations and integrated supply chains that centralize several functions at a regional or global level. Moreover, the growing importance of the service component of the economy, and the increasing centrality of intellectual property to value creation has made it much easier for businesses to locate both productive activities and legal rights in geographic locations that are distant from the physical location of their customers. These developments have been exacerbated by the sophistication of tax planners in identifying and exploiting the legal arbitrage opportunities and the boundaries of acceptable tax planning, thus providing MNEs with more confidence in taking aggressive tax positions.

The international tax rules similarly do not have an overall principle of coherence. In the domestic context, coherence is usually achieved through a principle of matching: a payment that is deductible by the payer is generally taxed in the hands of the recipient unless it is explicitly exempted. The lack of a similar principle to address the interaction between tax systems at the international level creates opportunities for cross-border arbitrage by taxpayers in which income can be made to disappear for tax purposes.

As a result, the current set of rules has proven to create unforeseen opportunities to artificially reduce taxable income or to shift profits to low-tax jurisdictions for base erosion and profit shifting (BEPS) by MNEs. BEPS relates chiefly to instances where the interaction of different tax rules leads to double non-taxation or less than single taxation. It also relates to arrangements that achieve no or low taxation by shifting profits away from the jurisdictions where the activities creating those profits take place.

Non- or low-taxation is not per se a cause of concern, but it becomes so when it is associated with practices that artificially segregate taxable income from the various activities that generate it. In other words, what creates tax policy concerns for countries participating in the BEPS project is that, due to gaps and frictions in the interaction of different tax systems, and in some cases because of the application of bilateral tax treaties and transfer pricing rules, income from cross-border activities may go untaxed anywhere, or be subject to unduly low taxation.

As a result, the current consensus-based international framework is at risk.

First, it no longer fully meets its objectives of allocating taxing rights between countries where companies operate. Instead, it facilitates the divorce between the location of the profit and the location of value creation. The consequence is that the existing international tax system in many cases allows structures and tax results *that no longer pass a basic test of common sense.* For example, as taxpayers increasingly rely on intangible assets as a value-driver, it has become easier for taxpayers to rely on existing principles to transfer legal ownership of those intangible assets to "cash boxes" in low-tax jurisdictions that receive a large share of profit but perform no or hardly any activity. Trillions of untaxed dollars are now located in such entities, in compliance with the existing rules. It is hard to imagine that this is what was intended when these rules were designed. Another striking example is where the features of a bilateral treaty cause investments in one country to be channeled through a particular jurisdiction by third-country investors. For example, as shown in IMF data, more than one quarter of direct investment into India was from Mauritius between 2010 and 2012.

Second, the current situation creates an uneven playing field in which some businesses, such as those which operate cross-border and have access to sophisticated tax expertise, receive unintended competitive advantages compared with enterprises that operate mostly at the domestic level or that use less aggressive tax planning techniques. This uneven playing field leads to an inefficient allocation of resources by distorting investment decisions towards activities that may have lower pre-tax rates of return, but higher after-tax rates of return. This also encourages resources to be spent on tax planning rather than productive business operations that could lead to job creation and innovation. These phenomena are by no means limited to U.S. multinational corporations: 74% of the Fortune Global 500 companies are non-U.S.-headquartered companies.

Third, these flaws in the current system undermine the sovereign right of countries to set tax policy. Countries must be able to set their own tax policy in the way they consider appropriate, in order to respond to their particular revenue needs. An international tax system that allows for unjustifiable results undermines this ability to exercise policy autonomy. BEPS activities threaten the tax bases of countries around the world. In the U.S., for example, a recent Congressional Research Service study reported that BEPS activities are estimated to reduce U.S. corporate tax revenue by $10-60 billion annually.

Finally, the fact that tax planning that complies with the technical tax rules can reach results that defy common sense has led to increased tax controversy and litigation with tax administrations frustrated with the implementation of the current rules. The increased number of international tax disputes also makes it harder for taxpayers to anticipate tax results, and can result in taxpayers being subjected to double taxation. This is exacerbated in some cases by the increasing prominence of emerging economies that did not participate in the development of the existing rules because they are not members of the OECD. The weaknesses of these rules make it harder for these countries to join the international consensus, which further increases uncertainty for taxpayers.

As a result of this growing concern over BEPS activities, many countries have considered action to protect their tax bases. Protecting the tax base is one of the recurrent features of corporate tax reform proposals in many countries, including the United States.

Unilateral action by countries on an uncoordinated basis, however, has the potential to replace the problem of non-taxation with the proliferation of uncoordinated legislative measures that will lead to excessive compliance costs for MNEs, as well as the potential for double or multiple taxation of the same income, undermining the existing consensus-based standards and replacing them with chaos. It also has the potential to encourage protectionist measures that would be detrimental to international trade.

In addition, the fact that BEPS arises from the interaction between different countries' tax systems means that unilateral action by individual countries is incapable of fully addressing the problem. If only a small number of countries attempt to solve BEPS, they may in fact further jeopardize their tax base as businesses move to jurisdictions that have not yet implemented preventive measures or that choose not to do so in order to gain a competitive advantage.

In the aftermath of the financial crisis, however, worldwide attention has been focused on international tax avoidance at the highest political levels and in many countries at the level of the man on the street. In some cases, this focus has increased pre-existing tensions, as individual companies have found themselves scrutinized by the media and by the public. *This increased focus, however, has also created a unique opportunity to modernize global standards, restore their coherence, and renew worldwide commitment to principled, consensus-based rules.*

A Coordinated Approach to Reform: The BEPS Project

Recognizing the threat to the existing standards for relieving double taxation, the OECD published its report, *Addressing Base Erosion and Profit Shifting*, in February 2013, which provided results of an in-depth analysis of BEPS identifying the problems and the different factors that cause them. The report was discussed at the February 2013 G20 meeting of finance ministers, who expressed strong support for the work done and urged the development of a comprehensive action plan.

In response to this request from the G20, the OECD published an Action Plan on Base Erosion and Profit Shifting in July 2013, which was fully endorsed by G20 finance ministers and G20 Leaders. The objective of the Action Plan, approved by consensus, is to restore coherence and common sense to the international tax system, keeping the overall approach, but updating it so that it continues to function in the modern context in which countries impose tax locally but businesses act globally. In this way, the fundamental goals of eliminating double taxation and providing certainty for business remains at the core of the work of the OECD in tax matters.

In order to achieve this objective, *the BEPS Project brings together 44 countries, comprising 90% of the world's economy, working on an equal footing*: all OECD members and accession countries as well as the 8 non-OECD G20 countries, i.e. Argentina, Brazil, People's Republic of China, India, Indonesia, Russia, Saudi Arabia, and South Africa. In addition, over 80 developing countries and other non-OECD/non-G20 economies have been consulted and their input has been fed directly into the BEPS process. This broad participation is aimed at reaching as broad a consensus as possible, creating a level playing field among countries so that countries that implement the measures do not risk losing their tax base to those that do not, or finding their MNEs placed at a competitive disadvantage. In this way, the work can restore the sovereign taxing rights of countries, giving them the tools to preserve their tax base.

The Action Plan is designed to take a principled, holistic approach to addressing BEPS. This is not a "revenue grabbing" exercise but one intended to fix existing deficiencies of the current standards. It focuses on ensuring the *coherence* of corporate tax systems in a cross-border environment, introducing *substance* requirements in the area of tax treaties and transfer pricing, and ensuring *transparency* while promoting certainty and predictability.

Recognizing that any discussion of tax changes raises uncertainty, *the Action Plan focuses not only on closing gaps that have led to tax avoidance, but also on improving dispute resolution* to ensure that new double taxation is not created and existing frictions are reduced. The worldwide and U.S. business community, as well as civil society and academics, have been extensively consulted throughout the process so far. This engagement will continue throughout the BEPS Project.

Addressing BEPS is critical for countries and must be done in a timely manner to be useful. Indeed, before the launch of the BEPS project, countries around the world had begun to explore ways to address BEPS unilaterally. Many have put those unilateral actions on hold in favor of participating collaboratively in the BEPS work. Failure to deliver concrete results in a timely manner thus would create a risk of unilateral actions, which would not only fail in many cases to address the core of the BEPS issue, but would lead to a risk of increased double taxation of businesses around the world. *This is why countries agreed to deliver on the Actions within a two-year time frame.* If it is important to come up quickly with detailed principles, it is also important to take some more time to provide detailed guidance for the implementation, so that technical quality and certainty are maximized. It is recognized that after guidance is developed, governments and taxpayers will need time for implementation.

The Action Plan takes the form of 15 actions, and calls for a series of concrete deliverables in response to these actions. A first set of deliverables is due in 2014, with a second set due in 2015. The 2014 deliverables are due to be delivered in September 2014, and will represent substantial progress toward providing countries with tools they can use to address BEPS.

The 2014 deliverables will help ensure the coherence of corporate income taxation at the international level by providing draft recommendations for new international tax and treaty standards to neutralize hybrid mismatch arrangements. They will show progress made in relation to work to tackle harmful tax practices. They will also help to restore the intended effects and benefits of international standards by providing recommendations to prevent the abuse of tax treaties and to address transfer pricing issues in the key area of intangibles. They will help to ensure better transparency and promote increased certainty and predictability by providing draft recommendations for improved transfer pricing documentation and a template for country-by-country reporting to be provided to tax administrators for high-level risk assessment. In addition, the 2014 deliverables will include a report on addressing the tax challenges of the digital economy, as well as a report on the feasibility of developing a multilateral instrument to amend bilateral tax treaties and enable swift implementation of treaty measures developed in the course of the BEPS work.

The need to provide certainty and limit the cost of compliance to businesses while providing useful instruments to countries is at the core of the work and has been fully taken into consideration. Country by country reporting is a good illustration of possible risks and tensions but also, at the same time, of the benefits of a multilateral approach. For several years now, many have advocated the need for more transparency in the reporting of MNEs. A number of countries, starting with the United States, have already enacted legislation to improve such reporting or intend to do so in the future. While this type of reporting increases the compliance burdens for MNEs, a common agreed framework is likely to limit this burden by taking a consistent approach that reduces the differences between country-specific requirements. Indeed, a number of countries have agreed to limit the scope of information requested from MNEs in order to pursue a multilateral approach that will guarantee efficient reporting while maintaining confidentiality. As a result of the multilateral approach, countries will run a more efficient reporting mechanism and businesses will face less burdensome compliance costs.

Completion of the work under the Action Plan will give countries the tools they need to ensure that profits are taxed where the economic activities generating the profits are performed and where value is created. It will also give businesses greater certainty. Finally, the international tax framework will make more sense, thereby strengthening consensus and reinforcing the ability of governments to eliminate double taxation.

CONCLUSION

Taxation remains at the core of national sovereignty, and each country must ultimately make its own tax policy choices. The BEPS Project developed out of the recognition that opportunities for BEPS arise from the interaction of different countries' tax systems, making it impossible for a single country acting unilaterally to effectively address BEPS. BEPS opportunities impair the ability of countries to achieve their tax policy goals, effectively undermining their sovereignty. Uncoordinated, unilateral action by individual countries to exert taxing rights over cross-border activity would only make the problem worse, resulting in double or multiple taxation, increasing disputes for business and among governments, and harming economic growth. The work on BEPS is intended to produce tools that countries can use to address BEPS, in order to ensure that the international tax system continues to function, and that a broader, more robust consensus to eliminate double taxation can be established.

The OECD has long recommended that countries reduce the distortive impacts of their tax regimes, and thus improve economic growth, by broadening the tax base (in which measures to address BEPS can be an important part) and lowering the rate. We hope that our work, including the work on BEPS, can support the ongoing tax policy reform discussions around the world and in the United States. BEPS is an important issue no matter what direction US international tax policy takes.

I would like to thank the Committee for the opportunity to provide testimony on this important work, and I look forward to answering your questions.

ANNEX: THE BEPS ACTION PLAN

The measures contemplated in the Action Plan will ensure the *coherence* of the international tax system by providing recommendations to neutralize "hybrid mismatch" arrangements that take advantage of differing treatment of entities or instruments in multiple jurisdictions to generate multiple deductions for the same payment, or deductions in one jurisdiction with no taxable income in another jurisdiction (*Action 2*). Coherence will be further improved by providing recommendations for the design of effective controlled foreign company (CFC) rules that tackle the issue of large amounts of untaxed income being routed through offshore affiliates in no-tax jurisdictions (*Action 3*), and for rules to prevent base erosion via excess interest deductions and other financial payments (*Action 4*). The work will also help jurisdictions counter harmful tax practices more effectively, particularly in the area of IP regimes, based on the recognition that tax competition through harmful preferential tax regimes left unchecked could ultimately lead to a "race to the bottom" that would drive tax rates on mobile sources of income to zero for all countries (*Action 5*).

The Action Plan is also intended to realign taxation with the *substance* of the activities of taxpayers. "Treaty shopping" by third country investors through shell companies in jurisdictions with broad tax treaty networks, along with other forms of treaty abuse, have allowed treaties to be used to generate double non-taxation. To prevent this abuse and allow tax treaties to serve their intended function of relieving double taxation, the Action Plan therefore calls for model treaty provisions to prevent the abuse of tax treaties (*Action 6*) and to prevent the artificial avoidance of taxation by abusing the permanent establishment standard used to determine taxing jurisdiction (*Action 7*). It will restore substance in the area of transfer pricing by ensuring that profits cannot be separated from the location in which economic activity occurs and value is created, in the key areas of intangibles (*Action 8*), risks and capital (*Action 9*), and other high-risk transactions (*Action 10*).

The Action Plan is also intended to ensure increased *transparency* in several respects. The work will recommend methodologies for collecting and analyzing data on the scale and effects of BEPS and on the impact of the actions to address it (*Action 11*). To ensure that tax administrations have access to comprehensive and relevant information on tax planning strategies, recommendations will be developed regarding the design of mandatory disclosure rules for aggressive or abusive tax structures (*Action 12*). In addition, the quality of information provided to tax administrations will be improved by developing improved and better coordinated transfer pricing documentation (*Action 13*). Finally, to ensure that actions to counter BEPS do not detract from certainty and predictability for business, solutions to ensure effective dispute resolution between jurisdictions will be developed (*Action 14*).

In addition to work in these three key areas, the work will address the cross-cutting issue of the tax challenges raised by the digital economy (*Action 1*). Recognizing the need for a way to implement agreed changes quickly and uniformly, particularly in the area of tax treaties, a multilateral instrument to enable jurisdictions to implement measures developed in the course of the BEPS work and to amend bilateral tax treaties will be developed (*Action 15*).

In: U.S. International Tax System
Editor: Holly Lanford
ISBN: 978-1-63321-976-2

Chapter 5

TESTIMONY OF MIHIR A. DESAI, PROFESSOR OF FINANCE, HARVARD UNIVERSITY. HEARING ON "THE U.S. TAX CODE: LOVE IT, LEAVE IT OR REFORM IT!"*

Chairman Wyden, Ranking Member Hatch, and Members of the Committee, it is a pleasure to appear before you today to discuss international tax reform. I am a Professor of Finance at Harvard Business School, a Professor of Law at Harvard Law School and a Research Associate of the National Bureau of Economic Research.

Recent merger transactions highlight long-simmering problems in the U.S. corporate tax, particularly with respect to its international provisions. My comments attempt to outline briefly the origins of these transactions, the range of alternative solutions, guidelines for evaluating alternative reforms and some reforms that should be avoided.

1. The last twelve months have witnessed a remarkable wave of merger transactions that facilitate the expatriation of U.S. corporations. Such transactions reflect the effects of policies and of the changing structure of multinational firms. From a policy perspective, the transactions highlight the increasing costs of employing a) a worldwide tax regime when most other large capital exporting countries no longer maintain such regimes and b) a corporate tax rate that stands well above rates employed by other OECD countries. From a firm point of view, the transactions highlight a) the increased mobility of activity in today's economy, b) the growing "decentering" of firms whereby headquarter locations have been split up and reallocated across the world, and c) the growing importance of non-U.S. markets for U.S. firms. Rather than questioning the loyalties of executives, it is critical to understand these underlying structural and secular forces. [See references 1, 2, 3, and 4]
2. While these transactions naturally attract growing attention, inversions are merely the most visible manifestation of these developments. In addition to inversions, these forces are giving rise to a) incorporation decisions by entrepreneurs that anticipate

* This is an edited, reformatted and augmented version of testimony presented July 22, 2014 before the Senate Committee on Finance.

the burdens of being a U.S. corporation, b) merger patterns that reflect the penalties of being domiciled in the U.S and the importance of offshore cash for U.S. corporations, c) investment patterns by U.S. and foreign companies, d) profit-shifting activities that are not value-creating and e) the consequent, negative impact of all of these distortions on the U.S. labor force. While it is tempting to limit attention to the more sensational effects and characterize them as tax-avoiding paper-shuffling, this would effectively be missing the forest for the trees. [See references 1, 2, 4 and 7]

3. Reforms should be focused exclusively on advancing U.S. welfare with particular attention on reforms that will improve American wages. These goals are mistakenly thought to be achieved by limiting the foreign activities of U.S. firms as foreign activities can be viewed as diverting economic activity away from the U.S. In fact, the evidence suggests the opposite as firms expand globally, they also expand domestically. Indeed, American welfare can be advanced by ensuring that investments in the U.S and abroad are owned by the most productive owner and that American firms flourish abroad, a goal advanced by the territorial regime that has now been adopted by most comparable countries. While the developments described above have crystallized the case for international tax reform with an increasing attention on switching to a territorial regime, there is still tremendous variation in proposals for territorial regimes. Some proposals, including those with an alternative minimum tax on foreign profits, are tantamount to a backdoor worldwide regime with even more complexity than today's system. Revenue considerations should figure largely in tax reform today but should be accorded secondary status in this setting given the very limited revenue provided by current international tax rules and the remarkable complexity and distortions required to secure any such revenue. Additionally, it is not clear that policies should prioritize revenue considerations in other countries. [See references 2, 5, and 6]
4. More broadly, the corporate tax is ripe for reform. In addition to international reforms and a rate reduction, reform should address the two other major developments in the corporate tax arena: a) the growing prominence of non-C corporate business income, and b) the disjunction between profits reported to capital markets and to tax authorities. A useful blueprint for reform would include a) moving to a territorial regime unencumbered by excessive complexity, b) a considerably lower tax rate in the range of 18-20%, c) better alignment of book and tax reporting of corporate profits and d) by some taxation of non-C corporation business income. This combination of reforms has the potential of addressing significant changes in the global economy in a revenue-neutral way that will advance U.S. welfare. More fundamental reforms, including those that replace a corporate tax with a consumption tax, are preferred if feasible. [See Reference 1]
5. Legislation that is narrowly focused on preventing inversions or specific transactions runs the risk of being counterproductive. These transactions are nested in a broader set of corporate decisions, leading to several unintended consequences. For example, rules that increase the required size of a foreign target to ensure the tax benefits of an inversion can deter these transactions but can also lead to more substantive transactions. More substantive transactions are likely to involve the loss of U.S. activity as American firms will be paired with larger foreign acquirers that demand the relocation of more activity abroad, including headquarters functions. Similarly,

specific regulations targeted at inverted firms may also lead to foreign firms leading such transactions to avoid those regulations. While it is tempting to address specific transactions in advance, or in lieu, of broader reform, it is useful to recall that the last wave of anti-inversion legislation likely spurred these more significant, recent transactions and reduced the prospect of reform in these intervening years. [See References 4 and 7]

Members of the Committee, I admire your foresight in addressing these issues. These highly visible manifestations of the structural problems in the corporate tax provide a significant opportunity for genuine reform. I'd be delighted to answer any questions.

References

[1] Desai, Mihir. "A Better Way to Tax U.S. Businesses." *Harvard Business Review* 90, nos. 7-8 (July–August 2012): 135–139.

[2] Desai, Mihir A. "Securing Jobs or the New Protectionism?" *Tax Notes* 123 no. 3 (July 2009): 315.

[3] Desai, Mihir A. "The Decentering of the Global Firm." *World Economy* 32, no. 9 (September 2009): 1271–1290.

[4] Desai, Mihir, and Dhammika Dharmapala. "Do Strong Fences Make Strong Neighbors?" *National Tax Journal* 63 (December 2010): 723–740.

[5] Desai, Mihir A., C. Fritz Foley, and James R. Hines Jr. "Domestic Effects of the Foreign Activities of U.S. Multinationals." *American Economic Journal: Economic Policy* 1, no. 1 (February 2009): 181–203.

[6] Desai, Mihir A., and James R. Hines Jr. "Evaluating International Tax Reform." *National Tax Journal* 56, no. 3 (September 2003): 409–440.

[7] Desai, Mihir A., and James R. Hines Jr. "Expectations and Expatriations: Tracing the Causes and Consequences of Corporate Inversions." *National Tax Journal* 55, no. 3 (September 2002): 409–440.

In: U.S. International Tax System
Editor: Holly Lanford

ISBN: 978-1-63321-976-2

Chapter 6

STATEMENT OF PETER R. MERRILL, PRINCIPAL, NATIONAL ECONOMICS AND STATISTICS GROUP, PRICEWATERHOUSECOOPERS LLP. HEARING ON "THE U.S. TAX CODE: LOVE IT, LEAVE IT OR REFORM IT!"*

I. INTRODUCTION

Chairman Wyden, Ranking Member Hatch, Members of the Senate Finance Committee, thank you for the opportunity to testify today. My name is Peter Merrill. I am a Principal in the National Economics and Statistics group of PricewaterhouseCoopers LLP (PwC). As a Ph.D. economist, the focus of my practice is primarily on the economic effects of tax policy. I am appearing here today on my own behalf, expressing solely my own views, not those of PwC, its clients, or any other entity.

Taxation is one factor that affects the ability of U.S. multinational corporations ("multinationals") to compete in foreign markets. The U.S. tax system currently diverges in a number of important respects from the policies and practices of other major industrial countries—often to the competitive detriment of U.S. businesses with international operations. With the one-third decline in the share of U.S. companies in the Forbes Global Top 500 list, dropping from 200 in 1998 to 135 in 2013, it is clear that U.S. companies face a far more competitive global environment and thus the effects of U.S. international tax rules on the competitive position of U.S. companies has become even more important (see Figure 1).

I have been asked to provide an overview of how the U.S. rules for taxing international income compare with other advanced economies. This statement provides a brief summary of the key U.S. rules governing the taxation of foreign source income, compares these rules with the tax rules of other OECD member countries, describes recent international tax reforms in Japan, the United Kingdom (UK) and New Zealand, and discusses some of the economic effects of these U.S. tax policies.

---

* This is an edited, reformatted and augmented version of a statement presented July 22, 2014 before the Senate Committee on Finance.

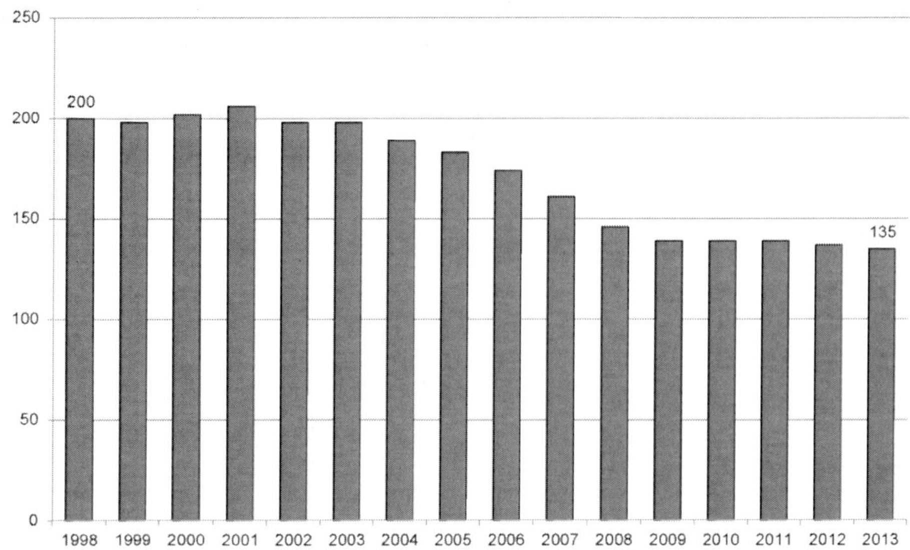

Source: Forbes 500s List, 1999-2003; International 800 List, 1999-2000; International 500 List, 2001-2003; Global 2000 List, 2004-2014.

Figure 1. U.S. Companies in Global Top 500 Companies, 1998-2013.

II. Overview of U.S. Taxation of Corporate Foreign Source Income

A. Worldwide System of Taxation

The United States has a worldwide tax system under which U.S. domestic corporations are subject to U.S. income tax on both their domestic income and their foreign source income. Thus, a U.S. corporation is subject to taxation by the United States on all of its income regardless of where the income is earned. The top U.S. corporate income tax rate, including state income tax, is 39.1 percent, the highest rate among Organisation for Economic Co-operation and Development (OECD) countries.

B. Deferral

While the United States has a worldwide tax system, the tax law recognizes the separate legal status of foreign corporations and generally allows U.S. shareholders to defer paying U.S. tax on foreign income until such income is distributed. However, U.S. shareholders may be taxed on certain types of undistributed profits of a foreign corporation, in particular, under the so-called U.S. subpart F rules that apply to controlled foreign corporations (CFCs) and the passive foreign investment company (PFIC) rules.

The subpart F regime, enacted in 1962, applies to U.S. shareholders that own 10-percent or more of the voting stock of a CFC. Under this regime, 10-percent U.S. shareholders must include in their taxable income their respective shares of certain types of CFC income (collectively referred to as "subpart F income"), regardless of whether that income has been distributed. Assuming the ownership requirements are met, U.S. corporate shareholders of CFCs may claim a foreign tax credit for the underlying foreign income taxes incurred by the CFC on its subpart F income. When a CFC distributes income that has been taxed under subpart F, it is not taxed again by the United States.

Subpart F income has numerous components, the most important of which is foreign base company income. Foreign base company income includes foreign personal holding company income (which consists mainly of passive investment income) and foreign base company sales, services, and oil-related income (generally active business income).

Subpart F also requires a 10-percent U.S. shareholder to include in income its pro rata share of any investments in U.S. property by a CFC. For this purpose, a loan to a related U.S. corporation is considered an investment in U.S. property.

Unlike domestic subsidiaries, foreign subsidiaries, other than certain Mexican and Canadian subsidiaries, cannot be included in a U.S. consolidated return. Thus, any losses of foreign subsidiaries cannot be used to offset other profits of the U.S. group. Also, the dividends received deduction, which partially or completely relieves corporations from taxation on dividends from domestic subsidiaries, generally does not apply to dividends from foreign subsidiaries.

C. Mitigation of Double Taxation

If a U.S. corporation conducts business outside the United States, it generally will be subject to taxation by the country or countries in which it conducts business. Because the United States taxes worldwide income, a U.S. corporation's foreign income also is subject to U.S. income tax. To mitigate double taxation of income earned abroad, foreign income taxes generally may be credited against U.S. income tax, with allowable foreign tax credits limited to the U.S. tax on foreign source income.

Specific rules are prescribed for identifying the source (domestic or foreign) of various types of income, such as interest, dividends, rents and royalties, services, and sales of purchased and manufactured goods. Other rules allocate and apportion expenses between domestic and foreign source income for foreign tax credit purposes. Expenses that are not directly allocable to a particular item of income, in particular, interest, research and development (R&D), and stewardship expenditures are subject to special allocation rules.

III. Comparison of How Other Countries Tax Corporate Foreign Source Income

A. Statutory Corporate Tax Rate

The top U.S. statutory corporate tax rate, including state corporate income tax, is 39.1 percent. This is the highest rate among the 34 OECD member countries, more than 14 percentage points higher than the average for the other OECD countries (24.8 percent), and almost 10 percentage points higher than the average for the other G7 countries (29.4 percent) (see Table 1).

Table 1. Top Corporate Tax Rate (Federal plus State), OECD Countries, 2014

Rank	Country	Rate
1	United States	39.1
2	Japan	37.0
3	France	34.4
4	Belgium	34.0
5	Portugal	31.5
6	Germany	30.2
7	Australia	30.0
8	Mexico	30.0
9	Spain	30.0
10	Luxembourg	29.2
11	New Zealand	28.0
12	Italy	27.5
13	Norway	27.0
14	Israel	26.5
15	Canada	26.3
16	Greece	26.0
17	Austria	25.0
18	Netherlands	25.0
19	Denmark	24.5
20	Korea	24.2
21	Slovak Republic	22.0
22	Sweden	22.0
23	Switzerland	21.1
24	Estonia*	21.0
25	United Kingdom	21.0
26	Chile	20.0
27	Finland	20.0
28	Iceland	20.0
29	Turkey	20.0
30	Czech Republic	19.0
31	Hungary	19.0
32	Poland	19.0
33	Slovenia	17.0
34	Ireland	12.5
G-7 average excluding U.S.		29.4
OECD average excluding U.S.		24.8

Source: OECD Tax Database.

The United States has not always had the highest corporate tax income rate among OECD economies. In 1988, as a result of the rate reduction made by the Tax Reform Act of 1986, the

U.S. corporate rate was more than five percentage points below the OECD average. Since then, the other OECD countries have reduced their corporate tax rates by an average of 19 percentage points, while the U.S. federal corporate tax rate has remained at 35 percent since 1993 (see Figure 2).

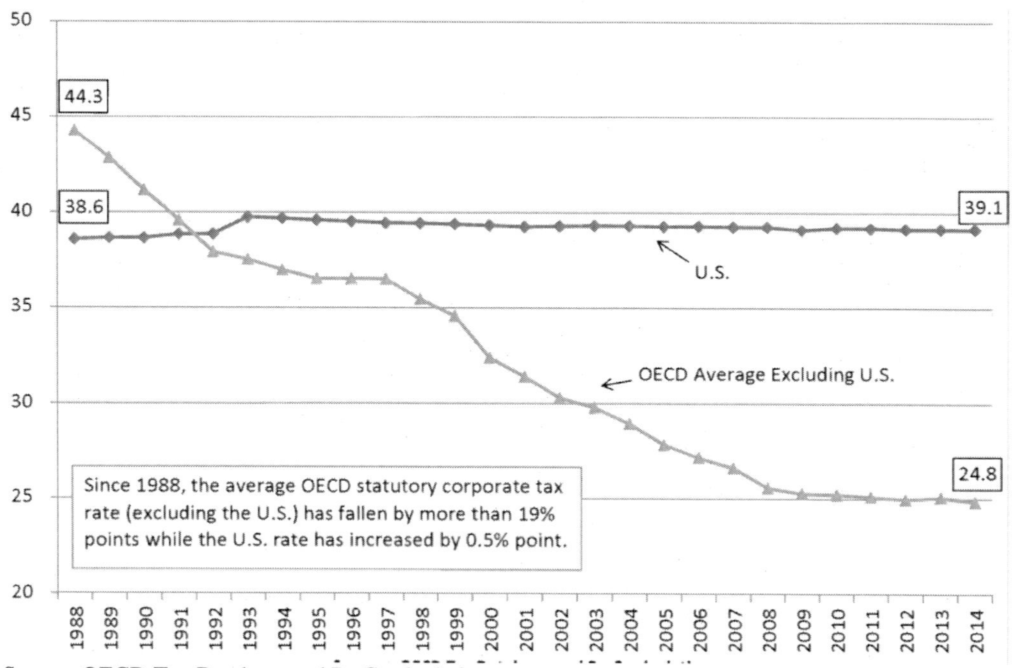

Source: OECD Tax Database and PwC calculations.

Figure 2. Top Statutory (Federal and State) Corporate Tax Rates, OECD Countries, 1988-2014.

The high U.S. statutory corporate income tax rate has a number of adverse economic consequences in an increasingly global economy. First, it discourages both U.S. and foreign companies from locating their most profitable assets and operations inside the United States. Second, it encourages both U.S. and foreign companies to locate their borrowing in the United States, as the value of interest deductions is greater against a higher corporate tax rate. Third, it discourages U.S. multinationals from remitting foreign profits to the United States and being subjected to the higher U.S. corporate tax. As a result, a growing share of the foreign earnings of U.S. subsidiaries may be more effectively invested outside the United States.

Effective tax rates take into account both the statutory tax rate as well as the breadth of the tax base. There are a number of ways to calculate effective tax rates including economic measures, such as marginal and average effective tax rates, and financial accounting measures, such as cash and book tax rates. Using a variety of different measures, international comparisons of corporate effective tax rates generally find that the U.S. corporate tax rate is higher than average (see Figure 3).

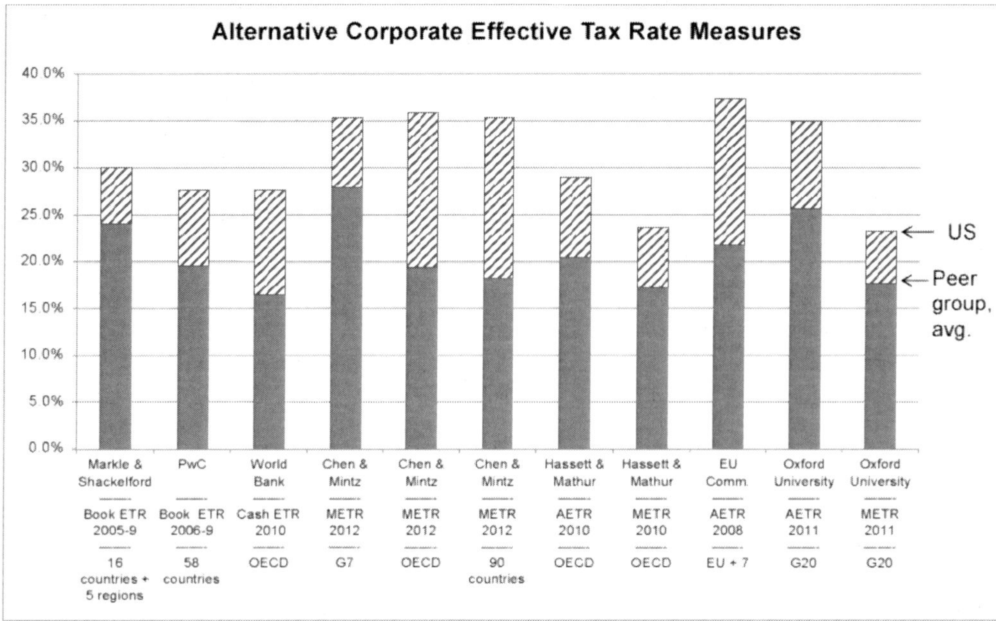

Sources:

K. Bilicka, M. Devereux and C. Fuest, "G20 Corporate Tax Ranking 2011" Oxford University, Centre for Business Taxation, July 2011.

D. Chen and J. Mintz, "Corporate Tax Competitiveness Rankings for 2012." Cato Institute, September 2012.

M. Devereux., C. Elschner, D. Endres, and C. Spengel, "Effective Tax Levels Using the Devereux/Griffith Methodology." Centre for European

Economic Research, October 2009 (Report prepared for the EU Commission).

K. Hassett and A. Mathur, "Report Card on Effective Corporate Tax Rates: United States Gets an F." AEI, February 2011.

K. Markle and D. Shackelford, "Cross-Country Comparisons of Corporate Income Taxes." NBER working paper 16839, February 2011.

PwC, "Global Effective Tax Rates." April 14, 2011 (Report prepared for Business Roundtable).

PwC, "Paying Taxes 2011: The Global Pictures," prepared for the World Bank and IFC Doing Business 2011 report.

Note: AETR = average effective tax rate. METR = marginal effective tax rate.

Figure 3. International Comparisons of Corporate Effective Tax Rates.

B. Relief of Double International Taxation

Unlike the United States, 28 of the other 33 OECD member countries and all other G-7 countries, have adopted dividend exemption (so-called "territorial") tax systems (see Table 2).

Under these territorial tax systems, the active foreign income of foreign subsidiaries generally is taxed only by the country where it is earned, and it can be distributed to the parent company with little or no residual taxation. By contrast, under the U.S. worldwide system, foreign income is taxed by the country where it is earned and then by the United States (with a foreign tax credit) when the income is remitted to the United States.

Table 2. OECD Countries with Territorial and Worldwide Tax Systems, 2014

Taxation of foreign subsidiary income	OECD Member Countries	Dividend exemption percentage
Territorial tax systems	Australia, Austria, Canada, Czech Republic, Denmark, Estonia, Finland, Greece, Hungary, Iceland, Luxembourg, Netherlands, New Zealand, Poland, Portugal, Slovak Republic, Spain, Sweden, Turkey, United Kingdom	100%
	Norway	97%
	Belgium, France, Germany, Italy, Japan, Slovenia, Switzerland	95%
Worldwide tax systems	Chile, Ireland, Israel, Korea, Mexico, United States	none

Source: PricewaterhouseCoopers, *Evolution of Territorial Tax Systems in the OECD*, The Technology CEO Council, April 2, 2013.

There has been a pronounced shift over the last 25 years toward the use of territorial tax systems. In 1989, only 10 OECD member countries had territorial tax systems and just two of the G-7 countries (Canada and France) had such a system (see Figure 4). Today, 28 OECD countries and all other G-7 countries have adopted some form of territorial tax system. Notably, over this period, only two OECD countries switched from territorial to worldwide tax systems (Finland and New Zealand) and both countries subsequently switched back to territorial tax systems.[1]

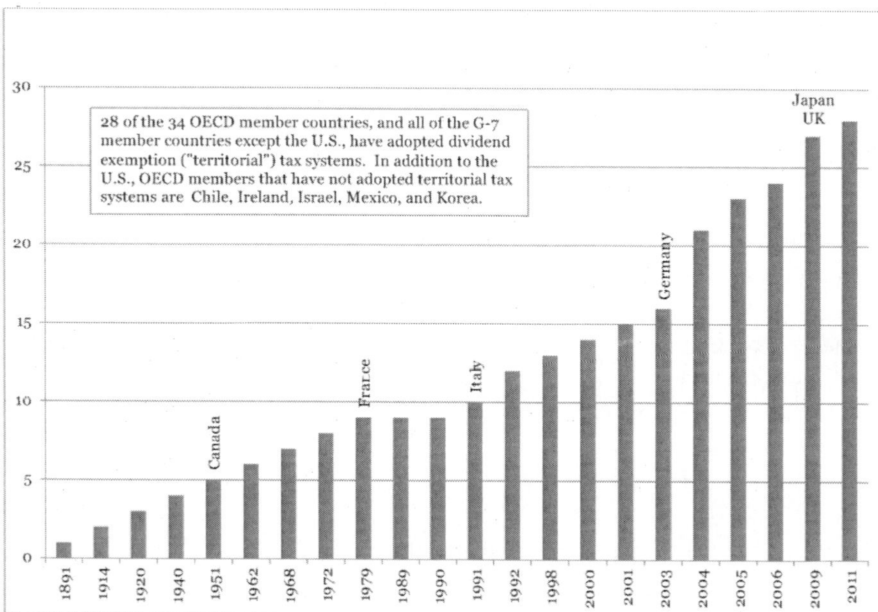

Source: Source: PricewaterhouseCoopers, Evolution of Territorial Tax Systems in the OECD, The Technology CEO Council, April 2, 2013.

Figure 4. Number of Countries with Dividend Exemption Systems among 34 OECD Countries, 1891-2011.

As a result of these trends, U.S. multinationals now compete against foreign competitors that overwhelmingly are taxed under territorial systems. Within the OECD, 93 percent of the non-U.S. parented companies on the Global Fortune 500 list in 2012 were located in countries that use territorial tax systems (Figure 5).

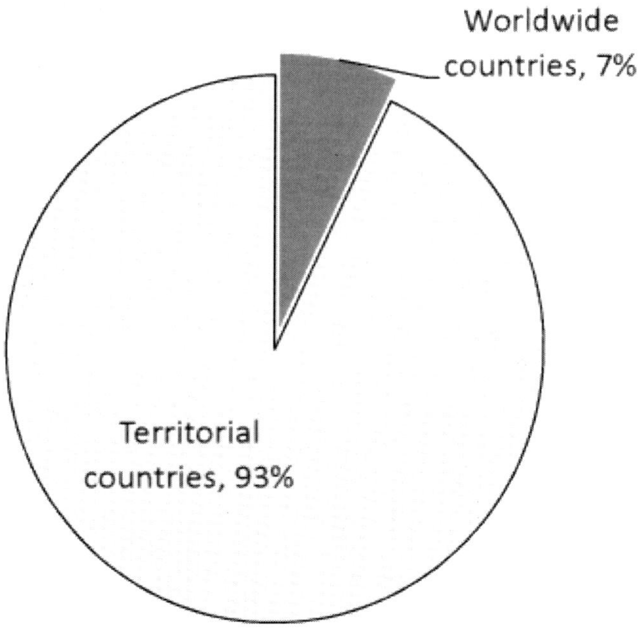

Source: Business Roundtable, *Corporate Tax Reform – The Time is Now*, April 15, 2013.

Figure 5. Headquarters location of non-U.S. OECD companies in the Global Fortune 500, 2012.

C. Allocation of Indirect Expenses

The U.S. rules for determining the source of income are unusual among OECD member countries in allocating and apportioning indirect domestic expenses, most importantly interest and R&D expenses, against foreign source income. As a result, when a U.S. company borrows money or conducts R&D in the United States, its foreign tax credit may be reduced.

In lieu of apportioning indirect expenses, eight of the 28 OECD countries with territorial tax systems exempt slightly less than 100 percent of foreign dividends, typically 95 percent (97 percent in Norway).

D. Controlled Foreign Corporation Regimes

The U.S. subpart F regime was enacted in 1962, and as described above, treats certain unrepatriated income earned by a CFC as if distributed to its U.S. shareholders and subject to current U.S. taxation. While the Kennedy Administration had proposed including all foreign subsidiary income within the scope of subpart F (other than income earned in less developed countries), Congress retained the general principle of deferral and limited the scope of subpart

F to certain passive and mobile income, with the goal to avoid unduly harming the competitive position of U.S. multinationals.[2]

Currently, 23 of the 34 OECD member countries have some form of CFC regime (see Table 3). In general, the scope of these CFC regimes is more limited than the U.S. CFC regime. Most countries restrict their CFC regimes to passive income and do not have provisions comparable to either the U.S. foreign base company sales, services, and oil-related income rules or the U.S. rules imposing current tax on foreign income invested in domestic property. Moreover, 12 of the 23 OECD member countries with CFC regimes are EU member states whose CFC rules (as they apply to EU corporations) are restricted by EU law to "wholly artificial arrangements."[3]

The potentially adverse competitive impacts of the relatively stringent U.S. CFC rules, however, have been mitigated by (1) the temporary enactment in 2006, and subsequent extensions, of the CFC look-through rules (which generally exclude from subpart F interest, dividends, rents, and royalties received from a related CFC and paid out of its active, non-subpart F income); (2) the temporary enactment in 1997 and subsequent extensions of the active financial services income exception from subpart F; and (3) the issuance by the IRS in 1996 of entity classification ("check the box") regulations that allow eligible entities (including foreign entities) to elect to be treated as corporations or as fiscally transparent.

Table 3. Controlled Foreign Corporation Regimes in OECD Countries, January 2014

Country	CFC Regime	EU member
Australia	Yes	
Austria1	Alternate	Yes
Belgium	None	Yes
Canada	Yes	
Chile	None	
Czech Republic	None	Yes
Denmark	Yes	yes
Estonia	Yes	Yes
Finland	Yes	Yes
France	Yes	Yes
Germany	Yes	Yes
Greece	Yes	Yes
Hungary	Yes	Yes
I celand	Yes	
Ireland	None	Yes
Israel	Yes	
Italy	Yes	Yes
Japan	Yes	
Korea	Yes	
Luxembourg	None	Yes
Mexico	Yes	
Netherlands2	Alternate	Yes
New Zealand	Yes	
Norway	Yes	

Table 3. (Continued)

Country	CFC Regime	EU member
Poland	None	Yes
Portugal	Yes	Yes
Slovak Republic	None	Yes
Slovenia3	Alternate	Yes
Spain	Yes	Yes
Sweden	Yes	Yes
Switzerland	None	
Turkey	Yes	
United Kingdom	Yes	Yes
United States	Yes	
OECD member countries		34
No CFC regime		11
EU member with CFC regime		12
Non-EU member with CFC regime		11

Source: Deloitte, Guide to Controlled Foreign Company Regimes, January 2014

[1] Austria's dividend exemption system excludes certain passive income.

[2] The Netherlands has a passive foreign investment company regime.

[3] Slovenia imposes withholding tax on payments for certain services and interest to persons established in certain low-tax jurisdictions.

IV. Recent Corporate Tax Reforms by Other Countries

A. United Kingdom

In 2009, the UK government replaced its worldwide tax system with a 100-percent dividend exemption (territorial) system.[4] Subsequently, HM Revenue and Customs and HM Treasury released the *Corporate Tax Road Map*, which set out a bold vision for a multi-year corporate tax reform package:

> "The Government wants to send out the signal loud and clear that Britain is open for business ... . In recent years too many businesses have left the UK amid concerns over tax competitiveness. It's time to reverse this trend. Our tax system was once viewed as an asset. And it needs to be an asset again. That is why the Government is prioritising corporate tax reform. Responding to the concerns of business, the UK is headed for a more competitive, simpler, and more stable tax system in the future, creating the right conditions for business investment."[5]

Chancellor George Osborne's 2011 budget accelerated the reforms with the goal to "create the most competitive tax system in the G20."

Since 2009, the UK government has enhanced the competitiveness of its corporate tax system by:

- Lowering the corporate income tax rate seven percentage points, from 28 percent in 2010 to 21 percent in 2014, with a further reduction to 20 percent scheduled in 2015.
- Extending the territorial system to foreign branches in 2011.
- Revising the UK CFC rules, effective in 2013, to be consistent with the territorial tax regime and focus more narrowly on foreign profits artificially diverted from the UK.
- Enacting a "patent box" system, effective in 2013, that phases in a 10-percent rate on patent-related income.
- Adopting a new 10-percent, non-incremental, refundable R&D credit.

In response to these corporate tax reforms, some multinationals returned to the UK and a number of other multinationals relocated their legal headquarters to the UK.

HM Revenue & Customs and HM Treasury (2013) used a computable general equilibrium model of the UK economy to simulate the long-term impacts of a reduction in the corporate tax rate from 28 percent in 2010 to a scheduled 20 percent in 2015. Relative to the baseline forecast, the study estimated that the rate reduction would increase GDP by between 0.65 percent and 0.82 percent after 20 years, and that these growth effects would offset between 45 percent and 60 percent of the static revenue cost of the tax rate reduction.[6]

Other researchers used data on 61,738 UK-owned foreign affiliates in 2008 and 2009 to estimate the impact of the UK territorial tax system, which took effect in 2009.[7] The authors found that UK parents of foreign affiliates responded to the adoption of the territorial tax system by increasing repatriations (by an average of over $2 million per affiliate) and reducing foreign affiliate investment.

B. Japan

Effective in 2009, Japan replaced its worldwide tax system with a 95-percent exemption for dividends received by Japanese corporations from foreign subsidiaries. The Japanese Ministry of Economy, Trade and Industry had advocated adoption of a territorial system to encourage repatriation of foreign earnings to Japan with a key goal of increasing domestic investment.[8]

In 2010, Japan liberalized and clarified its CFC rules, notably including within the scope of these rules only CFCs with an effective tax rate of less than 20 percent, as compared to 25 percent under prior law.

In 2011, Japan enacted a corporate rate reduction of five percentage points, but simultaneously enacted a temporary 2.5 percentage point surtax to aid in reconstruction work from the March 2011 earthquake. Both changes took effect in April 2012, resulting in the combined national and local corporate rate declining from 40.69 percent to 38.01 percent. The temporary surtax was to be in place for three years, but in 2014 was repealed one year early. As a result, beginning in April 2014, Japan's corporate tax rate declined to 35.64 percent. In June, Prime Minister Shinzo Abe's cabinet approved further reductions in the corporate tax rate to below 30 percent phased in over several years.

One report studied the effect of the adoption of territorial tax systems in Japan and the UK on cross-border mergers and acquisitions. The report estimates that elimination of the worldwide tax system in Japan increased the number of international mergers and acquisitions with a Japanese acquirer by 31.9 percent.[9]

Another report analyzed the effects of the UK and Japanese adoption of territorial tax systems in 2009.[10] The authors found that as a result of the adoption of territorial taxation, both UK and Japanese firms accumulated less cash, increased distributions to shareholders, and reduced foreign investment; however, they did not find a significant impact on domestic investment.[11]

C. New Zealand

Prior to 1988, dividends received by a New Zealand company from a foreign company were exempt from New Zealand income tax. Beginning in 1988, New Zealand resident companies were taxed on all income earned by their CFCs on a current basis with credits for foreign taxes (i.e., a worldwide system without deferral). No other OECD country has adopted a similar tax system. Instead, other OECD countries generally limit their anti-deferral regimes to passive income.

The New Zealand government ultimately determined that taxing all foreign subsidiary earnings on a current basis had adverse effects on their domestic economy. A 2006 New Zealand government report noted the following concerns with such an international tax system:[12]

1. "Since New Zealand taxes the income of its CFCs more heavily than other countries, it can be attractive for innovative and dynamic firms to migrate from New Zealand, establish themselves in other countries or simply stay small and local." [p. 7]
2. "Migration of even one or two of New Zealand's large dynamic firms could have a substantial negative effect on the economy ... Not only would migration lead to jobs within head offices being shifted offshore, so too would be the demand for associated professional services ... Firm migration also reduces the extent to which New Zealand could benefit from cluster effects." [p. 11]
3. "A foreign tax credit system can provide incentives for domestic firms to channel offshore investment into higher-tax foreign countries in ways which are not in New Zealand's best interest." [p. 9]
4. "Finally, higher taxes on offshore income may also make it difficult for New Zealand-based firms to expand out of local markets ..." [p. 12]

The 2006 report also noted that while the stock of outbound direct investment by New Zealand had remained relatively constant since the early 1990s, fluctuating between 10 and 15 percent of GDP, for the OECD as a whole, and Australia in particular, outbound direct investment increased from 10 percent of GDP to around 30 percent by 2004 (see Figure 6).

In response to the adverse economic effects of the change to a worldwide system without deferral, New Zealand switched back to a territorial system in 2009 (effective for tax years beginning after June 30, 2009). The New Zealand reform (1) restricted the scope of the CFC regime to passive income, and (2) exempted 100 percent of foreign subsidiary dividends.

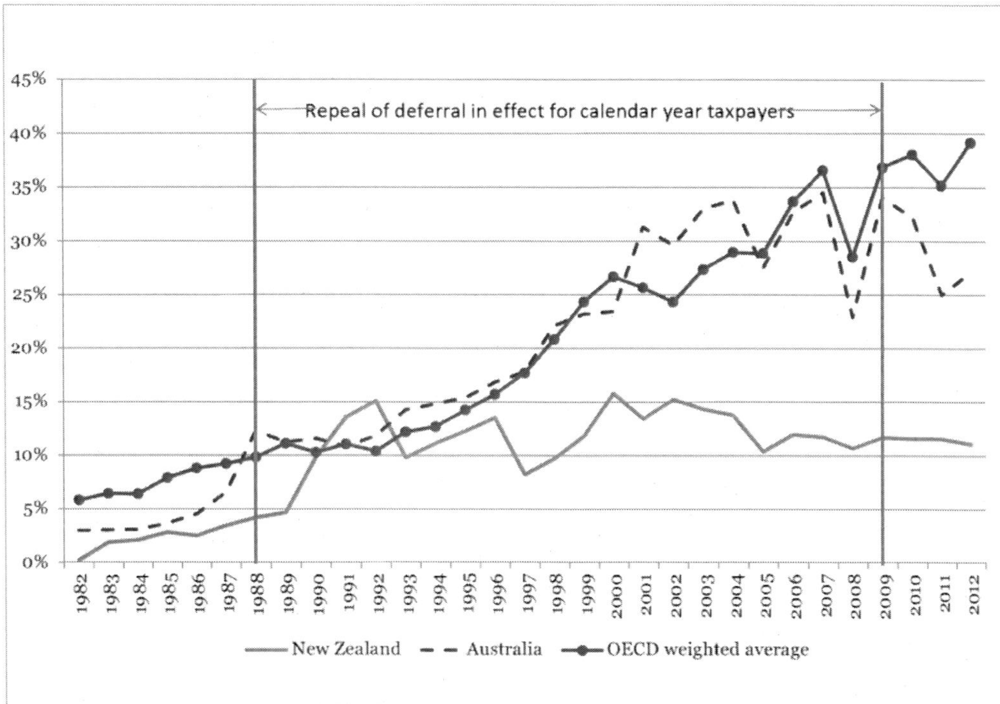

Source: UNCTAD (downloaded July 2014). Weighted average based on 2012 GDP from the IMF, World Economic Outlook, April 2014.

Figure 6. Outbound FDI Stock as a percent of GDP, 1982-2012 New Zealand, Australia, and the OECD.

V. Economic Effects of U.S. International Tax System

With the highest corporate tax rate among OECD countries and a worldwide tax regime, the U.S. corporate tax system falls far outside international norms for advanced economies, with possible adverse consequences for the U.S. economy. This section discusses the effects of U.S. tax policy on (A) foreign investment, (B) headquarters location, and (C) economic growth.

A. Foreign Investment

With the rapid growth in emerging market economies, the foreign share of U.S. multinational company earnings has increased. For all U.S. public companies, domestic and multinational, 48 percent of 2012 pre-tax book earnings was reported as coming from foreign sources.[13] The effect of U.S. tax law is to discourage companies from remitting these foreign earnings to, or investing it in, the United States, because doing so would result in imposition of U.S. tax at a federal rate of 35 percent, with an offset for associated foreign income taxes. As foreign income tax rates have fallen, the U.S. tax that would be incurred by repatriating foreign earnings has increased, in effect discouraging the repatriation of foreign income that is not currently needed for business purposes abroad.

One measure of the amount of earnings accumulated abroad that companies do not intend to repatriate or invest in the United States is the amount of income recorded on their financial statements as permanently or indefinitely reinvested abroad. Some of these earnings are reinvested abroad in active business assets, such as plant, property, and equipment, and some is invested in cash and equivalents.[14] Audit Analytics estimates that for the companies in the Russell 1000, permanently reinvested earnings reached $2.1 trillion in 2013, an increase of $1 trillion over the prior five years.[15]

One consequence of the U.S. tax rules with respect to repatriated foreign earnings is that it is more attractive for U.S. multinationals to invest abroad than at home. For example, if a foreign subsidiary earns $100 million and distributes $80 million of earnings, after paying $20 million of foreign tax, to its U.S. parent, there would be just $65 million available to invest after paying $15 million of U.S. corporate tax (35 percent of $100 million less a credit for the $20 million of foreign tax). By contrast, the entire $80 million would be available to invest if used to expand abroad or acquire a foreign company. In this example, the U.S. tax system effectively provides a $15 million tax incentive for investing *outside* the United States.

Walter Galvin, the retired Vice Chairman of Emerson, testified about a real-life example of how the U.S. tax system encouraged foreign investment:

> "Last year, Emerson bought a company in the U.K. called Chloride for about $1.5 billion with cash we had earned abroad and kept abroad. We considered other options for that cash, such as bringing it to the U.S., but the U.S. tax code would charge us an extra 10 to 15 cents in taxes on every dollar. Where is our return higher? A dollar invested in the U.K. or 85 cents in the United States?"[16]

Academic research confirms that U.S companies with foreign profits that would be subject to U.S. tax if repatriated are more like to invest abroad. Across a large sample of U.S. multinationals, one report found that both the probability and the number of foreign (but not domestic) acquisitions increases with the amount of foreign cash. [17] The authors also found that the stock market reaction to announced foreign acquisitions is more negative for firms with more locked out cash, suggesting that, "firms are both stockpiling cash and (poorly) investing overseas because U.S. policy hinders repatriation."

B. Headquarters Location

The combination of a high U.S. corporate tax rate and a worldwide regime which taxes foreign income when remitted to the United States is an important disadvantage to the selection of the United States as headquarters. If the United States is chosen as the tax home of the merged entity, distributions to the ultimate parent company of foreign income would be subject to the U.S. repatriation tax – a tax that does not apply if the parent company is headquartered in a country with a territorial tax system. Moreover, by establishing legal headquarters in a country with a territorial tax system, the company will be better positioned as an acquirer of businesses. This can be observed in a number of cross border merger and acquisition transactions in which the combined company has chosen to be legally headquartered outside of the United States.

Based on the experience of the UK and Japan, one study estimated that if the United States were to switch from a worldwide to a territorial tax system, the number of cross-border mergers and acquisitions in which the U.S. company was acquirer would increase by 17.1 percent.[18]

C. Economic Growth

A recent report by Laura D'Andrea Tyson and colleagues at the Berkeley Research Group analyzed the macroeconomic effects of eliminating most of the U.S. repatriation tax by adopting a 95-percent exemption for active foreign subsidiary earnings. The report estimated that such a territorial tax system (at the current U.S. corporate tax rate) would, on an ongoing basis, increase repatriations by $114 billion per year, increase U.S. GDP by $22 billion annually, and create an estimated 154,000 new jobs per year, with even larger effects during an initial transition from the current U.S. worldwide tax system.[19]

VI. Conclusion

U.S. companies are increasingly competing in foreign markets, which account for over 95 percent of the world's population and over 75 percent of global purchasing power. In many cases, a U.S. company's sales of goods and services overseas creates jobs and growth in the United States. For U.S. companies to succeed in the global marketplace, they must be able to provide goods and services that are competitive in terms of quality, innovation, and price.

Since the last major reform of the U.S. corporate income tax in 1986, the importance of foreign markets to the success of U.S. business has grown and international competition from foreign-based companies has increased. Over this same period, other advanced economies have reduced their corporate tax rates and moved from worldwide to territorial tax systems. As a result, the U.S. corporate tax system has become an outlier among OECD countries. Reform of the U.S. tax system to bring it more in line with international norms would enhance the ability of U.S. multinationals to continue to compete and succeed in global markets.

End Notes

1 Source: PricewaterhouseCoopers, Evolution of Territorial Tax Systems in the OECD, The Technology CEO Council, April 2, 2013.

2 National Foreign Trade Council, International Tax Policy for the 21st Century, December 15, 2001, pp. 37-57.

3 See Judgment of the European Court of Justice, Cadbury Schweppes plc and Cadbury Schweppes Overseas Ltd v Commissioners of Inland Revenue, Case C-196/04, September 12, 2006.

4 EU law restrictions on dividend taxation, CFC regimes, and on tax barriers to corporate expatriation were influential in shaping UK corporate tax reform.

[5] HM Revenue & Customs and HM Treasury, Corporate Tax Reform: delivering a more competitive system, November 2010, p. 7.

[6] HM Revenues & Customs and HM Treasury, Analysis of the dynamic effects of corporation tax reductions, December 5, 2013.

[7] Peter Egger, Valeria Merlo, Martin Ruf, and Georg Wamser, "Consequences of the New UK Tax Exemption System: Evidence from Micro-level Data," CESifo, Working Paper no. 3942, September 2012.

[8] Todd Landau, Takaaki Tokuhiro, Kinjun Muraoka, and Shuta Kobayashi, "Japan issues proposed 2009 tax reforms," Journal of International Taxation, March 2009, pp. 15-19.

[9] Lars P. Feld, Martin Ruf, Uwe Scheuering, Ulrich Schreiber, and Johannes Voget, "Effects of Territorial and Worldwide Corporation Tax Systems on Outbound M&As," Center for European Economic Research, Discussion paper no. 13-088, 2013.

[10] Matteo Arena and George Kutner, "Territorial Tax System Reform and Corporate Financial Policies," December 2013, available at: http://ssrn.com/abstract=2160954

[11] The global financial crisis, which occurred concurrently with the adoption of territorial tax systems in Japan and the UK, may have dampened domestic investment. Also, under the prior worldwide tax systems used in Japan and the UK, foreign subsidiary earnings could be lent to the parent company without triggering tax.

[12] Hon. Dr. Michael Cullen (Minister of Finance) and Hon. Peter Dunne (Minister of Revenue), New Zealand's International Tax Review: a direction for change, 2006.

[13] PwC calculations based on Compustat data.

[14] Ben Casselman and Justin Lahart, "Companies shun investment, hoard cash," Wall Street Journal, Sept. 17, 2011.

[15] Audit Analytics, available at: http://www.auditanalytics.com/blog/wp-content/uploads/ 2014/04/IRE-April-2014-Picture-1.png

[16] Testimony of Mr. Walter J. Galvin before the Committee on Ways & Means, U.S. House of Representatives, Hearing on "How Business Tax Reform Can Encourage Job Creation," June 2, 2011.

[17] Hanlon, Michelle and Lester, Rebecca and Verdi, Rodrigo S., "The Effect of Repatriation Tax Costs on U.S. Multinational Investment," May 23, 2014 (Journal of Financial Economics, forthcoming). Available at SSRN: http://ssrn.com/abstract=2441529 or http://dx.doi.org/10.2139/ssrn.2441529

[18] Feld et al. (2013), op cit.

[19] Eric Drabkin, Kenneth Serwin, Laura D'Andrea Tyson, "Implications of a Switch to a Territorial Tax System in the United States: A Critical Comparison to the Current System," Berkeley Research Group, October 2013.

In: U.S. International Tax System
Editor: Holly Lanford

ISBN: 978-1-63321-976-2

Chapter 7

TESTIMONY OF LESLIE ROBINSON, ASSOCIATE PROFESSOR OF BUSINESS ADMINISTRATION, DARTMOUTH COLLEGE. HEARING ON "THE U.S. TAX CODE: LOVE IT, LEAVE IT OR REFORM IT!"*

Chairman Wyden, Ranking Member Hatch, and distinguished members of the Committee, it is an honor to appear today to testify on the important topic of international corporate taxation. I am an associate professor at the Tuck School of Business at Dartmouth College. I teach financial accounting and taxation and my research centers on multinational corporations (MNCs). The views I am expressing are my personal views.

Abandoning our current approach to international corporate taxation in favor of one of the many alternatives would be a major policy move and deserves careful analysis. It is clear that reform is needed – the international system is one of the most technically complex areas of the U.S. tax code but raises little revenue.

In this testimony, I would like to offer my views on: (i) the problem(s) with the current system, (ii) some strengths and weaknesses of reform alternatives, and (iii) financial reporting considerations when formulating international tax policy. As my views are shaped by my own research and the research of my colleagues, I will summarize extant work guiding many of the assessments I offer in my testimony.

A. WHAT IS THE PROBLEM WITH THE CURRENT SYSTEM OF U.S. INTERNATIONAL CORPORATE TAXATION?

Comparative Tax Burdens

Public debate surrounding reform of U.S. international corporate taxation often features claims that the current system is not 'competitive'. The top U.S. federal corporate income tax rate is 35 percent. At present, this is the highest federal tax rate of all OECD countries, and

* This is an edited, reformatted and augmented version of testimony presented July 22, 2014 before the Senate Committee on Finance.

far exceeds the 23.5% average of all other OECD countries. Generally speaking, U.S.-based MNCs face this relatively high tax on worldwide profits, whereas non-U.S.-based MNCs face a relatively low tax on domestic profits and no residual home country tax on foreign profits. Thus, a common assertion is that U.S. MNCs are at a competitive disadvantage because they face larger corporate tax burdens than their competitors under a worldwide, rather than territorial, tax system.

Yet there is no evidence to support this assertion. Some studies compare global accounting effective tax rates (ETRs) across countries with the goal of informing the debate on competitiveness.[1] Markle and Shackelford (2011) finds that firms resident in countries with a worldwide tax system have ETRs that are 1.4% lower than firms resident in countries with a territorial tax system.[2] Avi-Yonah and Lahav (2011) finds that U.S. MNCs have ETRs that are 4% lower than MNCs based in the EU.[3] Finally, Maffini (2012) finds that, after controlling for statutory tax rates in the home country, there is no difference in ETRs of firms operating under a worldwide versus territorial tax system.[4]

The issue of competiveness is often raised when advancing reform towards adoption of a territorial system. Embodied in such a system is the concept of capital import neutrality that requires the same tax on firms with different nationalities that invest in a given location. Comparing global ETRs will not detect violations of capital import neutrality because they, in part, reflect differences in location decisions.

Since each MNC has a different geographic footprint, a comparison of ETRs within a single jurisdiction operated by MNCs resident in different countries would seem more appropriate. For instance, how does the tax burden (including both source and host country taxes) on operations in a given country compare between U.S. MNCs and nonU.S. MNCs?[5] We do not know the answer to this question, nor is there good data to answer it. At best, we observe the source country tax, but do not observe any home country tax imposed on profits earned in a specific country.

Both Markle and Shackelford (2011) and Maffini (2012) move closer to making the relevant comparison when they examine the impact of location decisions on global ETRs for firms resident in different countries. The former study finds that by operating a subsidiary in the Netherlands, a U.S. firm reduces its global ETR by 0.1% whereas a Swedish firm lowers its global ETR by 7.3%. The latter study finds that a tax haven subsidiary yields a greater reduction in the global ETR for territorial firms, relative to worldwide firms. The reality is that we know very little about how the tax burden in any particular jurisdiction depends on the parent company's country of residence.

There is no evidence that u.s. Mncs face greater tax burdens as a consequence of how foreign profits are taxed, relative to their competitors.

Further, Researchers cannot make comparisons by jurisdiction that would seem necessary to resolve the competitiveness issue. This is of particular importance when the public debate frames the problem with the current tax system as violating capital import neutrality and calls for the adoption of a territorial tax system.

The Implicit Cost of Tax Deferral

The burden associated with the current U.S. system includes both the explicit residual tax on actual repatriations and the implicit cost of avoiding repatriation. The explicit cost of the repatriation tax would show up in firms' ETRs, but the implicit cost of avoiding the tax would not. Such implicit costs might include high leverage in the U.S. to finance domestic investment, or making foreign investments with lower rates of return than could be earned domestically. Thus, it may be more fruitful to search for evidence that the U.S. tax system lacks competitiveness by examining implicit, rather than explicit, costs.

The implicit tax associated with avoiding repatriation is estimated at about 1% of pretax income (1.7% in tax havens).[6] However, the unexpectedly large repatriations under the 2005 tax holiday that reduced the repatriation tax rate to 5.25% suggests that these estimates are too low. The reason is that MNCs will not repatriate until the effective tax rate on locked-out earnings falls below the cost of deferral.

In light of the tax holiday, Grubert and Altshuler (2008) re-examines these estimates and finds that the implicit costs are increasing in the stock of deferrals, an issue that was previously not considered.[7] That is, the cost of using complex structures to avoid repatriation taxes increases as the amount of undistributed earnings rises. Consistent with this, Lewellen and Robinson (2013) documents a significant difference in both the size and age of foreign operations between U.S. MNCs that use complex internal ownership structures (i.e., affiliates are indirectly owned by the parent), relative to those that do not.[8]

An important implicit cost of deferral is the failure to allocate economic resources in an efficient manner. As U.S. taxation of foreign earnings only takes place when earnings are repatriated, firms have incentives to keep foreign earnings abroad. As a consequence, in times of limited foreign investment opportunities and high profitability, these funds are likely to be held abroad in the form of cash – referred to as the "lock out" effect or "trapped cash". Foley, Hartzell, Titman, and Twite (2007) finds that the repatriation tax helps explain cash holdings abroad in U.S. MNCs.[9] Hanlon, Lester and Verdi (2014) and Blouin, Krull, and Robinson (2014) develop proxies for trapped cash in U.S. MNCs and examine the economic effects of these cash holdings.[10]

Hanlon et al. documents that foreign acquisitions are more likely for firms with trapped cash, and that market reaction to the announcement of such acquisitions is negative. The inference is that foreign investments financed by trapped cash are value decreasing, possible reflecting agency issues. Blouin et al. documents that domestic investment of firms with trapped cash is less responsive to U.S. investment opportunities and is more sensitive to domestic cash flows than foreign cash flows. Further, this finding holds only in a sample of financially constrained firms (i.e., those with limited access to external capital markets). The authors conclude that trapped cash creates frictions in firms' internal capital markets.

There is also evidence consistent with the implicit cost of the lock out effect making U.S. MNCs less competitive in the market for corporate control. Huizinga and Voget (2009) finds that countries with worldwide tax systems are less likely to attract the parent companies of newly created MNCs following cross-border M&A transactions.[11] They estimate that U.S. adoption of a territorial system would increase the proportion of cross-border takeovers resulting in a U.S. parent firm from 53% to 58%. Feld, Ruf, Scheuering, Schreiber, and Voget (2013) finds that the number of cross-border M&A transactions featuring a Japanese or UK acquirer increased after these countries adopted a territorial system. Based on their results, they estimate that U.S. adoption of a territorial system would increase the number of cross-border transactions featuring a U.S. acquirer by 17%.

Balakrishnan, Blouin, and Guay (2012) documents another implicit cost by showing that firms engaging in more extensive tax planning have less transparent (internal and external) information environments due the organizational complexities associated with implementing various tax strategies.[12] Finally, Creal, Rogers, Robinson and Zechman (2014) fail to find evidence that the valuation premium in U.S. MNCs, relative to the value of a benchmark portfolio of firms operating independently in the same geographic footprint, is associated with the MNCs ability to shift income, suggesting that implicit costs reduce the value of tax benefits from shifting income.[13]

There is evidence supporting the notion that U.S. MNCs face non-trivial implicit costs of deferral that may put them at a competitive disadvantage, but there is no comparison of these costs to MNCs based in other countries. Competing firms operating under territorial tax systems may also bear implicit costs of avoiding home country tax through the need to navigate anti-abuse rules in the home country. The implicit cost is assumed to be low for non-U.S. MNCs, relative to U.S. MNCs. However, the validity of this assumption is not clear.

Corporate Inversions

A recent wave of 'inversions' is underway, urging policymakers to enact U.S. tax reform quickly. However, to my knowledge, there is no good data compiled indicating the extent of U.S. MNCs' involvement in inversion transactions as compared with nonU.S. MNCs, nor a thorough understanding of the precise tax motivations for the relocation choice. Voget (2011) reports that 6% of a sample of about 2,000 MNCs from 19 countries inverted over the period 1997-2007.[14] Interestingly, 10% of the sample relocated from the U.S. to another country, while the remaining firms were initially based in other EU countries, including EU tax havens. Thus, not all inversion transactions follow the fact pattern generally documented in the recent business press.[15]

Of the 27 firms that relocated from the U.S., 6 relocated to the U.K., 5 to France, 4 to Canada, and 4 to Germany. Though none of these countries has a particularly low statutory rate, they all operate a territorial tax system. Voget (2011) documents that both home country taxes on the repatriation of foreign profits and the introduction of controlled foreign corporation (CFC) legislation have a positive effect on the probability of relocation. Thus, it is not only the existence of a worldwide system that provides incentives for firms to relocate, but also the existence of anti-abuse legislation.

Similarly, Markle and Robinson (2012) examine the use of tax haven subsidiaries across MNCs based in 28 countries and document that both the existence of a worldwide system, and the existence of CFC legislation, reduces the probability of tax haven use. Moreover, Markle and Robinson consider the 'strength' of countries' CFC legislation by creating an index based on whether seven types of provisions contained in the legislation are likely to broaden the tax base. In subsequent analyses, the authors find that 'stronger' CFC legislation, as opposed to simply its existence, is associated with a lower probability of tax haven use. Interestingly, the U.S. ranks right in the middle, in terms of the strength of its CFC legislation, among the 18 countries in the sample with CFC legislation.

The significant number of recent actual or proposed inversions by U.S. companies is likely a signal that tax reform is needed soon. However, it would be useful to have comparative data on the extent to which non-U.S. firms are currently engaging in corporate inversions. This would be an indirect way of evaluating the implicit costs of avoiding home country tax on foreign source income across MNCs based in different countries. Note that even firms in territorial countries likely bear implicit costs associated with circumventing anti-abuse rules.

Overall, the problem is that a relatively high tax rate and worldwide system with deferral creates incentives to shift income (and real economic activity) to low-tax countries, and discourages repatriation. Research offers considerable support that the present system raises little revenue, is complicated, creates incentives for income shifting, and interferes with companies efficient use of capital as they try to avoid the repatriation tax. However, research offers little in the way of guidance as to how things would look under an alternative system. Moreover, comparisons of the U.S. to other countries, or worldwide countries to territorial countries, have only limited use because the U.S. differs from other countries along many important dimensions. Finally, all countries, in practice, use a hybrid system with anti-base erosion rules that broaden or narrow the tax base, limiting inferences made from comparisons between worldwide and territorial systems.

B. What Are Some of the Strengths and Weaknesses of Reform Alternatives?

Territorial Taxation Versus Worldwide Taxation

A recent KPMG survey of nearly 1,700 tax professionals and senior executives indicates that 49% are in favor of a relatively pure territorial tax system, 16% are in favor of the current system of worldwide taxation with deferral, 3% are in favor of a relatively pure worldwide system (without deferral), and 27% are unsure. It is not surprising to see many more members of the business community interested in a pure territorial system than a pure worldwide system, but preferences become less clear when proposals to lower the statutory rate under a pure worldwide system and introduce anti-based erosion legislation under a territorial system enter the picture.

Appropriately framing the objective of tax reform is important when choosing among alternative solutions. If the objective were to make U.S. firms more competitive by reducing the U.S. tax burden on their foreign income, then this would naturally lead one to want to support the adoption a territorial system. However, if the goal is to reduce the implicit costs of avoiding the repatriation tax, the path forward becomes less clear. That is because this goal can be achieved either by maintaining a worldwide system but eliminating deferral, or by adopting a territorial system.

It is also important to keep in mind that worldwide versus territorial systems are methods for alleviating double taxation of income. When framed in this fashion, it seems reasonable that a well-designed territorial system would appropriately limit eligibility for dividend exemption to income that has been subject to a robust tax system abroad. Thus, as eligibility becomes more and more restrictive on certain types of income taxed at low rates abroad, the pendulum swings back to that resembling a worldwide system without deferral.[16] Thus, it is possible for a well-designed territorial system to be more burdensome on a U.S. MNC than the poorly designed worldwide system we have now.

Territorial Taxation and Incentives to Shift Income

The first major concern with adopting a territorial tax system is that it will increase incentives to shift income to low-tax jurisdictions. The validity of this concern depends on (i) the new U.S. statutory tax rate, (ii) the anti-base erosion rules in place, and (iii) the extent to which U.S. firms are shifting income under the current tax system.

There is an extensive literature consistent with income shifting in MNCs. Estimates of the magnitude and trend in income shifting differ across studies that examine U.S.- based MNCs versus EU-based MNCs. In a sample of EU-based MNCs, a 10% decrease in the tax rate is associated with an increase in reported income ranging from 4% to 13%. These studies indicate that profit shifting is decreasing over time.[17] Research using a sample of U.S. MNCs paints a different picture. In particular, Klassen and LaPlante (2012) report a larger semi-elasticity of 17% and show that U.S. MNC profit shifting is increasing over time.[18]

Two studies attempt to compare income shifting by firms subject to a worldwide versus territorial system. Markle (2012) estimates the extent of income shifting in a sample of MNCs resident in different countries. Territorial firms engage in more shifting than *financially constrained* worldwide firms, while there is no difference between territorial firms and *financially unconstrained* worldwide firms.[19] If a firm can access external capital or generate sufficient internal domestic capital to fund their domestic investments, the repatriation tax should have no effect on the firm's investment. Using financially unconstrained U.S. MNCs as a proxy for how U.S. MNCs would behave under a territorial system, Dyreng and Markle (2013) estimate that constrained MNCs would shift up to 19% more income out of the U.S. under a territorial system.[20]

Incentives to shift income out of the U.S. would likely increase for financially constrained firms under a territorial system. Incentives to shift income would also still exist for firms with excess foreign tax credits under a worldwide system without deferral. However, these incentives would depend on the new U.S. statutory tax rate (under a worldwide system without deferral, the rate would determine the number of firms with excess foreign tax credits). Proposals differ on the new U.S. statutory tax rate – for instance, the Camp proposal sets the new rate at 25% while the Obama proposal sets the new rate at 30%. A reasonable rate would be one that approximates the actual effective tax rate on foreign income under the current system.

These incentives also depend on anti-base erosion legislation in place under a territorial system. The Camp proposal, for instance, appropriately introduces such anti-base erosion provisions. However, many of these provisions would be difficult to enforce, and would present new opportunities for tax planning.

Territorial Taxation and Intellectual Property

A second major concern with adopting a territorial tax system is that it will increase incentives to shift royalty income out of the U.S. in order to turn it into tax-exempt dividend income. This would most likely be accompanied by a shift in real R&D activities abroad. Moreover, this incentive will be stronger for U.S. MNCs shielding their royalty income using excess foreign tax credits under the existing system.

The Camp proposal appropriately addresses this issue with three possible anti-abuse rules. Options that reduce the effective tax rate on intangible income may be likely to keep R&D operations in the U.S. that are most likely to contribute to the U.S. economy. Christof, Richter, and Riedel (2013) finds that reducing income tax rates on R&D output (as opposed to other incentives) attracts relatively more innovative projects with higher earnings potential.[21]

Taxing the Existing Stock of Undistributed Earnings

A final issue, regardless of the new tax system, is how to treat the current stockpile of undistributed foreign earnings. Various proposals differ on this issue. For instance, under the Camp proposal, the undistributed earnings would be subject to tax at the rate of 5.25% and the tax obligation could be paid over 8 years. The foreign dividends, when repatriated under the new exemption system, would then be subject to an additional tax a the rate of 1.25% (25%*5%). The Baucus proposal would subject undistributed earnings to a one-time tax at a rate of 20%, as would the Obama proposal. Each proposal trades off being harsh compared to the current system (under which many firms may never repatriate) with providing unnecessary windfall benefits.

It is important, when deciding how to tax currently undistributed earnings, to understand (i) the size of the potential pool of earnings, (ii) the effective tax rate on those earnings, and (iii) the extent to which earnings are tied up in a non-liquid form. Blouin, Krull, and Robinson (2014) provide an analysis of permanently reinvested earnings (PRE) in a sample of 870 large U.S. MNCs and report that the aggregate ratio of PRE to foreign retained earnings is 59%, 24% of PRE is held in tax havens, and 45% of PRE is held in liquid assets. These descriptive data suggest that the pool of undistributed earnings that would be subject to tax is larger than PRE, not all PRE will have a significant residual tax liability associated with it, and the imposition of a transition tax on PRE is not likely to create a hardship on most MNCs.[22]

Finally, it is my conjecture that the recent build-up of undistributed earnings since the 2005 tax holiday is at least, in part, driven by the expectation of a potential future tax holiday. Thus, taxing undistributed earnings at any rate lower than 5.25% would seem to provide a windfall benefit to firms that have shifted income out of the U.S. in anticipation of such a holiday. That is, it is difficult to argue that much of this shifted income would have never been repatriated under the current system.

My view is that our current system of international taxation can be adequately reformed. We need not entirely abandon our current system in favor a fundamentally different system. Limiting deferral and lowering the statutory tax rate would generally reduce incentives to shift income, eliminate the implicit costs of avoiding repatriation, reduce complexity and uncertainty, be easier to enforce and administer, and lower the overall burden of the tax system on U.S. MNCs, relative to a territorial tax system that would necessarily feature anti-base erosion measures. That is, pleas for a more competitive tax system can be answered through a careful combination of base broadening and lower rates.

C. Are There Other Issues to Consider When Deciding on the Path to Reform That Might Not Have Been Considered So Far?

Accounting Principles Board Opinion (APB) 23

The accounting literature has recently documented a financial reporting cost of repatriation that is at least as significant to many U.S. MNCs as the cash tax cost – the decrease to financial accounting earnings related to the recognition of the residual U.S. tax. Under APB 23, accounting rules permit U.S. MNCs to defer recognition of the U.S. residual tax expense until repatriation, while the foreign income is recognized in accounting earnings immediately. All else equal, this creates a timing difference whereby accounting earnings increase in the period that foreign income is generated, and decrease in the year of repatriation.

Blouin, Krull and Robinson (2012) estimate that repatriations by U.S. MNCs would increase by approximately 17 - 20 percent annually if APB 23 were repealed, while Graham, Hanlon, and Shevlin (2011) survey executives who indicate that the importance of the tax expense recognition for accounting is as important as the cash tax when making repatriation decisions.[23] Either the elimination of deferral or the adoption of a territorial tax system would render APB 23 unnecessary. *Both revenue and rate estimates of various reform options should take into account the potential increase in repatriations attributable to changes in financial reporting costs.*

Adoption of International Financial Reporting Standards (IFRS)

Over 100 countries use IFRS as set by the London-based International Accounting Standards Board and U.S.-listed foreign firms have been allowed to file financial reports with the SEC in IFRS since 2007. Use of a common set of accounting standards in the EU expands the opportunity set of benchmark firms available to MNCs for substantiating tax-advantaged transfer prices. De Simone (2013) finds a positive association between IFRS adoption and income shifting in EU affiliates.[24]

There is no clear roadmap for adopting IFRS for U.S. firms. This may serve as a constraint on future income shifting out of the U.S. for U.S. MNCs, as the number of benchmark firms is limited to firms reporting under U.S. GAAP. *Any constraints on shifting income posed by the decision not to adopt IFRS in the U.S. should be considered when evaluating the extent of income shifting that might occur under a new tax system.*

Financial Reporting Disclosures and Tax Reporting

Financial reporting disclosures may affect firms' tax reporting decisions. Hope, Ma and Thomas (2013) find that firms voluntarily discontinuing disclosure of geographic earnings after the implementation of SFAS 131 have lower ETRs than other firms. SFAS 131 relaxed the requirement to reports earnings for geographic segments, and only required disclosure of sales and assets.[25] Akamah, Hope and Thomas (2014) find that disclosure aggregation for geographic operations is more prevalent in firms with tax haven subsidiaries. These findings imply that geographic segment data may facilitate the enforcement of transfer pricing rules, consistent with proposed regulations in the EU (OECD 2014).[26]

Dyreng, Hoopes, and Wilde (2014) examine a U.K. requirement to disclose the name and location of all subsidiaries. Firms that did not comply with these requirements, but were subsequently forced to do so, exhibit an increase in the accounting ETR and a decrease in tax haven usage relative to firms that were in compliance.[27] Gupta, Mills, and Towery (2014) find that mandatory disclosure requirements in the U.S. regarding tax uncertainty increase firms' state income tax expense as well as state income tax collections.[28]

The association between financial reporting disclosures and tax reporting behavior has two important implications. First, tax policy makers should consider any role of accounting disclosures in evaluating behavioral responses to various reform options. Second, tax disclosure requirements could be considered as additional policy measures to aid in the enforcement of tax policy.

Thank you. I would be happy to answer any questions that you may have.

End Notes

[1] Due to the ability to defer tax expense recognition for expected U.S. repatriation taxes under APB 23 in U.S. firms' financial statements, accounting ETRs will not reflect the expected residual U.S. tax, which may be indefinitely deferred. Thus, APB 23 puts U.S. MNCs 'on par' with MNCs based in territorial countries in terms of the accounting ETR.

[2] Markle, Kevin, and Douglas Shackelford (2011). Cross-Country Comparisons of Corporate Income Taxes, NBER Working Paper 16839.

[3] Avi-Yonah, Reuven, and Yaron Lahav (2011). The Effective Tax Rate of the Largest US and EU Multinationals. University of Michigan Public Law Working Paper 255.

[4] Maffini, Giorgia (2012). Territoriality, Worldwide Principle, and Competitiveness of Multinationals: A Firm-Level Analysis of Tax Burdens. Centre for Business Taxation WP 12/10.

[5] It is entirely possible that, for a given profit generated in a low-tax country, a non-U.S. MNC faces a higher tax burden due to 'strong' anti-abuse rules taxing those source country profits in the MNC's home country, while the U.S. firm faces indefinite deferral of home country tax under 'weak' anti-abuse rules.

[6] Grubert, Harry, and John Mutti (2001). Taxing International Business Income: Dividend Exemption versus the Current System. American Enterprise Institute, Washington DC.; Desai, Mihir, Fritz Foley, and Jim Hines (2001). Repatriation Taxes and Dividend Distortions. National Tax Journal 54 (4), 829-851.

[7] Grubert, Harry, and Rosanne Altshuler (2008). Corporate Income Taxes in the World Economy: Reforming the Taxation of Cross-Border Income. In Diamond, John W. and George R. Zodrow (eds.). Fundamental Tax Reform: Issues, Choices, and Implications, 319-354. MIT Press, Cambridge, MA.

[8] Lewellen, Katharina, and Leslie Robinson (2013). The Internal Ownership Structures of Multinational Firms. Tuck School of Business working paper.

[9] Foley, Fritz, Jay Hartzell, Sheridan Titman, and Garry Twite (2007). Why Do Firms Hold So Much Cash? A Tax-Based Explanation. Journal of Financial Economics, 86 (3), 579-607. However, this role of taxes is challenged in a recent working paper that compares cash holdings across firms resident in different countries. The authors find a number of results inconsistent with tax-induced cash holdings in MNCs resident in different countries. See Pinkowitz, Lee, René Stulz, and Rohan Williamson (2012). Multinationals and the High Cash Holdings Puzzle. Ohio State University working paper.

[10] Hanlon, Michelle, Becky Lester, and Rodrigo Verdi (2014). The Effect of Repatriation Tax Costs on U.S. Multinational Investment. Journal of Financial Economics, forthcoming; Blouin, Jennifer, Linda Krull and Leslie Robinson (2014). The Location, Composition, and Investment Implications of Permanently Reinvested Earnings. University of Pennsylvania working paper.

[11] Huizinga, Harry, and Johannes Voget (2009). International Taxation and the Direction and Volume of Cross-Border M&A. Journal of Finance 64(3), 1217-1249; Feld, Lars, Martin Ruf, Uwe Scheuering, Ulrich Schreiber, Johannes Voget (2013). Effects of Territorial and Worldwide Corporation Tax Systems on Outbound M&As. ZEW Discussion Paper 13-088.

[12] Balakrishnan, Karthik, Jennifer Blouin, and Wayne Guay (2012). Does Tax Aggressiveness Reduce Financial Reporting Transparency? University of Pennsylvania working paper.

[13] Creal, Drew, Jonathan Rogers, Leslie Robinson, and Sarah Zechman (2014). The Multinational Advantage. University of Chicago working paper.

[14] Voget, Johannes (2011). Relocation of Headquarters and International Taxation. Journal of Public Economics 95 (9-10), 1067-1081.

[15] E.g. Hoffman, Liz, and Hester Plumridge (July 14, 2014). "Race to Cut Taxes Fuels Urge to Merge" Wall Street Journal.

[16] In other countries, the scope of their territorial systems differs based on how broadly or narrowly the eligibility rules are for the exemption. Take Japan for instance, with a 20 percent minimum tax. This resembles a worldwide system without deferral, at least with respect to activity in low-tax jurisdictions.

[17] Huizinga, Harry, and Luc Laeven (2008). International Profit Shifting Within Multinationals: A Multi-Country Perspective. Journal of Public Economics 92 (5-6), 1164-1182; Lohse, Theresa, and Nadine Riedel (2013). Do Transfer Pricing Laws Limit International Income Shifting? Evidence from European Multinationals. CESifo working paper 4404.

[18] Klassen, Ken, and Stacie LaPlante (2012). Are U.S. Multinational Corporations Becoming More Aggressive Income Shifters? Journal of Accounting Research 50 (5), 1245-1285.

[19] Markle, Kevin (2012). A Comparison of Tax-Motivated Income Shifting of Multinationals in Territorial and Worldwide Countries. Oxford Centre for Business Taxation Working Paper 12/06.

[20] Dyreng, Scott, and Kevin Markle (2013). The Effect of Financial Constraints on Tax-Motivated Income Shifting by U.S. Multinationals. Duke University working paper.

[21] Ernst, Christof, Katharina Richter, Nadine Riedel (2013). Corporate Taxation and the Quality of Research and Development. CESifo working paper 4139.

[22] Note that the current stock of foreign earnings held abroad is often estimated for tax policy purposes by looking to PRE reported in firms financial statements. This will underestimate undistributed earnings.

[23] Graham, John, Michelle Hanlon, and Terry Shevlin (2011). Real Effects of Accounting Rules: Evidence from Multinational Firms' Investment Location and Profit Repatriation Decisions. Journal of Accounting Research 49 (1), 137-185; Blouin, Jennifer, Linda Krull, and Leslie Robinson (2012). Is U.S. Multinational Dividend Repatriation Policy Influenced by Reporting Incentives? The Accounting Review 87(5), 1463- 1491.

[24] De Simone, Lisa (2013). Does a Common Set of Accounting Standards Affect Tax-Motivated Income Shifting for Multinational Firms? Stanford University working paper.

[25] Hope, Ole-Kristian, Mark Ma, and Wayne Thomas (2013). Tax Avoidance and Geographic Earnings Disclosure. Journal of Accounting and Economics 56(2), 170-189; Akamah, Herita, Ole-Kristian Hope, and Wayne Thomas (2014). Tax Havens and Disclosure Aggregation. Rotman School of Management working paper 2419573.

[26] Discussion Draft on Transfer Pricing Documentation and CBC Reporting. 30 January 2014. http://www.oecd.org/ctp/transfer-pricing/discussion-draft-transfer-pricing-documentation.pdf

[27] Dyreng, Scott, Jeff Hoopes, and Jaron Wilde (2014). Real Costs of Subsidiary Disclosure: Evidence from Corporate Tax Behavior. Duke University working paper.

[28] Gupta, Sanjay, Lillian Mills, and Erin Towery (2014). The Effect of Mandatory Financial Statement Disclosures of Tax Uncertainty on Tax Reporting and Collections: The Case of FIN 48 and Multistate Tax Avoidance. The Journal of the American Taxation Association. doi: http://dx.doi.org/10.2308/atax-50766

In: U.S. International Tax System
Editor: Holly Lanford
ISBN: 978-1-63321-976-2

Chapter 8

STATEMENT OF ALLAN SLOAN, SENIOR EDITOR AT LARGE, FORTUNE. HEARING ON "THE U.S. TAX CODE: LOVE IT, LEAVE IT OR REFORM IT!"*

Chairman Wyden, Ranking Member Hatch, and Members of the Committee: thank you for inviting me to participate at this hearing. I'm honored to have a chance to address you directly rather than having to write a newspaper or magazine article and hope that you pick it up and read it. Before I proceed, please note that I am speaking for myself alone. I am not speaking for my editors; or for my employer, Fortune magazine; or for Fortune's parent company, Time Inc. I am also not speaking for the Washington Post, which has run my articles for many years.

Part of the way that I have made my living since becoming a business journalist in 1969 is by writing about strange and complicated transactions designed to allow corporations (and on occasion, individuals or families) to minimize or eliminate tax obligations. I try to do this by explaining these transactions in what I call "a language approaching English." For example, when the Smucker jelly company acquired Jif peanut butter from Procter & Gamble in a tax efficient transaction, I called it a merger of peanut butter with jelly, rather than a Reverse Morris Trust. When the RJR Nabisco tobacco-grocery conglomerate tried to turn its food company into an independent entity, I talked about RJR trying to separate cookies from cancer.

When I worked at the late, lamented New York Newsday, which was owned by the late, lamented Times Mirror Co., I specialized in writing nasty stories about the tax-dodging tactics of Times Mirror and its controlling family at the time, the Chandlers. After Tribune Co. bought Times Mirror, the Chandlers grew disenchanted and forced Tribune to sell out to Sam Zell. I knew the Chandlers were really angry with Tribune management, because they agreed to have the company do a taxable transaction with Zell. He calls himself the Gravedancer, but I took to calling him the Artful (Tax) Dodger.

I'm telling you this so you can see that I've been around the tax avoidance business for a long time and that I'm either intellectually honest enough or foolish enough to bite the corporate hand that feeds me. I used to consider corporate tax avoidance an indoor sport of

* This is an edited, reformatted and augmented version of a statement presented July 22, 2014 before the Senate Committee on Finance.

sorts. Up until inversions, many of the transactions I wrote about amused me—but I'm not amused now.

I consider inversions to be a threat not only to the public fisc, but to the public psyche. Enough of a threat for my editorial superiors at Fortune—who aren't exactly anti-capitalist—to have asked me to write what turned into Fortune's recent cover story about inversions, called "Positively Un-American."

One of the things I find most disconcerting about inversions is that many people aren't scared of them enough. These are something entirely different from the tax dodges I'm going to describe in a bit. They're different from the income-shifting games that companies like Apple and Caterpillar play that have gotten so much attention. Inversions have the potential to totally undermine the corporate tax system, because we're beginning to see the dynamic change from "what's an inversion?" to "sign me up."

I have watched corporations and financial markets for more than 40 years, with the eyes of an English major who has learned about business, as opposed to an economics student who started out with theories. I can sense the corporate stampede out of this country coming. And once it happens—which it will, absent some quick action, followed by fundamental corporate tax reform—it will be irreversible.

You don't have two or three or four years to look at this problem, consider it, listen to all the usual suspects, and legislate. If you don't do something quickly to halt inversions, by the time you get around to dealing with them as part of corporate tax reform, the corporate tax base will have been so diminished that it will be extremely difficult for you to come up with any sort of revenue-neutral program.

To be sure—which I consider the three most dangerous words in journalism--I don't have any statistics to support this. That's because we don't have any reliable statistics—at least, none that I'm familiar with—about how many inversions we've had, how many are pending, how much tax revenue inversions they have cost the rest of us and are likely to cost in the future. (I will elaborate on this problem later in my testimony.) If the projections you hear for individual companies are remotely accurate—I have no idea if that's the case, no one does—the JCT projection of $19.5 billion of tax revenue lost to inversions over the next 10 years absent legislation is way, way low. Make that way, way, way low. It's not the staff's fault—the dynamic has changed.

If I thought inversions were really only a $2 billion a year item—not that $2 billion isn't money—I wouldn't have written what I did. And if this committee thought it was such a relatively small problem, I would not be testifying here today.

Now, to my testimony. I will talk about some tax-dodging games that I have seen and written about over the years, and hope that they will put the current wave of corporate inversions into historical context. I will also try to demonstrate that these inversions are a vastly more serious threat to public well-being than even the most blatant of these transactions. And finally, I will give you my thoughts about how I would deal with the inversion problem if American voters took leave of their senses and elected me to public office.

MORRIS TRUSTS

Until 1997, these were used as a routine, tax-efficient way to separate companies into their component pieces. A company would stick a business it wanted to unload into a new corporation owned by its shareholders, which is a tax-free transaction. A nanosecond later, a buyer would acquire the new corporation in a tax-free stock-for-stock deal. Company holders would thus end up with shares in both the original company and in the buyer of the business being unloaded.

For example, Affiliated Publications, which owned the Boston Globe, had somehow ended up with a bloc of shares of McCaw Cellular, which was becoming more valuable than the newspaper. So Affiliated did a deal with McCaw, in which McCaw traded its shares in return for shares in an Affiliated subsidiary that owned more shares of McCaw than McCaw issued to acquire the subsidiary. So at the end of the day, Affiliated shareholders owned McCaw shares in addition to their Affiliated shares, and McCaw was able to reduce its number of shares outstanding. No harm, no foul, no capital gains taxes.

But instead of simply confining themselves to tax-efficient separations, which no rational person could oppose, Morris Trusters over reached. They created the "Cash-Rich Morris Trust," in which corporations got lots of cash in what in effect was a tax-free sale masquerading as a corporate split-up. Disney's sale of the newspapers it acquired when it bought Capital Cities Communications, and General Motors' sale of its defense business got the most ink, part of it from me. Congress tightened the rules. But loophole openers then created...

REVERSE MORRIS TRUSTS

These require that shareholders of the selling company end up with a majority stake in the acquiring company — a big disincentive to buyers. But P&G managed to find buyers for three such deals: Smucker in 2002 for Jif; and in 2008 for Folger's coffee, enhancing Smucker's breakfast brand presence; and in 2011, a company called Diamond Food for Crisco. I calculated that these transactions saved P&G a combined $2 billion in capital gains taxes. Fortunately for the public fisc, Diamond stock fell apart, the Crisco deal collapsed and P&G unloaded Crisco in what I think was a straight-up, regular sale.

SPLIT-OFFS

This is another common technique that morphed from being an efficient way to split up companies into something excessive.

A corporation that owned a business that it no longer wanted would turn that business into a new, independent company. Then it would offer shares in the new company to its shareholders in return for some or all of their shares. At the end of the day, the company would have disposed of the business it didn't want, and reduced the number of its own shares that were outstanding. It was really sort of neat. It was equivalent to a company selling the unwanted business for cash, and using the cash to buy in some of its own shares. But a sale would have generated taxes. A split-off didn't.

Some notable split-offs were Loews Corp., a conglomerate (in which I now own stock) that did a split-off with its big stake in Lorillard tobacco. McDonalds with Chipotle Mexican Grill. Bristol Myers Squibb with Mead Johnson, which makes baby food. These are all reasonable deals in which a company unloaded an unwanted business in a tax-efficient way, setting the business free to find its destiny.

But naturally, companies—and their advisors—weren't satisfied with a tax-free separation. So they created ...

Cash-Rich Split-Offs

These are much more like a sale than a simple, tax-efficient separation. The first one of these was in 1999, when the Janus mutual fund company swapped its 28% stake in DST Systems for a small DST business and $999 million of cash. It was a sale in a split-off's clothing, and the business, which was barely a rounding error in the overall transaction, was a necessary part of the deal to make it tax-free. Liberty Media swapped cash and a few properties to Comcast for $1 billion of Liberty stock that Comcast owned. Time Warner traded a bunch of money and the Atlanta Braves to Liberty for a big piece of Time Warner stock.

Congress got annoyed, and in 2006 passed legislation requiring that from May 17, 2006 through May 17, 2007, the business thrown into the pot had to be "somewhat more than a quarter" of the consideration being paid, and since then, it has had to be "somewhat more than a third." So now you've got deals tip-toeing right up to that line.

The one that comes screaming to mind involves Graham Holdings (the old Washington Post Co.) and Berkshire Hathaway (which needs no introduction). The exact numbers aren't yet available, but earlier this month, Graham swapped about $400 million of Berkshire Hathaway stock that it owned, plus about $388 million of cash, plus a TV station that it valued at something like $394 million, for about $1.2 billion of Graham Holdings stock that Berkshire had owned for 40 years or so, and in which it had an ultra-low cost basis. This saved the firms a total of close to $700 million of taxes. (I own shares in both companies, and I like and respect both Don Graham and Warren Buffett.)

The way to stop this silliness is to require that the operating business be at least 80 percent of the transaction. But that's not our topic today.

This Brings Us to .... Inversions

There's a huge, huge difference between these games that I've described involving Morris Trusts, Cash-Rich Morris Trusts, Reverse Morris Trusts, Split-Offs and Cash-Rich Split-Offs and inversions.

All of these transactions are generally one-time things. They don't involve a company renouncing its corporate citizenship to save money, but expecting to be treated as if it were a regular, legitimate American company.

The article I wrote, which underwent rigorous editing (unlike this presentation), explains the history and workings of inversions far better than I could in this testimony. It also has some telling examples of intellectual inconsistency—I don't want to violate Senate decorum by using the term "hypocrisy"—that the package's primary editor uncovered with the aid of several of our Fortune colleagues. Plus, the graphics are pretty good.

We've now got a tidal wave of inversions—or we will have them unless the people at the podium in this room and your colleagues do something about it. Quickly. Inversions beget inversions, both for competitive reasons and because there's now a critical mass of players such as corporate raiders (who like to call themselves "investor activists") who care only about getting a stock's price up today; investment bankers who get fees from these deals; and all sorts of hangers-on.

We will end up with almost every company capable of doing an offshore deal doing it, and putting increasing pressure on every corporate manager of an inversion candidate who wants to do the decent, economically-patriotic thing, and finds this kind of behavior abhorrent.

Let me offer up a telling piece of history.

The first inversion was in 1983 when McDermott International, a builder of offshore drilling platform and underwater pipelines, moved its domicile to Panama.

In its April of 1984 issue, Fortune carried a short story about McDermott, and mentioned that it had been thrown out of the Fortune 500 for no longer being an American company. It also noted that two Canadian companies—Inspiration Resources and Lafarge Corp.—had moved their domiciles to the U.S., and were added to the 500. You don't see companies inverting into the U.S. these days, which is a sign that things have changed.

One reason that inversions haven't attracted much attention until recently is that until Pfizer tried to invert, there hadn't been any big, household-name firm visibly trying to leave the country. Pfizer trying to go offshore by buying AstraZeneca shocked me into paying much closer attention to inversions, and I think it shocked a lot of people.

One of the problems I ran into almost immediately was answering a basic question: how many inversions have we had. Two of the major sources of lists—the Congressional Research Service and Bloomberg—are flawed. Tracking this stuff is extremely difficult. One of my colleagues at Fortune, a research librarian at a major law firm in his previous life, is trying to assemble a definitive database. But it is taking a lot of time and effort.

Part of the problem is what I call the "never-heres": companies whose ancestors were U.S. corporations, but that in their current incarnation have always been offshore. Therefore, they get upset when you call them inverters—which we at Fortune have decided to do. And that you should do, too. Examples include Accenture when it was spun off from Arthur Andersen; Seagate (in which I bought stock several years ago, not realizing it wasn't a U.S. company) when it was relocated after being acquired in a leveraged buyout; Delphi when it reorganized after its bankruptcy.

A contributing problem is that although we have overall Treasury numbers about how much federal corporate tax is collected, we don't know how much any individual corporation pays for a given year. That's not one of the dozen-plus tax metrics that publicly-traded corporations are required to disclose. That makes it impossible to do a rigorous analysis of the tax situation of any inverting or would-be inverting company. We can solve this problem—or you can—by asking the SEC or the Financial Accounting Standards Board to require publicly-traded corporations to disclose this information by taking two numbers from their corporate tax returns: taxable income for a given year, and taxes paid for that year. This is easily accessible to companies—though not to anyone else—because all they need to do is look at their tax returns. My estimate is that it would take one person-hour a year per company to generate this information, which companies have refused to give me when I asked. FASB and the SEC have basically blown me off, but they won't blow you off.

If you talk to companies about inversions, which my Fortune colleagues and I have been doing for several months, you hear things like "this is only part of our strategy, it's not why we're doing the transaction." Or, "we will continue to pay taxes in America."

This is, forgive me, misleading nonsense. Ask a company why, if inversion isn't a major purpose of the deal with the foreign company, it's not doing a straight-up acquisition. Ask how much it would be paying for the foreign company if inversion weren't part of the package. I haven't gotten answer to this, but you probably could, especially if you asked them these questions in public. You can also ask inverters if their contract with their inversion partners contains a clause giving the inverter to right to modify or cancel the deal if inversion rules change. I think you'll get a "yes."

As for the "we will continue to pay U.S. taxes" story, ask how much the company will pay in U.S. corporate income tax as an inverted company compared to what it would have paid had it not inverted. I can't get answers to this, but you can. I suspect the answers will upset you.

My Suggestions

I know little—almost nothing, actually—about the political dynamics that go into the making of tax legislation. The one thing I can see is that the inversion question is becoming even more politically toxic than most things that I write about.

I saw that House Democrats forced an up-or-down vote by trying to attach the Sander Levin legislation to the depreciation-extender bill. It got voted down on a party-line vote. Of course, I saw Secretary Lew's letter. And I saw Senator Hatch's response. With all due respect, this struck me as political theater, not substance. And we need to deal with substance. It would be absolutely tragic if we let the inversion question descend into soundbites, political rhetoric and attack ads.

Looking at this as an outside observer, I think it's glaringly obvious what need to be done. First, you pass the Levin legislation—I prefer the Senate version, for reasons you'll see in a bit—to enact changes that would require inversions to change management and shareholder control of inverting companies. You adopt the March 8 cutoff date. No, that wouldn't be unfair retroactive legislation. Ever since Senator Wyden's op-ed ran in the May 8 Wall Street Journal, corporate America has been on notice that a May 8 date is on the table. (An aside: when I saw that article in the Journal, I let loose a string of obscenities, because he had written what I had hoped to write as my Fortune-Washington Post column. Being beaten by a competitor is part of the game—but I'd never been beaten to the news by a Senator before.)

If I were you, I would adopt the Senate version of Levin legislation, so that there's a cut-off date, and so that averting inversions for awhile doesn't totally remove the pressure to do something about the corporate tax code reasonably quickly. I found aspects of Rep. Camp's proposal interesting, but I don't pretend to have any expertise in drawing up tax legislation. That's what you do. It's not what I do.

Lookit, as we used to say when I was growing up in Brooklyn. Tax reform has been kicking around Washington for years, but doesn't seem to happen. You have to do something. It's not a partisan issue, it's a national issue.

Inversions are a symptom of the underlying disease, which is the tax code. But as my daughter the ER doctor would tell you if she were testifying, sometimes you have to address the immediate symptom before going on to the cure. If you're bleeding out, you need to put on a tourniquet, then deal with the wound. You can't say, "there's no point in stopping the bleeding if the wound hasn't been healed." You can treat the symptom quickly, and spend some time—but not too much—trying to cure the disease. You shouldn't say that inversions and the code need to be treated simultaneously.

Inversions aren't an obvious emergency, the way that helping people and businesses recover from floods and hurricanes is. But they are an economic emergency whose outlines are becoming clear to anyone willing to see them. Despite the toxic climate around here, you have occasionally managed to surmount partisanship and spin and accomplish worthwhile things. Please do something about this looming financial disaster before it's too late.

Thank you.

INDEX

#

21st century, 90

A

abuse, 36, 41, 77, 84, 85, 86, 94, 95, 120, 121, 123, 125
access, 84, 91, 96, 119, 122
accounting, 14, 20, 76, 105, 117, 118, 124, 125
accounting standards, 124
acquisitions, 25, 44, 111, 114, 115, 119
adjustment, 15, 44
administrators, 33, 85, 86, 94
adverse effects, 112
affirming, 90
Africa, 89, 93
age, 86, 119
aggregation, 125
amortization, 16, 39, 45, 62
ancestors, 131
arbitrage, 36, 91
arbitration, 33, 85
Argentina, 93
Asia, 89
assessment, 36, 38, 85, 86, 94
assets, 3, 6, 7, 8, 12, 14, 15, 18, 20, 21, 29, 34, 37, 39, 63, 85, 86, 91, 105, 114, 123, 125
asymmetry, 33
audit(s), 33, 37, 86
Austria, 26, 40, 41, 78, 104, 107, 110
authorities, 30, 35, 85, 98
authority, 2, 3, 13
autonomy, 92
avoidance, 5, 29, 31, 32, 36, 41, 56, 65, 85, 92, 93, 96, 127

B

bankers, 82, 131
banking, 6, 13, 18, 19, 54, 55, 57, 60, 65, 67, 68, 69, 72
bankruptcy, 131
banks, 10
barriers, 115
base, 2, 3, 4, 17, 19, 25, 26, 28, 29, 30, 31, 32, 33, 34, 37, 42, 43, 44, 49, 51, 52, 53, 56, 59, 60, 61, 62, 65, 66, 67, 69, 75, 82, 83, 84, 85, 86, 87, 88, 89, 91, 92, 93, 95, 103, 105, 109, 112, 120, 121, 122, 123, 128
Belgium, 26, 37, 38, 78, 104, 107, 109
beneficiaries, 12
benefits, 2, 9, 11, 27, 29, 31, 36, 37, 51, 60, 69, 71, 74, 79, 86, 94, 98, 120, 123
bias, 29
bleeding, 133
blueprint, 98
bonds, 10
Brazil, 89, 93
bribes, 54, 79
Britain, 110
Bulgaria, 78
business income, 1, 9, 42, 47, 49, 51, 52, 58, 65, 67, 70, 98, 103
business model, 28, 30, 34, 86
Business Roundtable, 106, 108
businesses, 6, 33, 34, 37, 45, 69, 72, 86, 90, 91, 92, 93, 94, 101, 110, 115, 133
buyer(s), 129

C

cancer, 127
capital gains, 10, 38, 73, 74, 129
capital markets, 98, 119

case law, 12
case studies, 76
cash, 25, 51, 63, 76, 82, 87, 91, 98, 105, 112, 114, 116, 119, 124, 125, 129, 130
cash flow, 25, 119
category a, 50, 57, 62
category b, 21
challenges, 27, 30, 34, 77, 88, 94, 96
chaos, 92
Chicago, 126
Chile, 26, 104, 107, 109
China, 89, 93
chronic diseases, 81
citizens, 71
citizenship, 88, 130
civil society, 89, 93
classes, 14, 53, 80
classification, 4, 5, 6, 56, 72, 109
clients, 101
climate, 133
clothing, 130
CNS, 78
coffee, 129
coherence, 91, 92, 93, 94, 95
collateral, 19
commerce, 35, 75
commercial, 6, 39
commercial bank, 6
common sense, 91, 92, 93
community, 42, 93, 121
compensation, 7, 12, 19, 73
competition, 25, 37, 85, 95, 115
competitive advantage, 91, 92
competitiveness, 2, 42, 66, 81, 86, 110, 118, 119
competitors, 81, 82, 108, 118
complement, 33
complexity, 20, 58, 98, 123
compliance, 33, 91, 92, 94, 125
computation, 21, 49, 50, 62
computing, 39, 50, 62, 63, 68
conference, 38
confidentiality, 37, 86, 94
Congress, 2, 5, 73, 75, 78, 81, 88, 108, 129, 130
consensus, 30, 84, 85, 89, 90, 91, 92, 93, 94, 95
consumption, 7, 13, 25, 35, 48, 54, 61, 98
convention, 77, 84
coordination, 19, 20, 47
corporation tax, 79, 116
cost, 8, 24, 26, 28, 32, 40, 43, 72, 78, 79, 84, 94, 111, 118, 119, 120, 124, 128, 130
Council of the European Union, 41, 78
covering, 11, 74
creditors, 14
criticism, 1, 65, 66
Croatia, 78
cross-border income, vii, 1, 2, 66, 84
cure, 81, 82, 133
currency, 54, 55
customers, 13, 18, 29, 43, 65, 67, 69, 91
Cyprus, 78
Czech Republic, 26, 78, 104, 107, 109

D

database, 131
debts, 73
deduction, 4, 13, 15, 30, 35, 36, 38, 41, 44, 45, 46, 47, 48, 49, 50, 51, 52, 56, 57, 58, 59, 60, 61, 62, 63, 65, 67, 68, 69, 71, 78, 79, 80, 85, 87, 103
deficiencies, 87, 93
deficiency, 17
deficit, 63, 79
denial, 49, 62
Denmark, 26, 78, 104, 107, 109
Department of the Treasury, v, 71, 78, 83
deposits, 6, 10, 18
depreciation, 7, 16, 45, 62, 132
depth, 93
destiny, 130
detection, 33
developed countries, 108
developing countries, 93
direct investment, 24, 27, 74, 76, 91, 112
disaster, 133
disclosure, 33, 96, 124, 125
diseases, 81
disposition, 7, 13, 14, 44, 47, 48, 52, 53, 54, 55, 56, 61, 75
distortions, 90, 98
distribution, 14, 17, 50, 53, 58
District of Columbia, 6
domestic capital, 122
domestic economy, 112
domestic investment, 22, 23, 24, 25, 27, 37, 111, 112, 116, 119, 122
domestic laws, 4, 30, 83
draft, 30, 31, 33, 34, 35, 36, 37, 51, 53, 57, 58, 59, 60, 61, 62, 63, 64, 66, 67, 68, 69, 70, 71, 77, 79, 80, 94, 126
drawing, 133

E

earnings, 1, 2, 14, 15, 16, 18, 19, 20, 22, 23, 24, 25, 42, 44, 45, 46, 47, 50, 51, 52, 53, 56, 58, 59, 63,

66, 67, 69, 70, 71, 74, 75, 76, 78, 79, 80, 86, 87, 105, 111, 112, 113, 114, 115, 116, 119, 123, 124, 126
e-commerce, 35
economic activity, 30, 32, 33, 37, 85, 96, 98, 121
economic consequences, 105
economic development, 90
economic growth, 25, 90, 95, 113
economic resources, 119
economics, 128
editors, 127
election, 5, 20, 44, 46, 48, 51, 56, 64
emergency, 133
employees, 8, 19, 37, 43, 49, 55
employment, 25
enforcement, 2, 125
entrepreneurs, 78, 97
environment(s), 84, 90, 93, 101, 120
EPS, 84, 85, 92, 95
equilibrium, 111
equipment, 114
equity, 15, 29, 41, 61, 82
erosion, 2, 28, 29, 30, 31, 32, 33, 34, 37, 42, 44, 51, 56, 59, 60, 61, 65, 87, 89, 91, 95, 121, 122, 123
Estonia, 26, 78, 104, 107, 109
EU, 78, 106, 109, 110, 115, 118, 120, 122, 124, 125
Europe, 89
European Commission, 37, 40, 41, 78
European Court of Justice, 115
European Union, 2, 40, 41, 78
evidence, 78, 82, 98, 118, 119, 120
evolution, 34
exclusion, 18, 44, 52, 53, 55, 60, 66, 67, 68, 69, 71, 80
exercise, 2, 3, 90, 92, 93
expenditures, 14, 72, 103
expertise, 91, 133
exploitation, 28, 39, 46, 59, 60, 61, 78

F

fairness, 29
families, 127
FDI, 113
fever, 81
financial, 6, 11, 21, 31, 32, 35, 37, 45, 54, 57, 65, 72, 76, 84, 92, 95, 105, 109, 114, 116, 117, 124, 125, 126, 128, 133
financial crisis, 92, 116
financial institutions, 6, 11
financial markets, 128
financial reports, 124
Finland, 26, 78, 104, 107, 109
flaws, 92
floods, 133
food, 127, 130
force, 30, 34, 98
foreign companies, 25, 66, 98, 105
foreign direct investment, 27, 74, 76
foreign firms, 99, 124
foreign investment, 1, 3, 20, 22, 23, 24, 25, 36, 55, 66, 102, 110, 112, 113, 114, 119
foreign person, 1, 3, 4, 7, 8, 9, 10, 11, 12, 13, 14, 15, 17, 18, 19, 20, 54, 55, 57, 60, 61, 68, 74, 79, 80, 103
foreign subsidiaries, 1, 2, 3, 4, 24, 41, 44, 45, 64, 65, 66, 67, 71, 103, 106, 111
fragments, 31
framing, 121
France, 26, 37, 38, 40, 41, 78, 104, 107, 109, 120
funds, 20, 24, 53, 87, 119

G

G7 countries, 104
GDP, 90, 111, 112, 113, 115
General Motors, 129
Generally Accepted Accounting Principles, 87
Germany, 11, 26, 40, 41, 78, 104, 107, 109, 120
global economy, 22, 30, 90, 98, 105
global markets, 115
globalization, 30, 90
goods and services, 88, 115
governments, 25, 30, 33, 46, 83, 84, 94, 95
Greece, 26, 78, 104, 107, 109
growth, 24, 25, 27, 34, 82, 95, 111, 113, 115
guidance, 17, 31, 32, 36, 74, 88, 94, 121
guidelines, 3, 14, 31, 89, 97

H

Harvard Law School, 97
health, 8
hedging, 19
history, 73, 131
HM, 110, 111, 116
HM Treasury, 110, 111, 116
holding company, 17, 18, 19, 20, 54, 55, 57, 60, 61, 68, 75, 80, 103
host, 118
House, 2, 42, 79, 116, 132
House of Representatives, 116
housing, 71
Hungary, 26, 37, 38, 78, 104, 107, 109
hurricanes, 133

hybrid, 3, 5, 6, 29, 30, 35, 37, 40, 41, 42, 43, 44, 45, 46, 47, 49, 51, 52, 65, 68, 70, 77, 84, 85, 87, 94, 95, 121
hypocrisy, 131

I

Iceland, 26, 104, 107
identification, 3
IMF, 91, 113
imports, 72
in transition, 80
income support, 87
income tax, 2, 3, 4, 9, 10, 11, 12, 14, 16, 17, 19, 20, 21, 22, 25, 26, 39, 41, 44, 45, 47, 49, 50, 52, 54, 56, 58, 60, 62, 69, 70, 71, 74, 75, 76, 79, 82, 83, 85, 86, 88, 90, 94, 102, 103, 105, 111, 112, 113, 115, 117, 121, 123, 125, 132
India, 89, 91, 93
individuals, 3, 16, 20, 45, 74, 127
Indonesia, 89, 93
induced bias, 29
inefficiency, 81
inferences, 121
inflation, 60
information exchange, 86
institutions, 6, 11, 89
integration, 30
intellectual property, 2, 27, 28, 37, 38, 39, 40, 65, 78, 87, 91
intellectual property rights, 38, 39, 40
interface, 35
Internal Revenue Service, 5
international communication, 8
international competition, 25, 115
international law, 34
international standards, 30, 86, 89, 94
international trade, 92
internationalization, 78
inventions, 40
inversion, 4, 9, 46, 71, 73, 81, 82, 83, 88, 98, 120, 128, 131, 132
investment(s), 1, 3, 4, 14, 18, 19, 20, 22, 23, 24, 25, 27, 31, 33, 36, 37, 41, 42, 44, 52, 53, 55, 60, 65, 66, 67, 71, 75, 79, 81, 82, 90, 91, 92, 98, 102, 103, 110, 111, 112, 113, 114, 116, 119, 122, 131
investment bank, 81, 82, 131
investors, 10, 31, 72, 76, 91, 95
Ireland, 26, 27, 78, 104, 107, 109
Israel, 26, 104, 107, 109
issues, 12, 28, 30, 33, 34, 36, 37, 51, 65, 67, 83, 85, 88, 89, 94, 99, 116, 119
Italy, 26, 78, 104, 107, 109

J

Japan, 11, 26, 78, 101, 104, 107, 109, 111, 115, 116, 126
job creation, 92
journalism, 128
jurisdiction, 2, 3, 6, 17, 25, 29, 34, 35, 36, 37, 40, 42, 44, 74, 78, 86, 87, 91, 95, 96, 118

K

Korea, 26, 104, 107, 109

L

labor force, 98
landscape, 30
Latvia, 78
laws, 2, 4, 18, 29, 30, 35, 45, 47, 52, 72, 73, 77, 83, 84
lawyers, 81
lead, 23, 27, 29, 31, 86, 90, 92, 93, 95, 98, 112, 121
legislation, 2, 37, 40, 46, 50, 64, 66, 67, 68, 69, 70, 71, 78, 80, 81, 88, 94, 99, 120, 121, 122, 128, 130, 132
legislative responses, 42
lending, 54, 87
light, 119
limited liability, 5, 72
liquid assets, 123
Lithuania, 78
litigation, 92
loans, 18, 41

M

magnitude, 122
majority, 129
man, 92
management, 8, 15, 32, 72, 91, 127, 132
manufactured goods, 103
manufacturing, 2, 25, 54, 65, 82
market economy, 89
market share, 25
marketing, 84
marketplace, 115
mass, 131
matrix, 91
matter, 8, 69, 86, 95
Mauritius, 91
media, 78, 88, 92

median, 26
medical, 82
merchandise, 13
mergers, 111, 115
Mexico, 26, 28, 40, 83, 104, 107, 109
Microsoft, 76
migration, 4, 112
misuse, 86
models, 28, 30, 34, 38, 39, 86, 91
modifications, 49, 51, 54, 59, 64, 68, 80
monopoly, 34
morbidity, 17
mortality, 17
multinational companies, 1, 2, 64, 65, 74, 83, 84
multinational corporations, 24, 27, 92, 101, 117
multinational enterprises, 32, 33, 76, 90
multinational firms, 1, 22, 97

N

naming, 73
nationality, 2, 6, 8
negotiating, 73
Netherlands, 26, 37, 39, 78, 104, 107, 110, 118
neutral, 42, 85, 98, 128
New Zealand, 26, 101, 104, 107, 109, 112, 113, 116
non-OECD, 93
nonresident aliens, 1, 3, 10, 73
North America, 89
Norway, 26, 104, 107, 108, 109

O

Obama, 122, 123
obstacles, 33, 40
OECD, v, 2, 25, 26, 28, 30, 31, 32, 33, 34, 36, 37, 40, 77, 83, 84, 85, 86, 88, 89, 90, 92, 93, 95, 97, 101, 102, 103, 104, 105, 106, 107, 108, 109, 110, 112, 113, 115, 117, 125
oil, 17, 44, 46, 49, 53, 61, 103, 109
oligopoly, 34
operations, 3, 8, 15, 16, 17, 31, 49, 55, 69, 87, 92, 101, 105, 118, 119, 123, 125
opportunities, 24, 28, 33, 36, 74, 90, 91, 95, 119, 122
Organization for Economic Cooperation and Development, 83
overlap, 3, 20
overseas investment, 25
ownership, 2, 9, 18, 20, 28, 38, 39, 40, 48, 59, 73, 78, 91, 103, 119
ownership structure, 119

P

paints, 122
Panama, 131
parallel, 47, 52, 79
parents, 111
participants, 90
patents, 7, 13, 18, 38, 39, 40
peer review, 89
penalties, 37, 98
permission, 72
permit, 21, 71, 86, 124
personal views, 117
platform, 131
playing, 82, 87, 91, 93
pleasure, 97
Poland, 26, 78, 104, 107, 110
policy, 1, 2, 17, 18, 22, 31, 74, 84, 86, 89, 91, 92, 95, 97, 101, 113, 114, 117, 125, 126
policy choice, 89, 95
policy makers, 125
policy reform, 95
policy responses, 2
policymakers, 22, 24, 25, 27, 28, 120
pools, 62
population, 115
portfolio, 10, 14, 21, 56, 73, 120
Portugal, 26, 78, 104, 107, 110
predictability, 93, 94, 96
preferential treatment, 46, 68
preparation, 37
present value, 23, 25, 66
president, 85, 86
principles, 2, 20, 28, 29, 36, 38, 45, 49, 85, 89, 90, 91, 94
probability, 114, 120
professionals, 121
profit, 2, 4, 5, 28, 29, 30, 32, 33, 34, 35, 37, 40, 43, 65, 76, 86, 89, 91, 98, 122, 125
profitability, 119
project, 83, 84, 85, 86, 90, 91, 93
proliferation, 72, 92
property rights, 38, 39, 40
proposed regulations, 125
protection, 32, 38
public policy, 17
purchasing power, 115

Q

questioning, 97

R

race, 31, 85, 95
rate of return, 1, 22, 23, 24, 25
real estate, 14, 79
real property, 14, 73, 74
reality, 85, 118
recall, 99
recognition, 47, 56, 87, 95, 124, 125
recommendations, 30, 31, 32, 33, 35, 36, 37, 77, 83, 94, 95, 96
reconstruction, 111
recovery, 26
regulations, 4, 5, 6, 14, 50, 62, 63, 72, 74, 99, 109, 125
reinsurance, 11, 18, 44, 54, 56, 65, 70, 74, 78
relevance, 16
relief, 3, 4, 35, 36
rent, 55
repatriate, 24, 66, 80, 114, 119, 123
requirements, 17, 18, 19, 37, 48, 73, 79, 93, 94, 103, 125
researchers, 89, 111
reserves, 17
resolution, 33, 84, 85, 93, 96
resources, 5, 92, 119
response, 28, 30, 42, 73, 93, 94, 111, 112, 132
restrictions, 38, 68, 115
restructuring, 44
retail, 82
retained earnings, 123
revenue, 8, 27, 28, 30, 38, 42, 74, 85, 86, 92, 93, 98, 111, 117, 121, 124, 128
rhetoric, 132
rights, 27, 30, 38, 39, 40, 90, 91, 93, 95
risk(s), 11, 17, 29, 30, 32, 34, 36, 39, 43, 74, 85, 86, 91, 93, 94, 96, 98
risk assessment, 36, 85, 86, 94
Romania, 78
royalty, 38, 41, 45, 55, 73, 87, 122
Russia, 93

S

sales activities, 72
sanctions, 73
Saudi Arabia, 93
savings, 10
science, 38
scope, 42, 43, 49, 53, 59, 64, 66, 67, 79, 88, 94, 108, 109, 111, 112, 126
Secretary of the Treasury, 5
securities, 5, 12, 13, 19, 73
Senate, v, vii, 1, 2, 27, 42, 77, 79, 80, 81, 82, 83, 89, 97, 101, 117, 127, 131, 132
senses, 128
services, 7, 12, 13, 17, 21, 35, 39, 40, 43, 48, 49, 53, 54, 55, 57, 60, 61, 65, 66, 67, 69, 70, 72, 73, 75, 76, 80, 88, 103, 109, 110, 112, 115
shareholders, 8, 14, 16, 18, 20, 41, 46, 52, 57, 59, 63, 64, 66, 67, 76, 82, 87, 102, 108, 112, 129
showing, 27, 76, 119
Slovakia, 78
society, 89, 93
software, 39, 40
sole proprietor, 5
solution, 86
South Africa, 89, 93
sovereignty, 90, 95
Spain, 26, 37, 39, 78, 104, 107, 110
spillover effects, 31
spin, 133
St. Petersburg, 83
stakeholders, 89
state(s), 2, 29, 30, 31, 33, 34, 36, 38, 40, 41, 78, 102, 103, 109, 125
statistics, 128
stock, 8, 12, 13, 16, 17, 18, 19, 20, 24, 44, 45, 47, 48, 52, 53, 55, 59, 62, 72, 76, 78, 79, 80, 102, 112, 114, 119, 126, 129, 130, 131
stockpiling, 114
structure, 35, 36, 37, 43, 52, 73, 97
supply chain, 91
Supreme Court, 73
sustainability, 83
sustainable economic growth, 90
sweat, 82
Sweden, 26, 78, 104, 107, 110
Switzerland, 11, 26, 104, 107, 110

T

tactics, 127
target, 35, 60, 84, 98
tax base, 2, 3, 4, 25, 31, 39, 42, 43, 60, 65, 82, 83, 84, 85, 86, 88, 92, 93, 95, 105, 120, 121, 128
tax collection, 35, 125
tax credits, 6, 42, 49, 57, 58, 62, 103, 122
tax data, 76
tax deduction, 15, 30, 36, 41, 85
tax incentive, 26, 38, 114
tax policy, 91, 92, 95, 101, 113, 117, 125, 126
tax rates, 14, 25, 26, 28, 37, 54, 69, 73, 76, 81, 86, 87, 92, 95, 105, 113, 115, 118, 123

tax reform(s), 22, 42, 45, 56, 79, 81, 82, 83, 86, 87, 88, 92, 97, 98, 101, 110, 111, 115, 116, 120, 121, 128
tax rules, 1, 2, 9, 20, 22, 27, 29, 30, 34, 35, 42, 46, 64, 65, 66, 67, 68, 69, 75, 84, 85, 87, 90, 91, 92, 98, 101
tax system, vii, 1, 16, 25, 29, 42, 45, 51, 58, 83, 86, 87, 90, 91, 92, 93, 95, 101, 102, 106, 107, 108, 110, 111, 112, 113, 114, 115, 116, 118, 119, 120, 121, 122, 123, 124, 128
taxes, 3, 4, 9, 11, 14, 15, 17, 20, 21, 22, 24, 25, 29, 33, 37, 43, 44, 45, 46, 47, 49, 50, 51, 57, 58, 60, 62, 63, 71, 73, 84, 85, 86, 88, 90, 103, 112, 113, 114, 118, 119, 120, 125, 129, 130, 132
taxpayers, 4, 5, 9, 18, 30, 33, 35, 36, 37, 39, 71, 72, 80, 81, 87, 91, 92, 94, 95
technical assistance, 41
techniques, 27, 33, 92
technology, 34, 37
tensions, 92, 94
territorial, 1, 2, 3, 15, 25, 29, 42, 98, 106, 107, 108, 110, 111, 112, 114, 115, 116, 118, 119, 120, 121, 122, 123, 124, 125, 126
territory, 2, 3, 39
thoughts, 128
threshold level, 12
time frame, 94
Title I, 45, 58, 79
Title II, 45
Title IV, 58, 79
tobacco, 127, 130
tourniquet, 133
trade, 7, 8, 9, 10, 11, 12, 13, 14, 15, 18, 19, 30, 38, 40, 44, 46, 47, 48, 49, 55, 56, 68, 69, 70, 76, 79, 80, 90, 92
trademarks, 7, 38, 39
trading partners, 4
transactions, 4, 9, 15, 18, 29, 31, 32, 33, 36, 37, 43, 46, 54, 55, 56, 65, 67, 71, 73, 83, 88, 96, 97, 98, 115, 119, 120, 127, 128, 129, 130
transfer pricing, 4, 31, 32, 33, 36, 37, 43, 72, 84, 85, 91, 93, 94, 96, 125
transparency, 31, 33, 77, 93, 94, 96
transportation, 8
Treasury, 4, 5, 6, 71, 74, 78, 84, 88, 110, 111, 116, 131
Treasury Secretary, 6
treaties, 3, 4, 11, 12, 36, 56, 73, 77, 79, 85, 86, 90, 91, 93, 94, 95, 96
treatment, 4, 5, 6, 29, 30, 35, 36, 41, 43, 45, 46, 47, 52, 66, 68, 69, 80, 95
triggers, 75
Trust Fund, 63
Turkey, 26, 104, 107, 110

U

U.S. Department of the Treasury, v, 83
U.S. economy, 113, 123
U.S. international tax system, vii, 1, 42, 58
U.S. policy, 22, 27, 114
U.S. Treasury, 84
UK, 101, 110, 111, 112, 115, 116, 119
uniform, 73
United Kingdom, 11, 26, 37, 38, 40, 78, 101, 104, 107, 110
updating, 32, 85, 93

V

valuation, 53, 56, 72, 76, 120
value added tax, 86
VAT, 86
vein, 90
vision, 110
volatility, 34
vote, 9, 13, 17, 47, 132
voters, 128
voting, 20, 48, 59, 62, 63, 78, 79, 80, 102

W

wages, 98
war, 50, 62, 71
Washington, 125, 127, 130, 132, 133
welfare, 98
well being, 89, 128
withdrawal, 75
World Bank, 106
World War I, 89
worldwide, 1, 3, 9, 16, 21, 24, 27, 39, 40, 42, 61, 87, 92, 93, 97, 98, 102, 103, 106, 107, 110, 111, 112, 113, 114, 115, 116, 118, 119, 120, 121, 122, 126

Y

yield, 22, 23, 25